Adapting
Macbeth

SHAKESPEARE AND ADAPTATION

Shakespeare and Adaptation provides in-depth discussions of a dynamic field and showcases the ways in which, with each act of adaptation, a new Shakespeare is generated. The series addresses the phenomenon of Shakespeare and adaptation in all its guises and explores how Shakespeare continues as a reference-point in a generically diverse body of representations and forms, including fiction, film, drama, theatre, performance and mass media. Including sole authored books as well as edited collections, the series embraces a mix of methodologies and espouses a global perspective that brings into conversation adaptations from different nations, languages and cultures.

Series Editor:

Mark Thornton Burnett (Queen's University Belfast, UK)

Advisory Board:

Professor Sarah Hatchuel (Université Paul-Valéry Montpellier, 3, France)
Dr Peter Kirwan (University of Nottingham, UK)
Professor Douglas Lanier (University of New Hampshire, USA)
Professor Adele Lee (Emerson College, USA)
Dr Stephen O'Neill (Maynooth University, Ireland)
Professor Shormishtha Panja (University of Delhi, India)
Professor Lisa Starks (University of South Florida)
Professor Nathalie Vienne-Guerrin
(Université Paul-Valéry Montpellier 3, France)
Professor Sandra Young (University of Cape Town, South Africa)

Forthcoming Titles:

Women and Indian Shakespeares
Edited by Thea Buckley, Mark Thornton Burnett,
Sangeeta Datta and Rosa García-Periago

*Lockdown Shakespeare: New Evolutions in Performance
and Adaptation*
Edited by Gemma Allred, Benjamin Broadribb and Erin Sullivan

*'Romeo and Juliet', Adaptation and the Arts:
'Cut Him Out in Little Stars'*
Edited by Julia Reinhard Lupton and Ariane Helou

Shakespeare, Ecology and Adaptation: A Practical Guide
Alys Daroy and Paul Prescott

Adapting Macbeth

A Cultural History

William C. Carroll

THE ARDEN SHAKESPEARE
LONDON • NEW YORK • OXFORD • NEW DELHI • SYDNEY

THE ARDEN SHAKESPEARE
Bloomsbury Publishing Plc
50 Bedford Square, London, WC1B 3DP, UK
1385 Broadway, New York, NY 10018, USA
29 Earlsfort Terrace, Dublin 2, Ireland

BLOOMSBURY, THE ARDEN SHAKESPEARE and the Arden Shakespeare logo
are trademarks of Bloomsbury Publishing Plc

First published in Great Britain 2022
Paperback edition published 2023

Cover design: Tjaša Krivec
Cover image: Actors David Clavel Banquo's ghost, Adama Diop as Macbeth
and Chloe Rejo as Lady Macbeth perform on stage during a dress rehearsal
of the play Macbeth by Shakespeare (1564–1616) and directed by Stephane
Braunschweig at the Odeon Theatre de l'Europe in Paris on January 20, 2018.
(© JACQUES DEMARTHON/AFP via Getty Images)

A catalogue record for this book is available from the British Library.

A catalog record for this book is available from the Library of Congress.

ISBN: HB: 978-1-3501-8139-7
       PB: 978-1-3502-8854-6
       ePDF: 978-1-3501-8141-0
       eBook: 978-1-3501-8140-3

Series: Shakespeare and Adaptation

Typeset by Integra Software Services Pvt. Ltd.

To find out more about our authors and books visit www.bloomsbury.com
and sign up for our newsletters.

For Carol, David, and Rachel

CONTENTS

LIST OF ILLUSTRATIONS

The author and publisher gratefully acknowledge the permission granted to reproduce the copyright material in this book.

Every effort has been made to trace copyright holders and to obtain
their permission for the use of copyright material. The publisher
apologizes for any errors or omissions in the above list and would
be grateful if notified of any corrections that should be incorporated
in future reprints or editions of this book.

The third-party copyrighted material displayed in the pages of
this book is done so on the basis of 'fair dealing for the purposes
of criticism and review' or 'fair use for the purposes of teaching,
criticism, scholarship or research' only in accordance with
international copyright laws, and is not intended to infringe upon
the ownership rights of the original owners.

ACKNOWLEDGEMENTS

I began this book, although I did not know it at the time, when I was preparing the Bedford edition of *Macbeth*, published in 1999. The strange power of this dark play became increasingly evident, and I realized I wanted to write more about it. This impulse led in two directions: to an analysis of its historical context in 1606, but also to this book – the play's reproduction over the centuries, its transformation through adaptation. I found that studying the narrative of *Macbeth*'s adaptations was also a way, circling back, to understanding its historical moment as well.

Parts of some chapters began as conference papers or lectures at meetings of the Shakespeare Association of America, the European Shakespeare Research Association, the World Shakespeare Congress, the International Shakespeare Association, the Italian Association of Shakespeare and Early Modern Studies, and venues in Boston, Washington, DC, Padova and Bologna: my gratitude goes to those receptive hosts, audiences and stimulating colleagues. I would also like to thank my students at Boston University for their participation and interest in several courses on Shakespearean adaptation; I learned much from them and appreciate their openness to new things. One of those excellent students, Adrienne Rube, helped prepare a bibliography for this book. I also had the generous research support of a Bogliasco Foundation Fellowship, for which I am deeply grateful. I thank as well the Folger Shakespeare Library, which provided a month-long residency; the excellent staff in the Reading Room made everything simple, efficient, and friendly. It was the best place to work one could find.

Special thanks go to friends and colleagues who have provided conversation, comment, and generous support over the years: Rob Chodat, Diana Henderson, Coppélia Kahn, Jack and Sharon Matthews, George Park, and Jim and Alexandra Siemon. I am also deeply grateful to my local pandemic pod, a source of (distanced) support, stimulation, and flying prosecco corks over the past year when much of this book was written: Michael and Carol-Marie Mendillo, Robb Dixon and Barbara Snow. And I owe a very special debt of gratitude to Kent Cartwright, Pascale Drouet, Keir Elam, Lena Cowen Orlin, and Alessandra Petrina for their invitations, insights, suggestions, and support. Finally, I would be remiss if I did not mention, with great thanks, the anonymous readers for The Arden Shakespeare; Mark Dudgeon, the Publisher of Theatre and Shakespeare Studies at The Arden Shakespeare, who encouraged me to submit a proposal; his capable assistant, Lara Bateman; and Mark Thornton Burnett, who oversees this series, and whose own work on global Shakespeare has been inspiring.

Most inspiring of all, though, has been Carol, who has supported and encouraged me since we first met, especially during this past year. I owe everything to her.

The author and publisher gratefully acknowledge the permission granted to reproduce the copyright material in this book.

Part of the Introduction was originally published in *Shakespeare and the Supernatural*, eds. Victoria Bladen and Yan Brailowsky. Manchester: Manchester Univ. Press, 2020. I am grateful to Manchester University Press for permission to reprint.

Parts of Chapter One and Five, which were originally published in a French translation by Nathalie Rivere de Carles in the introduction to David Greig's *Dunsinane,* trans. Pascale Drouet, Nouvelles Scènes *anglais* series (Toulouse: Presses Universitaires du Midi, 2016), are used with kind permission of Presses Universitaires du Midi.

Part of Chapter Three was published in *Shakespeare on Screen: Macbeth*, eds. Sarah Hatchuel and Nathalie Vienne-Guerrin. Rouen: Publications des Universités de Rouen et du Havre, 2014. I am grateful to the editors for permission to reprint.

Part of Chapter Five was published in the online journal, *Borrowers and Lenders: The Journal of Shakespeare and Appropriation* 8.2 (2014); http://www.borrowers.uga.edu/26/toc. *Borrowers and Lenders* holds copyright on essays it publishes, but authors may share their essays freely. I am grateful to the Journal for permission.

Part of Chapter Six was published as 'Two Truths Are Told': Afterlives and Histories of Macbeths' in *Shakespeare Survey*

57 (2004): 69–80. Reproduced with permission of The Licensor through PLSclear.

Part of Chapter Seven was published in *Weyward Macbeth: Intersections of Race and Performance*, eds. Scott Newstok and Ayanna Thompson. New York: Palgrave Macmillan, 2010. I am grateful to Springer Nature Inc. for permission to reprint.

NOTE ON TEXT

All *Macbeth* quotations are from the Arden Third Series edition: *Macbeth*, Sandra Clark and Pamela Mason, editors, London: Bloomsbury, 2015. References to the 'Folio' are, for convenience, to the texts of typical modern scholarly editions of the play, while references to the 'First Folio' are to the specific 1623 volume of Shakespeare's plays, in which *Macbeth* first appeared. The distinction should be clear throughout. I have silently modernized some medieval and early modern texts for readability.

Introduction: *Macbeth* and Mackbeth, the prequel

This book will examine how the Folio text of the Scottish play has, from its first revisions by Thomas Middleton *c*. 1615 and by William Davenant in 1664, been continually transformed and adapted in attempts to clarify or explain its supposed lacunae, lapses, and inconsistencies. Since the play's first performance in 1606, directors, actors, editors, writers, and other artists have often felt compelled to write new scenes, dialogue, and stage directions, create new characters or provide prequels and sequels. Among those contemplating an adaptation but unable to complete their work were John Milton (1938: 245), who proposed 'Macbeth beginning at the arrival of Malcolm at Mackduffe. the matter of Duncan may be express't by the appearing of his ghost' (a ghost that does not appear in the Folio, as we will see, but shows up in various adaptations) and Beethoven, who from 1809–11 sketched out an opera based on the play (Lockwood 2003). Why does this compulsion exist for *Macbeth*: is there something in the nature of the play itself that compels a need or desire to reshape it?

Relatively few of Shakespeare's plays constitute the vast majority of appropriations and adaptations: *Hamlet, Romeo and Juliet, Julius Caesar, Richard III* – and *Macbeth*. Like these other plays, *Macbeth* has entered the cultural lexicon through iconic scenes (Lady Macbeth's hand-washing) and memorable lines ('Out, damned spot!'). The 'Tomorrow' speech is second only to 'To be or not to be' in fame. Indeed, some of *Macbeth*'s features have become so well-known in popular culture that famous lines are often wrenched out of context for advertising purposes: 'Out Damn Plaque', read an ad for the SoniPick ('the advanced flossing device powered by sonic frequency vibrations'), and a 1997 automobile ad headlined 'Something Wicked This Way Comes. Hell hath no fury like the seethings of a 300-horsepower' engine – the ad-writers apparently unconcerned about linking their product to a murderer or the demonic (or unwittingly borrowing faux-Shakespearean language from Congreve as well). The name 'Macbeth' alone is often appropriated with little or no linkage to the play itself. Thus, in Carmen Amato's 2017 novel, *Awakening Macbeth*, Brodie Macbeth is a university professor who falls in love with 'Joe Birnam, an Iraq War vet with his own demons'; 'not even Shakespeare', we are told, 'could have written the secret that will keep you up tonight'.[1] Mike Kostensky's 2014 novel *The Island of Macbeth* is set not in Scotland, but on 'a tight-knit island community off the coast of Massachusetts' that 'secedes' from the state,[2] while James Theres and Tim Schnese's 2014 *American Macbeth* is set in 1862, with 'Union General George McClellan' marching on Washington, DC, to overthrow President Lincoln 'not to save the country, but to save his wife'.[3] There are many more such borrowings.

Inevitably, in 2005, the one-thousand year anniversary of the historical Macbeth's birth, Scottish MSP Alex Johnstone sponsored a motion that 'regrets that Macbeth is misportrayed when he was a successful Scottish king ... [Johnstone's] attempt to overturn Macbeth's image as a murderous villain [was] supported by 19 other MSPs'. The motives behind this sentiment were less fidelity to historical truth than promoting commercial tourism: 'It might be fitting if we used this to build up interest in tourism in that part of Scotland and counter some of the difficulties Scottish tourism has had', Johnstone commented.[4] The cause has been taken up by such Scottish heritage projects as 'The Real Macbeth Tour', which includes 'a wonderful tour of Glamis Castle to discover how Shakespeare wrongly placed it in Inverness, how Glamis is linked to the real Macbeth and how the story continues to this day. Entry fees and a light lunch are included' in the £95 fee.[5] Not to be outdone are the creators of 'A Tour of Macbeth's Scotland in 13 Places', from Dingwall ('This is where historians believe the real Macbeth may have been born, and the town is certainly old enough to warrant this suspicion') and Moray to Cawdor Castle and Glamis Castle. We are told 'it does not really matter if Shakespeare was not historically accurate in his portrayal of Macbeth and Glamis' (a dismissal that might call into question the whole enterprise), and then, in a non-sequitur: 'Today, Glamis Castle features on the reverse of some Scottish £10 notes.'[6] A more serious-sounding tour, 'The Archaeology of Macbeth', covers eight days of exploration, promising 'to untangle the history of Macbeth and the truth behind the play' for the serious rate of $3,640.[7] The Swiss firm *Macbeth International* 'is a boutique luxury lifestyle management company providing global bespoke advisory services'[8] ('Beware the Thane of Fife'?).

Commodifying Macbeth – the play and/or the characters – has been particularly extensive since the Second World War. Today, the Metropolitan Opera gift shop sells 'Lady Macbeth's Guest Soap. Out, Damned Spot!' which one should 'Try … in the Macbath!'[9] The 'Macbeth Bracelet', on sale for $74.25, 'features the famous witches' incantation, "Double, double, toil and trouble," … engraved in a decorative script adapted from 17th-century handwriting'.[10] The Etsy website contains dozens of homemade and commercial items, from T-shirts, framed quotations, and more soap to Lady Macbeth candles, witches' hats, and, in response to the current pandemic, face masks bearing the witches' cauldron chants.[11] Choosing between the 'Eye of Newt Mug' and the 'All Hail Macbeth Water Bottle'[12] might be difficult for some, but surely no thane could resist the 'Macbeth "Damned Spot" Cufflinks' carried at Shakespeare's Globe Theatre in London.[13] This kind of Shakes-pop (Lanier 2002b: 148) occurs for all Shakespeareana, of course, but the ruling themes for Macbeth seem to be the witches, Lady Macbeth, blood, and a handful of the more famous speeches. No one needs to know Shakespeare's play to understand such broad cultural references. Indeed, the owners of 'Macbeth Footwear' offer this account of their company's genesis, in which the name seems wholly detached from its context: 'Macbeth, the names [sic] comes from one of Shakespeare's literary creation [sic], aiming to meet the demand for fashion forward shoes that illustrate the customs and culture of rock music and an active lifestyle in Southern California.'[14]

Macbeth's enormous popularity stems from several of its formal and thematic features: the play's openly political nature; its inclusion of supernatural elements; its parable of the dangers of ambition; its setting in Scotland, useful for 'heritage' versions; its violence; its focus on tyranny; its 'domestic' focus on a husband and wife; its extraordinary language and rich characterization. Interpretations easily pivot from a personal focus on the Macbeths as a couple virtually begging to be psychoanalysed, to political themes of authoritarian rule, to – improbably – the play as a contemporary tool ('Shakespeare's tale of ambition gone awry') for teaching business leadership ('Business'; see Lanier 2002a). Yet each of these features has also, at one time or another, been construed as a flaw or mistake that requires correction and, often, re-writing.

When I began this project, I knew that there would be too many adaptations (to say nothing of the mugs and T-shirts) to read or view and properly assess, but I confess to astonishment at the vast array that confronted me – I can only imagine the numbers for *Hamlet*. Although I refer to many different versions, I suspect that virtually every reader of this book will complain that I have left out a favourite adaptation: I can only plead guilty as charged. My analysis is, for example, woefully short on international versions, particularly the plenitude of materials from Asian sources. The MIT Global Shakespeare website alone lists thirty-five films or productions, from India, Thailand, Korea, Japan, China, Yemen, Brazil, Mexico, and others. Seminars at the Shakespeare Association of America and the European Shakespeare Research Association conferences are usefully extending the play's afterlives 'beyond its original Anglophone context'[15] in yet further directions. Some of these versions are inaccessible to me, quite literally as well as linguistically. I can also imagine that some readers will lament the absence of a detailed analysis of a particular work, and it is true that I have spent less space on some well-known versions – Kurosawa's great film *Throne of Blood*, for example, has a rich archive of analytic essays by some of the most eminent critics in our field, and I saw little point in trying to outgo them. On the other hand, I suspect that some of the versions I examine at length here – such as the *Secret History* or *La Señora Macbeth* – are less well-known, and are worth the space.

The examples that follow are not entirely arbitrary, then, but in truth they do depend in great part on accessibility, my own language capabilities and some serendipity (cf. *Joji* in the **Epilogue**). Dozens of innovative stage and opera productions could have been included, but instead I have chosen to show the breadth of adaptational strategies rather than plumb the depths of particular genres. Limitations of length also meant that some forms – comic books or computer simulation games, for example – did not receive sufficient attention. The range and number of adaptations here will nevertheless, I believe, provide a real sense of the possibilities that adaptation creates.

The First Folio text

The nature of *Macbeth*'s text provides one reason for the play's susceptibility to transformation: the shortest of the tragedies, it exists as a Folio-only text but with evident signs of revision (perhaps only minor additions) by Thomas Middleton, probably around 1615, perhaps earlier.[16] In recent years scholars have renewed efforts to understand the text's origin(s) and features. After reviewing some of its logical problems (such as the sequence from 3.6 to 4.1, where Macbeth seems to know, and then not know, about Macduff's flight to England), Arthur Kinney comments that 'this notably imperfect text denies the organicism desired by critics using the earlier New Critic [*sic*] paradigm of organicism; such basic coherence is not now available to any reader, student, or performer' (2001: 280–1). Kinney's enlightened view of 'what was essentially an unfixed text' (282), however, seems undermined in the language of his account of other editors' discoveries: some, he said, found 'corrupting practices', including compositional 'error' (282) and 'the text may be further contaminated by at least one other hand' (283). The Folio text, he concludes, 'is itself sufficiently corrupt that it denies total reintegration without the participation of actors, spectators, or readers'. We must, he concludes 'admit the necessity, *to make sense* of the play, of a reordering of parts and by our own amending imaginations' (284; my emphasis). The rhetoric of 'corruption', 'error' and 'contamination' implies, in spite of Kinney's post-modern gestures, an authentic original, somewhere, that once was healthy and whole, but now is contaminated and diseased, so that we are justified in 'reordering' some of it 'to make sense [what kind?] of the play'.[17]

In his reconsideration of the First Folio text and its perceived problems, Anthony B. Dawson suggests that the play's shortness has been overemphasized: 'the differences in length between it and the rest of the tragedies are often exaggerated' (2014: 19), citing *Timon of Athens* and *Titus Andronicus* for comparison. The copy that reached the printer, Dawson argues, '(probably a transcript and not the play-book itself) was in a sense palimpsestic, the result of different stagings with different directions, additions or cuts' (22), and that 'it's just as likely that the inconsistency [the 3.6 to 4.1 issue], such as it is, was there in the original version' (23).

Brett Gamboa has argued 'that *Macbeth* is built to fail' from the perspective of performance (2014: 33). The play's structure 'intensifies the engagement of audiences by exploiting their attachment to what is progressively denied them .... failure is central to the play' (33). Such traditional perceptions of failure as the play's less-dramatic second half, the disappearance of Fleance, the awkwardness and length of 4.3, and the lack of a death speech for Macbeth could, he suggests, be part of a design by which the audience 'might experience tragedy as Macbeth does. In other words, audiences face their own powerlessness before a play that had formerly super-empowered them, and their own disappointment in a character that had electrified them, in order to experience a fall that parallels Macbeth's own after being crowned a king' (47).[18] Gamboa thus thematizes the text's commonly perceived logical and structural problems as part of a larger aesthetic design, and in effect accepts the Folio text as is, without feeling Kinney's 'necessity' of 'reordering' some of it.[19]

Does the Folio text of *Macbeth* in fact contain more errors of chronology, logic, or plot than Shakespeare's other plays? Anyone who examines the textual discussion sections of the Arden, Oxford, or New Cambridge editions will find similar problems in all of them, I would argue, from the confusions of the masking scene in *Love's Labour's Lost* and the geographical errors in *The Two Gentlemen of Verona* to the vexed theories of the transmission of *Hamlet*'s texts to the puzzling chronological elements and logical issues in *Cymbeline*. *Pericles* is of course a textual island unto itself. Yet the desire for completeness and for answers (just how many children *did* Lady Macbeth have?) to unanswerable questions persists through editing practices – and adaptations.

No doubt few adapters have felt entirely comfortable with G. K. Hunter's assertion that 'the text as we have it is entirely intelligible, orderly and coherent' (Hunter 2005: 94), or Nicholas Brooke's that the 'text is a good one, overall' (Brooke 1990: 49). Certainly many elements of the First Folio *Macbeth* puzzle the will. But the alternative to acceptance, in terms of editorial practice, is to repair the problematic speech prefixes, verbal cruxes, or illogical stage directions, for example, while the alternative, in terms of critical and imaginative response, is to adapt – rewrite – the text. Not all the adaptations considered in this book originate in a critique of the Folio text, to be sure; anti-colonialist discourse, to take one example, seeks to rewrite the play in order to resist the hegemony of English (or more broadly Western) culture, while other adaptations want to borrow some of Shakespeare's cultural capital to enhance their projects' prestige. And some, like Bertolt Brecht, see *Macbeth* as 'a good story not of far away and long ago but recurring again and again in common life without losing its profound appeal' (Brecht 1997a: 143) (see Chapters **One** and **Four** for more on Brecht), and thus well worth retelling.

Adaptation and revision

Three recent examples of adaptation indicate some typical critiques and repairs of the First Folio text. First, the authors of a 2012 novelization of the play declared that 'we decided to like the Macbeths, not to excuse their actions, but to try to explain them, to afford them an inner life that went beyond whatever the play could tell us, and then to watch them make a series of bad choices that escalate' (Hartley and Hewson 2012: 319), so they proceed, as many adapters do, by 'filling out what is passed over' in the play (311). Second, in his 'Genetic Text' of the play, in his edition of Middleton, Gary Taylor imagined that in the pre-Middleton-revision text of the play, Shakespeare had actually shown Edward the Confessor enter, rather than remaining offstage in 4.3. Taylor produced this invented stage direction: '*Solemn music. Enter at the other door Saint Edward the Confessor with Siward and monks. He touches the sufferers and hangs a golden chain about their necks and they arise healed and exeunt*' (2007: 1195). Taylor argues that Middleton (but not Shakespeare) *may* 'have been uncomfortable with the celebration of a Catholic saint, especially if his appearance here were accompanied by any kind of religious ritual' (1194) and so cut it (the implication being that Shakespeare *was* comfortable with it). And so, without any evidence beyond an indistinct feeling about both Shakespeare's and Middleton's religious comfort levels,

Taylor produced it. Finally, unsatisfied not only with the ending of the play but with a variety of its elements, Noah Lukeman in 2008 announced that '*Macbeth* is unfinished' (v), and so wrote a sequel, *The Tragedy of Macbeth, Part II: The Seed of Banquo*, in which he supplied what he felt had been 'omitted from the play' (vi). These adaptations rewrite the Folio text in a manner so that it will 'make sense' in a particular way – the perceived problems are the lack of a sufficient 'inner life', scenes said to be cut from an original that does not exist, and the play fails to resolve the Fleance plot. Similar examples could be provided 'til the crack of doom.

The play's overall structure, especially Macbeth's part, has often been said to be flawed. In praising Laurence Olivier's 1955 production, for example, Kenneth Tynan in effect made Olivier's triumph the exception to the general rule, and succinctly expressed what many theatre professionals had said over the years: 'As the play proceeds, the hero shrinks; complex and many-levelled to begin with, he ends up a cornered thug, lacking even a death-scene with which to regain lost stature' (Kliman 2004: 73–4).[20] Orson Welles went even further, claiming that

> no actor in the history of theater has ever been a great Macbeth. Why? Because there has never been an actor who could perform the first and second parts of the play. For this play has a great defect, an imperfection: the Macbeth who is the victim of Lady Macbeth is not the one who then becomes king. No actor has ever been able to play both parts equally well. The actor must be brutally simple and completely natural to play the first part, and extremely cerebral to play the second part.

In other words, Welles concluded, 'Laurence Olivier would have to play in the first part, and John Gielgud in the second' (Miola 2014: 113). Note that Tynan's 'complex and many-levelled' Macbeth in the first part is contradicted by Welles' 'brutally simple and completely natural' version, and Macbeth is either a 'cornered thug' or 'extremely cerebral' in the second half. Macbeth's very nature, then, often defies categorization even within similar concepts of the play's structural flaw.

Many scholars and directors have criticized the lack of a death scene for Macbeth – a dying speech such as Hamlet and Lear have – but this lack would soon be remedied, as we will see in

Chapter One. And Bertolt Brecht ventriloquized earlier complaints, as we will see, about the asymmetry of the witches' prophecies, which fail to be realized in the case of Fleance. The Porter Scene, too, has frequently been faulted for its irrelevance to the rest of the play (or its impropriety: thus 'when Schiller adapted *Macbeth* for Goethe's stage, he replaced the porter scene with a pious morning song' [Höfele 2016a: 216]).[21] Critics, directors, and actors have been especially drawn to supposed 'missing' scenes because the 'incongruities and gaps in the narrative', as Mariangela Tempera points out, suggest that 'something is missing, scenes from the original play have not survived'. But, as she goes on to note, the 'suspected cut may indeed simply point to a more sophisticated strategy of writing than critics are prepared to hypothesize' (1993: 61); she quotes H. W. Fawkner's astute comment that the cut 'is a productive and constitutive *feature* of the play – not merely something external that may (or may not) happen to the text after the time of its completion' (1993: 61; my emphasis). Stephen Orgel, on the other hand, notes that 'arguments that make the muddles not the result of cutting but an experiment in surreal and expressionistic dramaturgy only produce more questions, rendering the play a total anomaly' (1999: 145). Neo-classical and post-Romantic theories of the unified and coherent text, in addition to modern proclivities towards psychoanalysis and causal order, may have warped our perceptions of the play's features – or rather, attempted to unwarp them, to straighten out and regularize the play's features.

I will engage the play's adaptation history not through a linear narrative, but through several tropes of interpretation that have recurred since 1606, analysing how translations and adaptations have understood or explained the play, particularly in repeated attempts to regularize elements of the play that are, by formalist, realist, and modern psychological standards, admittedly quite irregular. To borrow Foucault's phrase (if not his exact concept) from *Discipline and Punish*, I see these attempts to fill in gaps, resolve plot-lines, and expand on characters' 'inner lives' as part of a normalizing process designed to produce 'docile [dramatic] bodies' susceptible to logic and obedient to linear plots with coherent psychological motives. I argue that the play's supposed irregularities have been one of the major forces drawing adapters to their work, and that many, perhaps most adaptations attempt to 'make sense' by rewriting the apparent irregularities.[22]

My choice of interpretive tropes crosses various genre boundaries, modes of media, and elite/popular culture divides, from historic productions to contemporary novelizations and young adult literature, opera, and gangster *noir* films. Some versions, such as Davenant's, appear in more than one chapter. Some chapters focus on a single character as an index to the play's changing shape, but my approach is in no way a character analysis. I use the terms 'version', 'adaptation', and 'appropriation' more or less interchangeably. I assiduously seek to avoid the fallacy of 'fidelity' while necessarily pointing out how a given adaptation reimagines the Folio. The works of art considered – plays, novels, films, operas, symphonies – are *all* 'unfaithful', which is to say that they are all interpretations of one kind or another. Some will seem more outlandish than others, some simply the product of their times, some mindlessly banal, some a violently original intervention. The versions of the play found in the immersive, deconstructed *Sleep No More* and in the one-man performance by Alan Cumming (as a patient in a mental hospital) may seem radical to audiences accustomed to what has been termed the 'brand' of the 'normative MACBETH': 'There is at any given time a prevailing consensus which informs what readers will consider to be a *Macbeth*' (Fedderson and Richardson 2008: 301). In her influential work on adaptation (2013: 9), Hutcheon argues that 'sequels and prequels are not really adaptations either, nor is fan fiction', but I have taken a wider view here, and consider several prequels and sequels, some of them among the most interesting and provocative responses to *Macbeth*.

Developments in aesthetic theory from the nineteenth to the twenty-first century have dramatically shifted how various elements of the play could be perceived; today's 'normative' version of the play differs in many ways from, say, the version seen by Samuel Pepys in 1667. The concept of the unitary formal text, which some adapters hold as an underlying assumption, ignores the hybrid nature of this and so many other early modern plays, as Jeremy Lopez (2017) has demonstrated. All Shakespearean texts are hybrid in the sense that they are mediated, but some texts are more hybrid than others, and some texts are critiqued more than others through later analysis. The kinds of textual difficulties discovered by editors, scholars, actors, directors, and readers of *The Comedy of Errors*, for example, are quite different from the 'problems' attributed to *Macbeth*. This is both self-evident, since they are very different plays, but also crucial to my sense that *Macbeth* has been revised and adapted far more than most of Shakespeare's plays. But revision and adaptation of the story of Macbeth did not begin with Middleton or Davenant: it began soon after the historical Macbeth's death in 1057. The pre- and post-Folio accounts of the witches reflect the earliest adaptations of *Macbeth*.

Creating the supernatural

While the First Folio is the starting point for this book, more than five *hundred* years of Macbeth discourse existed prior to 1606: Shakespeare's play is itself an adaptation of preexisting narratives that differ in many ways from the Folio, especially in terms of the supernatural. Indeed, the development of the supernatural over the five hundred years before Shakespeare rewrote the various traditions that he inherited is an exemplary case of what Douglas Lanier has described (invoking Deleuze and Guattari) as the 'rhizomatic' network of adaptations of Shakespeare: a rhizomatic structure is 'a horizontal, decentered multiplicity of subterranean roots that cross each other, bifurcating and recombining, breaking off and restarting' (2014: 28). Thus, while the brief history that follows proceeds chronologically, the various texts have often developed not through action-reaction causal links, but through several different 'subterranean' paths.

The earliest Scottish chronicles of the historical Macbeth's reign (1040-57 CE) never mention witches, witchcraft, the supernatural, prophecies, Banquo, Fleance, Macduff, or Lady Macduff. The first of these histories, the *Chronicle* (*c.* 1082) of Marianus Scotus, states the entire story in the briefest terms: 'Duncan, the king of Scotland, was killed in autumn (on the nineteenth day before the Kalends of September,) by his earl, Macbeth, Findlaech's son; who succeeded to the kingdom, [and reigned] for seventeen years'(Anderson 1922: 1.579).[23] Other early accounts say even less: 'Macbeth, Findlaech's son, reigned for seventeen years. And he was killed in Lumphanan, by Malcolm, Duncan's son; and was buried in the island of Iona' (Anderson 1922: 1.600). Granted that these chronicles are primarily king-lists, still, the stories of Duncan's death and Macbeth's reign and death are terse. Later versions invent episodes, motivations, and characters, including the witches. John Fordun's fourteenth-century *Chronica Gentis Scotorum* – apparently the first full-length narrative of Macbeth – describes Duncan's overthrow as in part his own fault: 'He was, it seems, too long-suffering, or rather easy-going, a king … He was so gentle and mild that he punished no one at all', hence he was an easy mark for Macbeth, 'by whom he [Duncan] was privily wounded unto death at Bothgofnane' (Fordun 1872: 4.180). Macbeth was 'hedged round with bands of the disaffected and at the head of a powerful force', and so 'seized the kingly dignity in A.D. 1040, and reigned seventeen years' (4.180). No prophecy, no witchcraft, no Lady Macbeth, no Banquo or Fleance, no supernatural elements to the story: just the same straightforward narrative of treachery and murder that – according to the English – had characterized the Scottish monarchy for centuries.

But then Andrew Wyntoun's *Original Chronicle of Scotland* (1406) says that Macbeth murdered Duncan – not simply slew him in battle – after he had a dream:

> One night he thought in his dreaming / That sitting he was beside the King, / … He thought while he was so sitting, / He saw three women then, thought he, / Three weird Sisters most like to be; / The first he heard say going by, / 'Lo, yonder the Thane of Cromarty!' / The other woman said again, / 'Of Moray yonder I see thee Thane'. / All this he heard in his dreaming. (Wyntoun 1872: 2.1850–70)[24]

The nature of the three women he thinks he sees remains ambiguous – they were 'most like to be' 'Three weird Sisters', but it was all a dream. Macbeth's motive for killing Duncan, then, originates (in Fordun) in 'the wickedness of a family … the head of which was Machabeus' (Fordun 1872: 4.180), and in Wyntoun, in Macbeth's own mind, where he dreams the prophecies ('The fantasy thus of his dream / Moved him most to slay his eme [uncle]' [Wyntoun 1872: 2.1875–6]). Similarly, in his *Historia Majoris Britanniae Angliae quam Scotiae* (1521), John Major says that Duncan was 'secretly put to death by the faction which had been till then in opposition. He was mortally wounded by one Machabeda at Lochgowane … Now those kings showed a grave want of foresight, in that they found no way of union and friendship with the opposing faction ... for to gain a kingdom many a wicked act is done' (Major 1892: 120–1). Wickedness, dreams of ambition, factional conflict: the secular nature of the crime, even though it is against royalty, could not be clearer.

It should be noted that Wyntoun first (apparently) introduced a supernatural element into the narrative, for Macbeth's mother, we are told in a later section, one day walking in the woods for the air, met a handsome man, 'proportioned well in all measure', slept with him, 'and on her that time too soon got / This Makbeth', and 'he the Devil was that him got' (Wyntoun 1872: 2.1911–8, 1925), who then made the prophecy that 'no man should be born of wife / Of power to rewe [rob, deprive forcibly] him his life' (2.1929–30). As several scholars have noted, Wyntoun's story has many elements of Norse and Celtic mythology, such as Macbeth's conception. According to Cowan, 'The story of MacBeth's father is basically a Celtic *compert* or conception tale and so is that relating to Malcolm's birth. MacBeth thus joins the ranks of other "fatherless" heroes' (1993: 132).[25] Dreams and visitations of course often derive from supernatural sources, but Wyntoun's 'thre wemen' are not further described, and are a 'fantasy' in Macbeth's head that moved him to commit the crime.

Hector Boece's 1527 narrative *Historia Gentis Scotorum* is a landmark (not necessarily a positive one) in the adaptation of the Macbeth narrative: it is full of new, invented scenes and events, ranging from the characters of Banquo and Fleance to the names and dates of the mythical first forty-five kings between Fergus I and Fergus II.[26] Boece also greatly developed Wyntoun's dream of the 'Three weird Sisters' into actual mysterious figures. Now, they are 'clothed in elrage [i.e. "eldritch"=unnatural] and uncouth weed [garment]', who 'suddenly vanished out of sight' (2.259) after delivering the prophecies (now not in a dream).[27] After killing Duncan, Macbeth recalls 'the prophecy of the foresaid witches' and would have slain Macduff had not 'a witch, in whom he had great confidence, said, to put him out of all fear, That he should never be slain with man that was borne of wife; nor vanquished, until the wood of Birnam were come to the castle of Dunsinnane' (2.269). Boece thus formalized the second set of prophecies, adding the one about Birnam Wood, all of them the product of 'false illusions of the devil' (2.269; repeated 2.274). Boece also produced a Lady

Macbeth that greatly amplified the sparse (and in the earliest cases, non-existent) references to her in the preceding narratives:

> His wife, impatient of long tarry, as all women are, especially where they are desirous of any purpose, gave him great artation [urging] to pursue the third weird, that she might be a queen: calling him oft timid, feeble coward, and not desirous of honours; since he durst not assail the thing with manhood and courage, which is offered to him by benevolence of fortune; howbeit sundry others have assailed such things before, with most terrible jeopardy, when they had not such certainty to succeed in the end of their labours as he had. (2.260)

Macbeth, 'be [by] persuasion of his wife', gathered his allies (now including an invented Banquo), and 'slew King Duncan' forthwith.

Boece's account was largely taken over by Raphael Holinshed, Shakespeare's main, direct source for his play. Holinshed describes 'three women in strange and wild apparel, resembling creatures of elder world' who give the first set of prophecies, then 'vanished immediatly' ([1587] 1808: 5.268). Holinshed then adds an interpretation of these figures: 'afterwards the common opinion was, that these women were either the weird sisters, that is (as ye would say) the goddesses of destiny, or else some nymphs or feiries, endued with knowledge of prophesy by their necromantical science, because everything came to pass as they had spoken' (5.269). Yet the well-known illustration of the three witches in the 1577 edition of Holinshed shows something less than 'strange and wild apparel', as the three women are more dowager-like than the typical period illustrations of witches.

In his account of the attempt on Macduff, Holinshed's Macbeth hesitates: 'but that a certain witch, whom he had in great trust, had told that he should never be slain with man born of any women, nor vanquished till the wood of Bernane came to the castle of Dunsinane' (5.274). This (single) 'witch' seems, at least in Holinshed's phrasing, to be distinct from the three weird sisters and from yet another prophecy by 'certain wizards, in whose words he put great confidence (for that the prophesy had happened so right, which the three fairies or weird sisters had declared unto him) how that he ought to take heed of Makduffe, who in time to come should seek to destroy him' (5.274). Holinshed concludes Macbeth's reign by noting, as Boece had, that after Macbeth's ten years of good rule, 'by illusion of the devil, he defamed the same [deeds] with most terrible cruelty' (5.277). Boece's elaborate portrait of Lady Macbeth, however, is boiled down to a single sentence in Holinshed: 'his wife lay sore upon him to attempt the thing, as she that was very ambitious, burning in unquenchable desire to bear the name of a queen' (5.269).

John Leslie's 1578 history, *De origine, moribus et rebus gestis Scotorum* (see **Figure 5**), also following Boece, initially relates that 'vainglory of spirit puffed up Macbeth, filling his mind with an insane lust for rule, insomuch that (his wife urging him on, when he was fearful, with hope of a happy outcome) he impiously murdered the saintly (*sanctissimum*) King Duncan' (Bullough 1975: 7.518). But Leslie returns in a later chapter to the reign of Macbeth when he sets forth the origin of the Stewarts in Banquo's descendants: Macbeth 'understood, by the prophecy of some women – or rather Demons who assumed the likeness of women and were the sure causes of treason, hatred and strife – that after his line was extinct that of Banquo would flourish and reign for a long time etc.' (7.519). Leslie is so concerned to demonize Macbeth that in his main entry on Macbeth's reign he dismisses the entry in Marianus Scotus (otherwise considered an authority) that 'The king of Scotland, Macbeth, scattered money like seed to the poor, at Rome' (Anderson 1922: 1.588) on the grounds that Macbeth's tyranny was too great for such a religious pilgrimage; instead, in the kind of revision we see throughout Macbeth narratives, he says, '[I] am persuaded rather to believe the same to have been of whom now we shall make mention, to wit Malcolm', who during Macbeth's reign of terror, 'obtained both the ornament and glory of a Prince most godly and righteous, in visiting religious and holy places' (Leslie 1888: 1.308). A misplaced speech prefix, then, to borrow language of the theatre. Leslie thus dramatically enhanced the exaltation of Malcolm (to be further examined in **Chapter Two**) through his revisionist history.

A few years after Holinshed's first edition of 1577, George Buchanan's *History* of 1582 developed a parallel secular reading of the narrative in depth, blaming both the victim and the murderer, while also reporting that the prophecies came just through a dream:

Mackbeth, who had always a Disgust at the un-active Slothfulness of his Cousin; and thereupon had conceived a secret

Hope of the Kingdom in his Mind, was further encouraged in his Ambitious Thoughts, by a Dream which he had: For one Night, when he was far distant from the King, he seemed to see Three Women, whose Beauty was more August and Surprizing than bare Womens useth to be, of which, one Saluted him, *Thane* of *Angus* [etc.] ... His Mind, which was before Sick, betwixt Hope and Desire, was mightily encouraged by this Dream, so that he contrived all possible ways, by which he might obtain the Kingdom. (Buchanan 1690: 7.210)

Given his 'Sick' mind, and 'spurred on, by the daily Importunities of his Wife' (who was Privy to all his Counsels'), Macbeth murdered Duncan. Buchanan's 'Three Women' are of 'Surprizing' beauty, and the dream only 'further encouraged' the 'Ambitious Thoughts' that already possessed him. Indeed, Buchanan completely dismissed the supernatural moments of the earlier chronicle histories: 'Some of our Writers do here Record many Fables, which are like Milesian Tales, and fitter for the Stage, than an History; and therefore I omit them' (7.214). 'Milesian fables', he said in an earlier note, were 'so far from being true that they had not the least shadow of Truth in them' (2.77).

In Buchanan's narrative, Duncan is an 'effeminate and slothful King' (7.207), incapable of effective rule, as a result of which '*Mackbeth* ... had conceived a secret Hope of the Kingdom in his Mind' (7.210), prior to the dream. Moreover, when Duncan made his son '*Malcolm*, scarce yet out of his Childhood, Governor of *Cumberland*, *Mackbeth* took this matter mighty Hainously; in regard, he look'd upon it as Obstacle of Delay to him, in his obtaining the Kingdom' since 'the Government of *Cumberland* was always look'd upon, as the first step to the Kingdom of *Scotland*' (210). Duncan's naming of Malcolm, an attempt to reinstitute King Kenneth's change in the system of succession, is thus a prime but typical example of the perils of the new system, in which an incompetent (e.g. a childlike Malcolm) could become king; moreover, the violation of the old system offends those who rest their belief in tradition. (We will see this aspect of the narrative taken up by later adapters.) In Buchanan's version, Macbeth is certainly a violent warrior and an ambitious man, as he is in Shakespeare's, but he is also more clearly wronged, and in some ways had, as David Norbrook has noted in an important essay, 'half-buried associations with constitutionalist traditions', a figure in whom 'vestiges remain of a worldview in which regicide could be a noble rather than an evil act'.[28]

Well before Shakespeare's play, then, the story of Macbeth had become a token in competing political and religious narratives; his story received 'correction' and 'adjustments' almost from the beginning, as the political winds shifted direction. The earliest accounts of Macbeth do not include women, witches, prophecies, the supernatural, or (until 1527) Banquo and Fleance at all; in these versions, Duncan is a weak king, Macbeth's ambition is his own, arising partly from the power vacuum that seemed to invite him, and the witches are nothing more than a dream or even an outright invention. With Wyntoun and especially Boece, however, the process of demonization begins, supernatural elements are added and the good deeds of the first ten years of Macbeth's seventeen-year reign are erased. Holinshed provided a version of this narrative that Shakespeare, for the most part, followed. But it is clear that many strands of the Macbeth story were in circulation through adaptation and revision, and available for Shakespeare's appropriation.

A few years after Shakespeare's play premiered, Simon Forman saw it at the Globe in 1611, remarking 'howe Mackbeth and Bancko, 2 noble men of Scotland, Ridinge thorowe a wod, the{r} stode before them 3 women feiries or Nimphes, And saluted Macbeth, sayinge' the prophecies to him (Chambers 1988: 2.337). As Braunmuller (1997: 58) and others have noted, Forman seems also to have read Holinshed's narrative, not only because of the episode with the horses (the men 'Ridinge'), which are not in the Folio text, but also because of the echo of Holinshed's reference to 'some nymphs or feiries'. Forman, in any event, never mentions the witches again, and if they were shocking or unusual, they impressed him less than the other supernatural element in the play, the ghost of Banquo.

Sir William Davenant's adaptation for the Restoration stage (1663–4) reflected different aesthetic preferences from those of 1606, and a (partly successful) intensification of pro-royalist sentiments in the play. Thus he amplified the roles of Lady Macbeth and Lady Macduff (even having them meet and speak together), in order in part to produce some structural symmetry; introduced a new figure, the ghost of Duncan, that had seemed lacking; and fulfilled the missing prophecy by bringing Fleance back at the end (see **Chapter Three**).

He paid special attention to the witches, adding new scenes and, more importantly, new aspects of their representation. Now they both fly (*'Enter three Witches flying'* [1674: 3]) and are highly musical, singing several songs (from Middleton's *The Witch*) and dancing (*'Musick. The witches Dance and Vanish'* [49]), and their number has multiplied, the traditional three in some scenes, four in others, plus Hecate, and possibly two others at the end of the second act. The witches appear to the Macduffs, moreover, with further ominous prophecies, making the play even more insistently about 'Title', or legitimacy:

> *3 Witch*. Many more murders must this one ensue,
> As if in death were propagation too.
> *2 Witch*. He will.
> *1 Witch*. He shall.
> *3 Witch*. He must spill much more bloud,
> And become worse, to make his Title good. (26)

The *Chorus* that follows expresses more directly the witches' anti-royalist nature: 'We shou'd rejoice when good Kings bleed. / When cattel die, about we go, / What then, when Monarchs perish, should we do?' (27) and their Second Song follows suit: 'We gain more life by *Duncan*'s death' (28). After Davenant, singing and dancing witches became the norm in productions throughout the eighteenth and nineteenth centuries, their numbers ever increasing: Kemble had a chorus of fifty or more singing witches in his 1794 production (Donohue 1967).[29] This trend continued well into the twentieth century, though more recent adaptations have featured sinister, uncanny, and threatening witches,[30] while others have offered such eccentric representations as two corrupt policemen (the film *Maqbool*), three innocent-seeming schoolgirls (Wright's film), three scruffy bin men (Brozel's *Shakespeare ReTold* film), or three 'nurses' (**Figure 1**).

The Macbeth narrative, over a period of time, was thus transformed from a typical Scottish account of secular ambition, rival factions, and weak or strong kings, to a narrative of supernatural intrusion, demonic prophecy, secret murder, and the disruption of lineage. R. J. Adam has argued that the demonization may have sprung from local politics: 'Moray [Macbeth's home] remained the great danger to the Normanizing, Anglicizing house

FIGURE 1 *The witches.* Macbeth *directed by Rupert Goold* © *PBS Home Video/WNET.org 2010. All rights reserved. Screen grab.*

of Malcolm Ceann-mòr for almost a century after his death', and so the story of Duncan received a post hoc 'tragic colour which contemporaries had not seen' and 'projected on to the greatest maormaer of Moray something of the hatred and fear which the stubborn Celtic rearguard inspired' (1957: 387).

No doubt many chroniclers indebted to the Scottish throne felt the pressure to demonize Macbeth and associate him with the supernatural, particularly through prophecy, which had been associated by many writers with witchcraft, King James among them (in his *Daemonology* [1597]). But there were parallel sceptical (secular) discourses in which prophecy was the product of fabrication and illusion, with distinctly political implications, as Keith Thomas has shown.[31] Howard Dobin, Jr., has noted that 'In practical terms, all prophecies voiced outside the auspices of crown and church were treated as demonic or fraudulent' (1990: 45), thus identifying the demonic prophecies in *Macbeth* as 'intentionally duplicitous … [which] preserved, by contrast, the ideology of univocal meaning; the devil's lies only validated God's truth' (76). When King James and his court journeyed to Oxford on 29 August 1605, they witnessed an academic play by Matthew Gwinn, and were greeted after its performance with a brief, staged prophecy fawning over the relatively new king's power ('Hail, whom Scotland serves!

Whom England, hail!' etc.) and his supposed lineage ('Thou dost restore the fourfold glory of Canute') (Bullough 1975: 7.470–2).[32] In terms of the present argument, the main item of interest is that the prophecies were spoken by *'three (as it were) Sibyls ... as if from a wood'* ['*tres quasi Sibyllae, sic (Ut é sylva)*'] who identify themselves as 'We three same Fates'.

Any such prophetic figures associated with or emanating from sovereign power would be construed as Sibyls, beautiful women, fairies, dream-like, while any such figures associated with opposition to sovereign power would be demonized, represented as the frightening, seditious creatures. Kings, it seems, may have sybils prophesy to them, but tyrants would have only witches.[33] As a supreme example in the play, Malcolm reports to Macduff (who has come to the English court to appeal to Malcolm in 4.3), that the saintly King Edward the Confessor not only possesses the miraculous 'touch' that heals the 'Evil', but 'With this strange virtue, / He hath a heavenly gift of prophecy' (4.3.148–59). You say demonic, I say heavenly.

Like much else in Macbeth-discourse, the witches have been invented, then once established, radically transformed across the centuries, their supernatural natures undermined and overdetermined in turn, as the political or religious moment suggests. By the late twentieth century, Terry Eagleton could argue that 'to any unprejudiced reader – which would seem to exclude Shakespeare himself, his contemporary audiences and almost all literary critics – it is surely clear that positive value in *Macbeth* lies with the three witches. The witches are the heroines of the piece, however little the play itself recognizes the fact' (Eagleton 1986: 2). Eagleton's notorious comment reflects the attempts in recent decades to recast the witches in a more positive light, usually as demonized projections of patriarchal anxieties in contexts of patriarchal, religious, social, and political discourses.[34]

Shakespeare's representation of the witches in his play reflects the multiple, often contradictory associations of the previous narratives – chronicle adaptations, as it were. But the witches are only a part of the considerable adaptation that Shakespeare made of Holinshed and the other narratives he knew. Among the many key differences are Shakespeare's enormous expansion of Lady Macbeth's role, from the scant references; the erasure of Macbeth's ten years of enlightened rule and the twenty-five laws of equity that Macbeth introduced; the introduction of Banquo's ghost; and the erasure of Banquo's role as co-conspirator with Macbeth against Duncan. Although he shows Duncan to be a fatally passive king, Shakespeare also suppresses the more openly contemptuous comments on Duncan in Holinshed. While this book's focus will now be on adaptations and appropriations after 1606, it is important to note that Shakespeare was only one – the preeminent one, in retrospect – in a long line of adapters of the Macbeth story. The common theme evident in the following examples of adaptation is the ongoing effort to 'make sense' of the play's features. These examples most often look back to the play itself for inspiration, but it also seems evident that 'Macbeth' as a cultural idea has long since floated free of its moorings in any particular early modern text or even a modern 'normative' version. Rather, *Macbeth* is in a state, as Lanier says, of endless becoming, of 'non-unitary multiplicity' (2014: 27).

* * *

The chapters that follow are grouped and organized in different ways – perhaps something of a rhizomatic structure itself. The most prominent trope of interpretation is the political, broadly conceived. The first three chapters concern how various adaptations have overtly negotiated or appropriated its elements for political ends. But almost every chapter reveals a political or ideological agenda at work, whether knowingly or not by the adapter. Many of Shakespeare's plays can claim to be highly 'political' in terms of their themes and characters, and *Macbeth* is securely among them.

1

Political *Macbeth*

Writing to David Garrick in 1774 about his difficulties in adapting *Macbeth* for French audiences, Jean-François Ducis complained that 'I am dealing with a nation which demands no end of accommodating adjustments when one wants to lead them along the blood-drenched roads of terror' (Golder 1992: 163). Two centuries later, Heiner Müller commented that 'One can say a lot of things about Stalin with a production of *Macbeth*' (Weber and Young 2012: 4). It would be difficult to find writers more dissimilar than the ones quoted above, but both Ducis and Müller, otherwise so different, sought to counter what has been called the royalist interpretation of *Macbeth* – also known as the 'King James' or 'Authorized' version – in which the political ideologies embedded and enacted in the play are read as a defence of monarchical power and dynastic succession.[1] Such contrasting interpretations of *Macbeth* reflect larger arguments about Shakespeare's own politics, his affinity for republicanism on the one hand,[2] or his royalist inclinations (as one of the King's Men) on the other.[3] The earliest adapters of *Macbeth* generally reinforced the royalist interpretation.

Both Ducis and Müller, like other adapters, rewrote the play to reflect their political readings of it. But what does the word 'political' mean in such a context? Either: (1) the play's costume/setting/scenery has been updated to suggest or allegorize other time periods or political events, like Rupert Goold's 2010 'Stalinist' film version (which began as a stage production at the Chichester Festival in 2007); (2) the director/editor has emphasized some textual elements and suppressed others to make a particular point; (3) the play's plot and/or characters have been substantially rewritten to form a different 'message'; or (4) even the most traditional production, depending on its historical context, becomes 'political' simply for being performed. If one play could represent all of these categories, it is certainly *Macbeth*.

Here I will analyse how some adaptations revised the Folio to support or undermine political structures and regimes outside the play. This survey is admittedly limited in various ways and does not analyse individual actors' performances. Rather, I consider how a given adaptation revised the play's structure, plot, or characterization to support or resist a particular political position, with a special focus on how Macbeth's moral condition and Malcolm's succession are represented.[4] *Macbeth*'s plot opens up major questions about the nature of power and authority – whether sovereign power derives from the authority of God, or from the actions of man.[5] Michael Hattaway has noted (2013: 111) that the plot itself – its representations of tyranny and regicide – constituted a danger at its first production *c.* 1606: 'The very fact of placing a tragic action at court was, because of the particular decorum of English tragedy, likely to demystify the authority of prince and courtiers.' The demystification of state power through representations of regicide on the early modern stage may well have prepared the king's way to the scaffold, as Franco Moretti (1982) and others have argued. For later royalist adapters, the depictions of regicide might provide an unpleasant reminder of Charles I's execution. Yet even when Macbeth's murder is justified as tyrannicide, the play has seemed equally dangerous. In many post-1945 countries, totalitarian authorities condemned plays which, in their interpretation, seemed to reflect all too closely critiques of their rule as authoritarian, or failed to portray 'progressive ideas' of the dominant ideology. If the plays (they believed) mirrored their own actions, then they could not be staged or seen; such censorship is often premised on simple and unambiguous interpretations of the plays themselves. *Macbeth* sets its regicides in a foreign land, a violent, primitive Scotland, but this land of thanes and witchcraft has served as a screen through which aspects of the social and political order outside the play have been viewed.

Macbeth himself, over the centuries, eventually transformed from a violent warrior in a near-savage feudal society – the apex of masculine action – into an anguished, increasingly weak husband dominated by his wife, full of guilt and remorse over his misguided ambition, and even mentally ill. Some modern adaptations enhance this interpretation by making Macbeth the product and victim of an oppressive social system, and attention often refocuses away from Macbeth's character to larger conceptions of political-historical process. Some modern adaptations, such as Goold's film, represent Macbeth as a fascist sociopath, calmly making a sandwich while ordering the murder of Banquo and Fleance, while others, like Branagh's 2013 staging, offer a kilted Heritage-heroic figure striding through the playing space, a deconsecrated church. Shakespeare's play is not a Rorschach test, with Macbeth the ambiguous figure on whom is projected a given culture's political anxieties, but there is no denying that the play has been rewritten and adapted in ways that represent culturally specific political fears and desires.[6] Although the play's politics may *seem* infinitely malleable, at the centre there is always murder.

England: Davenant, Garrick, and royal succession

The principle of royal succession in *Macbeth* – the 'line of kings' in 4.1[7] – has seemed self-evident to many readers, especially to those invested in the Authorized Version: Malcolm is the rightful king, and his crowning at the end represents a restitution of the legitimate, almost sacred line that Macbeth has interrupted.[8] Certainly most directors deployed this interpretation of the play in the first three centuries of the play's afterlife. Davenant's version of 1664 – the first full adaptation – produced a more conventional and patriotic final scene than the Folio provided. Macduff enters not with Macbeth's head, but 'with *Macbeths* Sword' (signifying Macduff as a minister of Justice), heralds Malcolm as King, and presents him with

> The Tyrants Sword, to shew that Heaven appointed
> Me to take Revenge for you, and all
> That suffered by his Power.
> ...
> Now *Scotland*, thou shalt see bright Day again,
> That Cloud's remov'd that did Ecclipse thy Sun,
> And Rain down Blood upon thee. As your Arms
> Did all contribute to this Victory;

So let your Voices all concur to give
One joyful Acclamation.
Long Live Malcolm, King of Scotland. (1674: 66; Klv)

In Malcolm's invented response, Davenant enhances the principles
of royalty and succession:

And may they [the titles of 'Earl'] still Flourish
On your Families; though like the Laurels
You have Won to Day, they Spring from a Field of Blood.
Drag his Body hence, and let it Hang upon
A Pinnacle in *Dunsinane*, to shew
To shew [sic] to future Ages what to those is due,
Who others Right, by Lawless Power pursue. (66; Klv)

The new titles, like the kingship itself, should follow through lineal
descent, and there is no question about 'Right' and legitimacy;
the unnamed Macbeth's body will become an exemplary semiotic
spectacle like the grisly description of the regicide Damiens'
execution in Foucault's *Discipline and Punish*.[9]
    Most strikingly, the final words of the play are now some freshly
written moralizing spoken by Macduff:

So may kind Fortune Crown your Raign with Peace,
As it has Crown'd your Armies with Success;
And may the Peoples Prayers still wait on you,
As all their Curses did *Macbeth* pursue:
His Vice shall make your Virtue shine more Bright,
As a Fair Day succeeds a Stormy Night. (66; Klv)

Now a morality fable, the play becomes a binary struggle between
the 'Crown' and Macbeth, between 'Virtue' and 'Vice', between
crowning and cursing, with the 'Fair Day' inevitably following (as
in Polonius's platitude[10]) the 'Stormy Night'. Loaded with royalist
buzz-words (crown, reign, crowned, prayers, virtue, succeeds), the
speech rhetorically sweeps away both the unpleasant violence that
has produced this moment but more importantly any conceivable
doubts about the legitimacy and moral authority of Malcolm's reign.
Earlier, in the 'show of kings' scene in 4.1, Davenant's revisions
of the Folio enhanced the racial and blood-lineal aspects of what

he saw to be the play's ideological framework, for after asking if Banquo's 'Issue' will 'succeed / Each other still till Dooms-day?', Davenant's Macbeth sees Banquo smiling, as seeming 'to say / That they are all Successors of his race' (48, 49); the Folio reads, more ambiguously, 'Banquo smiles upon me / And points at them for his' (4.1.122-3). The 'race' of future kings will 'succeed' in a naturalized progression that reveals no gaps or fissures. Still, as Lois Potter has shown, even Davenant's version rests on unstable ideological legs: the play now 'justifies both those who act and those who merely wait for the prophecies to be fulfilled. What it does *not* justify is Divine Right; Macbeth ... is not a fiend from hell, but a man who has pursued "others Right, by Lawless power"' (Potter 1989: 207).

Davenant had also added a dying moralizing line for Macbeth, whose Folio death comes silently in a stage direction; by contrast, Davenant's Macbeth gasps out 'Farewell vain World, and what's most vain in it, /*Ambition*' (65). A century later, when David Garrick prepared his version of the play, he kept some of Davenant's changes, and amplified Macbeth's dying final speech into full melodrama:

'Tis done – The scene of life will quickly close,
Ambition's vain delusive dreams are fled,
And now I wake to darkness, guilt, and horror –
I cannot bear it – Let me shake it off –
It wo'not be – My soul is clog'd with blood,
And cannot rise – I dare not ask for mercy! –
It is too late – Hell drags me down – I sink –
I sink – Oh! my soul's lost for ever. [*Dies*] (1753: 86)[11]

Garrick followed Davenant, too, in depicting subservience to monarchical authority with his stage direction: '*Enter* Macduff *with* Macbeth*'s sword, which kneeling he presents to* Malcolm' (87). Garrick (and the many who followed his lead) normalized Macbeth's death into a cautionary tale of misplaced 'Ambition', followed, in a moral chain, by 'guilt' and what seems to be a Faustus-like eternal damnation. The punishment for treasonous 'Ambition' is clearly acknowledged by the now-beaten Macbeth. Davenant and Garrick thus began the process of correcting what they perceived as the play's flawed aesthetic-political themes and structure, especially its ending, and bolstering what they interpreted as the play's support of kingship and succession.

Garrick's alterations also led, in both stage performances and contemporary scholarship, to an increasing attention centred on the character of Macbeth and the relative amount of sympathy an audience might feel for him.[12] The character/psychological emphasis inversely relates to the play's political issues: thus in Garrick's version, Macbeth was dominated 'mentally and physically by his wife', hence 'divested of responsibility for instigating evil …. [Macbeth] reiterate[d] ideals of masculine nobility through the expression of sensitive remorse', as seen in the new final death speech (Prescott 2004: 85). The drive for political power thus devolved into the story of a sensitive soul's personal ambition and punishment. Nietzsche, for one, saw the inadequacy of this interpretation: 'The man who imagines that the effect of Shakespeare's plays is a moral one, and that the sight of Macbeth irresistibly induces us to shun the evil of ambition, is mistaken, and he is mistaken once more if he believes that Shakespeare himself thought so' (Nietzsche 1974: 237). Yet the play's politics were, until the twentieth century, invariably interpreted as royalist (with some complications) and adaptations focused on character and emotion.

Ducis and European adaptation in the late eighteenth and nineteenth centuries

On 22 April 1798 – his last evening in Paris before departing to lead the invasion of Egypt – Napoleon Bonaparte attended a performance of Shakespeare's *Macbeth*. But it wasn't a play by 'Shakespeare' so much as one by Jean-François Ducis – the key figure in introducing Shakespeare to non-English speaking Europe – who had freely adapted the play from earlier translations by Pierre-Antoine de la Place (1746) and by Pierre Letourneur (1776). Ducis struggled with *Macbeth* for years, writing David Garrick in 1774 about his frustrations in finding a way to present 'the blood-drenched roads of terror' within a decorum suitable for his age. It evidently wasn't easy: Ducis continued rewriting the play for years following the inaugural 1784 production's failure after only seven performances.[13] The three versions I will refer to here – 1784, 1789, 1798 – reflect Ducis's evolving relations to royal power.

No matter how earnestly Ducis excised the play's considerable bloodshed and revised its structure – deleting the Lady Macduff scenes, for example, and pushing violent scenes into descriptions or even mere summaries – he could not eliminate the play's central action of regicide. Although the murder of Duncan 'is always referred to as parricide, never regicide' (Golder 1992: 204), Ducis's transformations of the plot circled closely around issues of sovereignty and rule. Frédégonde (=Lady Macbeth), for example, has a son Clotaire, for whom she will do anything. In the final act of the 1789 revision, Frédégonde enters the play's sleepwalking scene carrying a taper and dagger, walking 'blindly into the wings to stab her sons [now two of them] to death as they lie asleep' (214), in a morally symmetrical punishment for having deprived the kingdom of a father. The rightful son and heir, Malcôme, is crowned in both the 1784 and 1789 versions, and Macbeth is somewhat rehabilitated, stabbing himself after hailing Malcôme as the rightful king in 1784, and even dying while defending Malcôme from hired assassins in 1789 (171, 214).

In the revision perhaps most linked to the theme of sovereign rule, Ducis transformed the play's banquet scene into a coronation scene, and replaced Banquo's ghost with Duncan's. In the 1784 version, Duncan's ghost had appeared three times during the coronation ceremony, pushing Macbeth away as he tried to sit on the throne. The stage direction reads:

[Macbeth] sees the spectre or shadow of King Duncan... standing and bloody before the door and on the level of the chamber where this Sovereign and the Prince Glamis have been massacred. From the top of this stage the spectre reveals itself in the eyes of Macbeth and the spectators, but the theater is arranged in such a way ... [that] only Macbeth... can see it. (185)

In the 1789 production, however, the coronation scene was cut, and as Macbeth 'reaches for the crown, Duncan's ghost reappears in his mind's eye' (212).

When Ducis revised the play for the 1798 performance before Napoleon, Ducis had to attack the text once again, removing as many references to royalist discourse as possible – kings, princes, crown, sceptre, all in all a considerable percentage of a play that contains three Scottish kings, refers to a fourth (the off-stage English king), stages two regicides, and alludes to nearly every theory of kingship available in the early modern period. Moreover, the coronation scene was back, though Ducis had scrubbed the text and turned the scene about as far from Divine Right theory as possible. In earlier versions, the character Loclin (a man of the people) had offered the crown to Macbeth, but now in 1798, 'instead of offering Macbeth a crown, Loclin lifts an impressive folio volume from an ornate cushion, and holds it out to him':

> Macbeth, Duncan is no longer, I bring before you
> This sign of power, the book of the law.
> If it assures you that it gives you the empire,
> Of your sacred duties it must also instruct you. (219)[14]

Displacing the crown, 'the book of the law' signals Ducis's resistance to potential tyranny.

In all of Ducis's versions, Macbeth suffers from an extraordinary, crippling guilt which eventually leads to his partial redemption; one of the actors in the initial version had taken to referring to the play as the 'Traité du Remords' (165). In the 1798 version, Loclin, in handing the 'book of laws' to Macbeth, had commanded him to swear 'That your heart will be sensitive to the good of the state, / That you are nothing here but a first citizen, / Who will do all by law, who without the law is nothing' (219-20). Turning the 'dead butcher' into a man of law, a *'premier citoyen'*, would be a neat trick if it could be done. But it couldn't, neither for Macbeth nor for Napoleon.[15] (The reaction of Napoleon – no stranger to blood or terror himself – is not known.) For this eighteenth-century French audience, the play needed to be de-royalized and its politics domesticated; by contrast, for twenty-first-century audiences, dealing with their own Bonaparte-tyrants, appropriations and adaptations recognize and often enhance its terror. Many other countries would follow Ducis's lead in the eighteenth and nineteenth centuries, indeed his was often the only version of the play available and served to introduce *Macbeth* throughout Europe.

In Spain, for example,[16] Ducis's *Macbeth* reached the Spanish stage in 1803 (Gregor 2010: 42–3). After that, the Napoleonic and other political upheavals led to a long hiatus, and *Macbeth* – found to be 'disgusting' and 'absurd' by some critics adhering to neoclassical models (41) – finally appeared again in 1838 in Madrid, but without success. Gregor quotes the single surviving review which critiqued the irrelevance of Scotland to Spain but also: 'There are too many discords between the exteriors of the English dramatist and of our own opulent playwrights to ever bring them into line with our manner of feeling' (43).

Shakespeare's plays came to Italy even later than to Spain – rather ironic, considering Shakespeare's enormous interest in Italy, at least in the locations of many of his plays, and the unfounded speculations that he might have travelled to Italy himself. The introduction came, once again, through the adaptation of *Hamlet* by Jean-François Ducis, near the end of the seventeenth century (Carlson 1985: 15). And as in France and Spain, adherents of neoclassicism – principally deploying Voltaire's critique of Shakespearean drama as consistently violating the 'unities' – struggled with the wildness and hybridity of much of Shakespearean drama, with the original texts unplayed or drastically modified. The history of Shakespearean tragedy in Italy, as Shaul Bassi notes, 'is one of multiple displacements and dislocations' (2016: 694).

New translations of the plays began to appear in the mid-nineteenth century, Carcano's of *Macbeth* in 1848, 'only a few days before the 1848 uprising against Austrian rule in Milan' (Carlson 1985: 20), and a year after Verdi's opera. Marvin Carlson describes in detail the performances of Lady Macbeth by the Italian actress Adelaide Ristori, based on Carcano's translation, though with so many modifications enhancing Ristori's role (she specialized in the sleep-walking scene, often detached as a kind of epilogue to other plays) that the play was frequently referred to in reviews as *Lady Macbeth* (36). Ristori's version drained the text of any political associations – the second prophecy scene (4.1) and the murder of Lady Macduff and her children were cut (as they usually were in neo-classically inflected productions) so that the focus became the sleepwalking scene, and even there, 'all political references were removed from the doctor's lines' (45). After this scene, the rest of the play was compressed and swiftly played, giving Macbeth himself 'little time to reflect upon his fate' (46). As Carlson notes, 'the central conflict of her *Macbeth* was in the soul of her character' (44), which she had attempted to enhance even further by asking Carcano if it would be possible for him to add a scene 'so that she might die on stage' (26), but he refused.

Tommaso Salvini was of course best known for his intense performances of *Othello* and, close behind, *Hamlet*, but when he began to perform *Macbeth* (on his 1880–1 tour in New York[17]), the results were praised, in part because he 'presented the play almost uncut', with the costumes designed by Gustav Doré (93, 94). His Macbeth was not in thrall to Lady Macbeth, inverting Ristori's dominance over her Macbeth. Still, like Ristori's, this version was a star vehicle designed to emphasize the greatness of Salvini's acting though the final scenes – evidently more or less intact – included no dying speech. Salvini's own political misfortunes (including imprisonment after having fought the French army under Garibaldi [Salvini 1893: 45–62]) may have led him to avoid openly political implications and an emphasis on great, sublime, even terrible heroes: Macbeth, Salvini said, was 'ambitious, venal, and sanguinary' (Salvini 1893: 211). Like many other productions in the eighteenth and nineteenth centuries, Ernesto Rossi's versions cut not only the murders of Lady Macduff and her children, but also the sight of Macbeth's severed head. The emphasis on character first in these productions, and the elimination of some of the play's most egregious violence, in effect ensured non-political interpretations in which Macbeth was the 'dead butcher', however powerful and sympathetic he might have appeared earlier, and Malcolm the rightfully restored king at the end. The culmination, indeed the perfection, of nineteenth-century Italian approaches to Shakespeare would be found in Verdi's *Macbeth* (**Chapter Eight**).

For earlier directors, the question had been whether it was possible to generate any kind of sympathy for Macbeth, while still upholding a royalist stance; hence, the sentimentalization of Macbeth as (almost) a victim of Lady Macbeth, the witches, or fate.[18] But in the twentieth century, the interpretation of tyranny and power in *Macbeth* pivoted and the perception would become, for many, that the play's violence really did reflect or explain the political violence of the culture around it. No longer an individual responsible for the evil in the play or even merely a conduit for the witches' power, Macbeth would become the product of a corrupt and evil socio-political culture, with the corollary result that figures such as Duncan and Malcolm were not just de-royalized, but became much more complex, even malevolent. At the same time, the settings for many post-Second World War productions became dystopian or fascist worlds of the sort just seen throughout Europe.[19]

Brecht, Kott, and totalitarian Europe to 1989

In terms of a conceptual shift in political productions of *Macbeth*, the importance of Bertolt Brecht cannot be exaggerated, even though little of Brecht's writing on *Macbeth* survives. Brecht produced a radio play version for Berliner Rundfunk in 1927. The performance script has been lost, and only a brief summary of the production's elements exists in a 1938 book by Erich Schuhmacher. The account describes a revolutionary approach for the time, with Brecht's 'alienation' techniques such as scene titles:

> From the noise of a modern battle could be heard the voices of the 'Field Preachers', the 'Pacifist', a 'Stage [or Dashing] Hero', the 'Dashing Officers', the 'Traitors', the 'Cowards', an 'Occultist', and a 'Dying Man'... The noise merged with the nagging of the witches. The text is always very freely and arbitrarily compressed from the original.[20]

The object of these transformations was to deliver these battle scenes from the traditional stagings – to 'deface' (or disfigure: *verunstaltete*) them (254). 'Music' by Edmund Meisel (Brecht 1997b: 1160) was used to emphasize important dialogue, and 'as in a film', one scene often faded into another. After the second act, the Announcer reminded the audience of the king's murder and then explained the content of the entire third act. Brecht replaced the Ghost with a description spoken by the narrator. Like many hostile conservative critics of the time, Schumacher faulted Brecht for being unable to find a 'substitute for Shakespeare's impressive plot and language, even in the slightest' (255) – not that this was Brecht's intention. The scenes at the end, Schumacher noted, are 'summarized in a simplified manner and – like the whole piece – cut short, connected and supported by musical accents and interspersed with conversations that should give the illusion of space and time. The arrangement is completely incomplete' (*ganz und gar unvollkommen*; 254). The overall effect, Schumacher lamented, was 'typical of the fanatical and irreverent intention to place the poetic work in the service of petty and subversive party propaganda' (254).

Brecht's dramaturgy thus, as one might expect, defamiliarized the play's plot and characters, and so overturned conventional assumptions about both its interpretation and staging (assuming the details reported by this one listener are accurate). But something concrete does survive from the occasion of this radio play: the introduction, or *Vorrede zu 'Macbeth'*, given before the broadcast, about the structure and plot of *Macbeth* and its contemporary reception.[21] Brecht begins by quoting 'friends' who assert that Shakespeare's text 'cannot stand up to modern dramatic criticism …. purely *qua* play it leaves a great deal to be desired … [including] a frightening lack of logic'. These critics' chief example of a flaw, Brecht reports, is that the audience would be 'mentally prepared for the fulfilment of the prophecies', and

> has every right to expect Banquo's son [sic] to become King before the curtain falls.[22] Instead of that Malcolm, son of the murdered King Duncan, becomes King, and the audience, having been led to think that it will see Banquo's son come to the throne, is left rather ignominiously placed …. [Macbeth] is just as convinced as the audience that the prophecy will be fulfilled. Yet after all this fuss about Fleance's escape he never appears again. It can only be assumed that the playwright forgot about him or that the actor who took the part wasn't good enough to be included in the final curtain call.

Brecht's sardonic ventriloquism of such criticisms continues with the more interesting observation that many aspects of the play's dramaturgy 'are impossible to represent in the theatre as it now is', because 'at one time a theatre … had quite a different relationship to life' than in the present. Only 'the epic style' can realize Shakespeare's 'philosophical' content now. Brecht's understanding of Shakespeare's dramaturgy reflects both a profound interpretation and the necessity for the kind of staging that his radio play seems to have had:

> With [Shakespeare] the audience does the constructing. Shakespeare wouldn't dream of giving a suitable twist to a human life in Act 2 so as to prepare the way for Act 5 … With him everything develops naturally. In the inconsequentiality of his acts we can recognize the inconsequentiality[23] of a human

life, as reported by somebody without any interest in making a pattern of it so as to lend arguments not drawn from life to a principle that can only be prejudice. There is nothing sillier[24] than producing Shakespeare so that he becomes clear. He is naturally unclear. He is absolute matter.

It seems we will never have Brecht's full script to consider, but everything known about it indicates a radical adaptation.[25]

It may be, however, that a fragment of one scene survived; though its origin may be unrelated to the radio broadcast, it dates from the same period. The scene rewrites Shakespeare's 1.3, beginning with the three witches speaking cryptic prophecies different from those in the Folio. Brecht 'disfigures' the scene, as Schumacher said of the radio play, by turning it into the most artificial kind of scene, borrowed from early modern drama, in fact – an Echo scene.[26] The witches' words are heard by Macbeth and Banquo as follows (most of the scene requires no translation here). After the first two stanzas ('When the noise of slaughter is silent' and 'Brother, I know these coasts'), the scene proceeds:

3 [Witch]

Blutiges Tier und blutiges Tier	[Bloody animal and bloody animal
Rauft sich dort und rauft sich hier	Struggles there and struggles here
Und was übrig bleibt, sind wir	And what remains left is us]

Echo	Sind wir.
Macbeth	Ist da was? Wer seid Ihr?
Echo	Wer seid Ihr?
Macbeth	*stellt sich vor* Macbeth! Macbeth!
Echo	Macbeth!
Banquo	Ist da was, was Antwort gibt? [gives an answer]
Echo	Das Antwort gibt. (Brecht 1997b: 550)

Brecht thus pushes the witches out of any pseudo-realistic framework, and ultimately Banquo, not the witches, speaks the key prophecies (using his helmet as a witches' cauldron [*Hexenkessel*] to make an 'ominous' or 'unholy' [*Unheilssuppe*] soup (551). Macbeth then returns the favour to Banquo, speaking his prophecies:

Macbeth	Heil, heil, heil!	
	Kleiner als Macbeth	
Banquo	Kleiner als Macbeth.	
Macbeth	Und doch grosser	
	So glücklich nicht	[not as happy]
	Und doch glücklicher	[and yet happier]
	Selbst König nicht	
	Doch du zeugst Könige.	
Echo	Könige. (552)	

The scene's cascades of 'Heil' seem proleptic, in 1927–8, but the main effects are, first, the distancing of the scene, and second, the dispersal of the witches' voices; in the *Vorrede*, Brecht is far more interested in the nature, theatrical effects, and logic of the prophecies than in the witches *per se*.[27]

Paired with Brecht's revolutionary influence and the ravages of the Second World War, the 1962 publication of Jan Kott's *Shakespeare, Our Contemporary* (English translation, 1964) produced a great shift towards a new politics of *Macbeth*, though some productions had anticipated Kott's views. Kott's conception of Shakespeare has been so completely absorbed into contemporary theatrical practice that it is easy to forget how revolutionary it was.[28] Kott read Shakespeare's plays in the light of apocalypse and Auschwitz. His most famous and influential chapter may have been 'King Lear or Endgame', but his thoughts on *Macbeth* – in a chapter ominously named 'Macbeth or Death-Infected' – completely changed, for many, their view of the play. For Kott, *Macbeth* was 'a nightmare … which paralyses and terrifies' (Kott 1964: 85–6): 'A production of *Macbeth* not evoking a picture of the world flooded with blood, would inevitably be false' (87). Kott saw only one theme in the play – not 'ambition', or 'terror', but 'murder': 'History has been reduced to its simplest form, to one image and one division: those who kill and those who are killed' (87). Long before historicist investigations into Scottish history and its tangled theories of royal succession, Kott understood its essence: 'The new king will be the man who has killed a king' (87). Macbeth, Kott says, has reached 'the Auschwitz experience' (92). All Macbeth can do is murder, and the end of the play 'produces no catharsis … Macbeth does not feel guilty, and there is nothing for him to protest about. All he can do before he dies is to drag with him into nothingness as many living beings as possible .... Macbeth is still unable to blow the world up. But he can go on murdering till the end' (97).

This view of the play and its relation to twentieth-century history is about as far from Garrick's invented final speech as can be imagined; understandably, many readers and directors have not warmed to Kott's dark vision, and some others have offered critiques from the left (Sinfield 1985) while many ostensibly 'modern' productions still reproduce the traditional thematics of the Authorized Version. But Kott made possible a world-wide shift in conceiving the play. A 1988 production at the Royal Exchange Theatre in Manchester, in fact, actually set the play in a concentration camp. The director Braham Murray had the 'prisoners [of the camp] rehearse a production of *Macbeth* to try to understand how the evil that envelopes them had come about' (Murray 2007: 212). Their props were what would have been available in a camp: 'barbed wire crowns' and so on. Scotland became 'a nuclear winter area ... The last act is pure Hitler in the bunker' (212). At the end, when Malcolm 'made his speech about a new future, the doors opened, searchlights played on the prisoners and they left to go to their deaths' (213).

Recent scholars have documented at length how Kott's readings of the plays revolutionized the staging and interpretation throughout post-Second World War Europe. Nicole Fayard (2006: 55–7), for example, documents at length how Kott's readings of the plays revolutionized the staging and interpretation in post-Second World War France, leading to such productions of *Macbeth* as Guy Rétoré's 1964 production set 'in what looked like a metallic box, with steel walls of oppressive hues of lead and brass', suggesting, one reviewer said, 'the conniving intervention of nature at war, the implacable mechanism of human history, and Macbeth's powerlessness' (59); in 1973, Rétoré returned to the play with a set of 'dark, austere walls spiked with threatening girders, against which the spotlights tracked individual characters and set them into relief" – in short, a 'tragedy of fear' (90–1). For Jacques Rosner in 1994, *Macbeth* is 'today the play which best describes the last years of our twentieth century' (132), and for Bernard Sobel (in 1986), the play depicting an eleventh-century Scottish king was ironically 'a play about the future, therefore about today' (282). On the other hand, Ariane Mnouchkine's 2014 production at the Théâtre du Soleil featured Macbeth as a victorious modern general, heralded by a crowd of reporters with flashing cameras, who in the final scene was reduced to a frightened face peering through a small opening in a mobile Hitler-bunker. The production was visually splendid, but in spite of its updating, remained rather traditional in its curious optimism. Modernizing settings and making historical allusions to known dictators do not always add up to a political interpretation radically different from earlier periods.

When the play was first performed in Spain after the Civil War, for example, the Franco regime – themselves masters of terror – had already nationalized some of the theatres and backed productions that aligned the 'royalist' views of the play in support of the regime's legitimacy. In Luca de Tena's production of *Macbeth* in 1942, the medieval trappings of the production were 'complemented by the militaristic black and white "period" costume ... which suggested both Norman chain-mail and Scottish kilt, with most of the uniforms bearing insignias that mingled pseudo-Celtic iconography with the symbolism of Fascism' (Gregor 2010: 90). Even more to the point, the production's ending deleted both the scene of Macduff holding Macbeth's severed head aloft and the play's final speech, presumably, Gregor speculates, 'on the grounds that Malcolm's plans to recall "our exiled friends abroad / That fled the snares of watchful tyranny" could be construed as a reference to Franco's own persecutions' (165 n.5.) Thus, a typical political confusion: the play's internal politics, in a regime like Franco's, require Malcolm to be seen as the legitimate heir who has overthrown his corrupt predecessor, yet the Folio's ending muddies the message considerably and so must be jettisoned.

In Portugal, as Francesca Rayner (2014) has demonstrated, the country's isolation after the Second World War greatly impacted the development of theatre. Throughout his paranoid regime, António Salazar prohibited any public performance of *Julius Caesar* (128), in stark contrast to Mussolini in Italy, yet permitted censor-approved performances of *Macbeth*. Rayner raises the question of how *any* performance of *Macbeth* could have been permitted, speculating that the play's ambiguity permitted 'both regime and opposition to cast each other as the tyrant and themselves as the heroic opposition without having to make such partisan readings explicit in performance' (128). Productions that attempted a more radical re-imagining of the play and 'linked the political violence of life under a moribund regime with a deliberate deconstruction of the canonicity of the Shakespearean text were met with the full force of the tyranny of political censorship' (136). Rayner's formulation here highlights how, in virtually every post-war European country, the elements of a particular play could be superseded, or reinforced, by positioning Shakespeare himself and his texts as emblematic of order – of the conservative political order of the state that sanctioned or censored performances. By the end of the Salazar dictatorship, the ideological construction of *Macbeth*'s politics had swung in a clear direction, as it became '*the* Shakespeare political play, where moral and political opposition to tyranny expressed growing discontent with a regime that came increasingly to resemble Macbeth's paranoid and doomed attempt to hold onto power' (136). In the post-revolution period, Jan Kott's work began to have a similar impact on productions in Portugal as in other countries (137).[29]

In post-Second World War Slovenia, Communist functionaries – like their blinkered colleagues in similar Soviet-occupied countries – criticized Shakespeare's politics, based on ironically conservative readings of the play. One writer, in an unsigned memorandum of 7 March 1947, asserted that 'While Shakespeare is considered one of the world's greatest playwrights, he was working within a feudal social order which he did not criticize but, more often than not, even affirmed'. In the plays, moreover, this writer complained that Shakespeare 'delights in portraying the triumph of violence and tyranny over innocent people; for the most part, the victims in his plays belong to the deprived classes, but Shakespeare does not clearly indicate where the solution lies or portray progressive ideas in the struggle for a more just social system' (Poniž 2014: 189). In many countries, totalitarian authorities condemned certain plays which, in their interpretation, seemed to reflect all too closely the critiques of their rule, or failed (as here) to portray 'progressive ideas' of the dominant ideology. Such censorship is premised on simple and unambiguous interpretations of the plays themselves. The Slovene condemnation of Shakespeare would be repeated, or inverted, in many European countries suffering totalitarian rule after the War.

The works of Shakespeare became tokens of ideological positioning, none more so than *Macbeth*, with its display of tyranny, regicide, and systemic political violence. Artists, writers, directors, and actors in fascist and Stalinist totalitarian societies learned, often at their peril, how to survive and create. The effects of their political conditions often manifested in profound artistic compromises and, for those who did not simply capitulate to their masters, in bitter psychic damage. In his analysis of these phenomena in *The Captive Mind* (1951), Czeslaw Milosz describes how artists learned a kind of psychic/spiritual doubleness or acting that he termed 'Ketman' (after a Persian practice): 'Ketman means self-realization *against* something. He who practices Ketman suffers because of the obstacles he meets; but if these obstacles were suddenly to be removed, he would find himself in a void which might perhaps prove much more painful' (Milosz 1981: 80). Attila Kiss describes how this practice of complete submission plus inner resistance functioned in the theatre: 'Before 1989, the theatrical scene in East-Central Europe was the field where perhaps the most intensive artistic experimentations were always combined, through the "double talk" or double coding of covert intellectual messages, with political awareness and subversive ideological critique' (Kiss 2013: 113). The reception history of *Macbeth* in Hungary, Kiss notes, 'revealed that its popularity increased after the political changes of 1989', though 'the tradition of double coding continued to reflect on the political intensities of a society in transition, but in which the spectators were also compelled to bear witness to the questions of individual and collective responsibility'. The play was often staged 'as deeply tragic and ironically pathetic at the same time' (2013: 132).[30] As Milosz noted, Shakespeare had a special status in pre-1989 Eastern Europe, and thus his works could be staged under a regime's ideological conditions:

> A play that introduces 'strangeness,' revealing the author's interest in the tragedy of life, has no chance of being produced because the tragedy of human fate leads to thoughts about the mystery of human destiny. One forgives certain writers like Shakespeare these predispositions, but there is no question of permitting any contemporary author to harbor them. (Milosz 1981: 73–4)

Thus *Macbeth*, like other 'dangerous' works about regime change such as *Hamlet* and *King Lear*, once more had to be domesticated and transformed, with mixed results. As Anna Worthen notes of pre-1989 performances in Czechoslovakia, 'Under the watchful gaze of the censors, the theater only at times may have intended to share a certain "coded" or veiled meaning with its audience; at other times, the audience took the active role, spontaneously creating an ironic or critical element of the production in an unexpected way' (Worthen 2007: 118).

Cold War and post-1989 Europe

Shakespeare's importance in central Europe is hardly recent – the transcultural traffic between English and European actors dates from the 1590s – but since 1989 'more than anywhere else, Shakespeare's plays have ... been appropriated for political interpretations' (Stříbrný 2000: 1).[31] Perhaps the best-known version of *Macbeth* from a central European author (via Singapore, India, and the UK) is Tom Stoppard's *Cahoot's Macbeth*, designed to be performed after *Dogg's Hamlet* (1979). Stoppard's play may not be particularly representative of Czech politics,[32] but Stoppard certainly understands the various artistic and linguistic forms that political resistance can take. After watching *Dogg's Hamlet*, the audience of *Cahoot's Macbeth* has learned how to interpret 'Dogg' language, and so is able to decipher a speech from the first play and recognize that, as a linguistic code, it has become a language of political resistance. The Porter becomes a threatening secret policeman knocking at the door, and a sense of dread overcomes all the 'actors'.

When the actors relate 2.4.31–2 ('He is already named, and gone to Scone / To be invested'), a stage direction shows Macbeth crowning himself, which the police inspector applauds, assuming it is the end of the play: 'Very good. Very good! And so nice to have a play with a happy ending for a change' (Stoppard 1993: 190). He continues with a critique of Shakespeare that precisely reflects how, as Milosz and Kiss show, Shakespeare was deployed in resistance to and co-opted by totalitarian regimes:

Shakespeare – or the Old Bill, as we call him in the force – is not a popular choice with my chief, owing to his popularity with the public... The fact is, when you get a universal and timeless writer like Shakespeare, there's a strong feeling that he could be spitting in the eyes of the beholder when he should be keeping his mind on Verona... He didn't know he was doing it, at least you couldn't prove he did, which is what makes the chief so prejudiced against him.

The authorities, the Inspector continues, would prefer to counter a direct rather than a submerged resistance: 'But what we don't like is a lot of people being cheeky and saying they are only Julius Caesar or Coriolanus or Macbeth. Otherwise we are going to start treating them the same as the ones who say they are Napoleon. Got it?' (192–3). In short, he concludes, this living room 'performance of yours goes right against the spirit of normalization' (194). The prospect of normalizing *Macbeth* verges on a *reduction ad absurdum*, but many adapters have attempted just that.

Pavel Drábek notes that 'the modern Eastern European tragic protagonist is typically imagined as a failure', and he describes a 1999 *Macbeth* production in Nitra, Slovakia, by Vladimir Morávek as typical of this mood:

> Macbeth and Lady Macbeth entered the play in pyjamas and shabby nightgowns, watching TV and drinking bottled beer from their fridge. As if by miracle, they entered the dreamy 'big world' they knew from the TV screen, and performed nightmarish deeds of cruelty in a desperate attempt at maximizing the gains of their new-found ambitions …. [they were juxtaposed] with the grand world of aristocracy… [playing] off the cultural sentiment of disenfranchisement and the powerlessness of the 'small person' in confrontation with the power players of the 'big world'. (Drabek 2016: 754–5)

The play was thus turned into 'a tragedy of degeneration' (755). Throughout Drábek's survey, Shakespearean tragedies, because of their political nature, have served 'as metaphors of desired freedoms' (759), even in Morávek's production, where the tyranny and violence of social class work reciprocally. Or, put another way, Drábek argues that

> After 1989, political readings of Shakespeare in Central and Eastern Europe mushroomed. Shakespeare was shown "painted red", politically subversive, almost as if he was an accomplice in the political dissent surreptitiously voiced onstage …. the identity crisis of the countries of the now dilapidating Soviet bloc had

important symptoms[, among them] were the turncoat narratives of paradise regained – or the tyranny defeated (Drabek 2017: 7)

In Poland during the war, as Williams notes, Shakespeare was 'repossessed' by secret theatres and theatres in exile, while after the war, Shakespeare 'became a part of the postmodern discourse of recycling the past, its values, and myths', a discourse that advances a belief in 'progress' that (partly) erases 'the idea of significant loss' (Williams 2012: 290).

In post-war Communist Romania, productions of *Macbeth* 'internalized the inflexible determination in the pursuit of power', according to Matei-Chesnoui, sending 'explicit messages to an audience that had experienced the obdurate extravagance of the Communist leader Ceauşescu and his ambitious wife' (2006: 162).[33] According to Florian Nicolau (sympathetic to the regime), the 1962 production at the Bucharest National Theater, 'denouncing the bloody tyrants' despotic autocracy ... the central concept of the spectacle', showed Shakespeare – supposedly on the side of 'the hero who protests and fights against the social evil' – demonstrating that Macbeth, 'though gifted with great psychological force and noble attributes, lost his humane qualities' because 'he thought that he could achieve the full potential of his humanity by becoming a king' (Matei-Chesnoiu 2006: 167); Lear, by contrast, regains his humanity when he loses his kingship. Coming just five years after the abolishment of monarchy in the country (168), and given that kingship was generally considered the 'least desirable of all social hierarchies of power' (167), the play, according to Nicolau, asserted 'the legitimate right of the people to rise against their tyrannical kings' (168). It's doubtful that Ceauşescu and his wife had time to meditate on the phenomenal ironies of their links to the Macbeths, given the speed of their one-hour trial and execution five minutes later on Christmas Day, 1989.

Productions of Shakespearean tragedies (those that 'could yield political interpretations') during the 1970s had begun conveying 'a covert political message under the appearance of theatrical innovations' (172). A 1976 production, influenced by Kabuki theatre, erased traces of the supernatural, and the witches' prophecies became one of the hallucinating Macbeth's inner voices (176); moreover, 'Everybody looked like Macbeth in this evil world, and the king was different only through the fact that he visualized his hallucinations' (176). Thus, the shift from locating evil within the two central characters onto a larger social map. A 1982 production 'was a *danse macabre* in the pursuit of power', in which a revised ending showed 'that Malcolm was much more dangerous for Scotland than the murderous couple' (183); the director, Matei-Chesnoui observed, had 'anticipated a political situation that would settle in Romania after the fall of the Communist regime' (184). After Ceauşescu's death, a 1990 performance of Alfred Jarry's *Ubu Rex with Scenes from Macbeth* made even clearer, in Mr and Mrs Ubu, the link between the Macbeths and the late dictator and his wife, as did several other post-1989 productions. As we have seen before, the same play that in 1962 had seemed to replicate the values and politics of the contemporary regime was a few years later read as its ideological inversion – now subverting the regime rather than sustaining it.

In Bulgaria, the first translation of *Macbeth* appeared in 1885, and through 1996 it was the most frequently translated Shakespeare play, even more than *Hamlet*. Shurbanov and Sokolova (1996) note that there were relatively few productions, however, and by the 1980s, *Hamlet* 'became once again the central Shakespearean tragedy' (Shurbanov 1998: 142). Shurbanov notes that after 1989, directors and critics were intent 'on using his [Shakespeare's] work as a mirror of our time, sometimes even adapting it quite freely for the purpose. As Shakespeare was employed in the service of dissidence, negation and destruction became the norms of his interpretation ... Something has been gained, something has been lost' (143). This aesthetically conservative lament ('even adapting it quite freely') about postmodernist interpretations privileges the Shakespearean text as if it were a stable and known essence.

Demonstrating that even some dictatorships have limits, the film *Severed Heads* – directed by Glauber Rocha, a Brazilian (that country also under military dictatorship at the time) – premiered in Spain four years before Franco's death. A film 'against dictatorships, and the funeral of dictatorships' (Fuentes and Vera 2014: 266), Rocha said, the film refracts *Macbeth* through the tyrant Diaz, who has gone to Spain in exile; he is killed by a shepherd, who represents the oppressed people. The title refers to decapitated statues as well as to the fate of the tyrant, in an obvious link to the end of Shakespeare's text (267). One scene in the play script but deleted in the film suggests that the film's analysis of tyranny is in some ways retrograde; the Shepherd says

Lady Macbeth was the one to blame
Poor Macbeth had no ambition
He was a faithful vassal of the King
But Lady Macbeth had dreams of grandeur
And with her charms she awakened in poor Macbeth's heart
The wish to become a King. (268)

Locating the impulse to evil within character – Macbeth's weakness and Lady Macbeth's 'dreams of grandeur' – hearkens back to Romantic readings of the play, and not to any systemic critique of the social order.

Perhaps the most freely reimagined politicized version of the play in Spain was Calixto Bieito's Catalan (hence linguistically transgressive) version in Barcelona, which ended with 'all the characters [including the "dead" Macbeth] gather[ing] on stage to sing a Nick Cave song that runs: "When you're sad and lonely and you haven't got a friend, remember death is not the end."' Billington (2002) took this 'to be Bieito's own ironic comment on the sentimentality of a world that rejects God but craves an afterlife …. as the cast sang this Cave number surrounded by the dirty debris of materialism'. Bieito said that

Macbeth has to be a new piece by a new writer. We changed the text all the time. The fifth act is my favourite. It is like the last days in the bunker. We gave Lady Macduff five children.[34] Macbeth did not die at the end. He stays with all his ghosts. Death, we know, is for heroes. Always with Shakespeare you can do whatever you want. All you must do is surprise the audience. The text is not the limit. This is theatre. There is no limit. (Coveney 2004)

In a more or less gangster-mafia world, Bieito's production wasn't about the politics of the state, as the play has so often been to support or refute (even though his reference to 'the bunker' alludes to Hitler) but about the broader public sphere. Another recent production (2006) by Helena Pimenta took place in Galicia; Spain's regional strains have proven fertile ground for oppositional productions (no matter who controls Madrid). Pimenta's version, according to one reviewer, brought into play 'the emotional imbalance … and multifaceted personality of someone who ends up confusing the exercise of power with something that actually belongs to them' (Gregor 2010: 154).

Germany is *Macbeth*: Heiner Müller

While *Hamlet* has always been *the* Shakespearean play in German culture,[35] the nation's association with *Macbeth* has been nearly as strong. As early as the First World War, the English playwright Henry Arthur Jones wondered, 'What evil angel of their destiny tempted the Germans to choose Macbeth for their anniversary [1916] offering to Shakespeare, in this year of all others? It is the very picture of their own character marching to its ruin' (Höfele 2016a: 3). Later, throughout the Nazi regime, the GDR regime, and post-1989 politics, *Macbeth* proved an irresistible paradigm, depending on how the play was read, for both the legitimacy of State power and resistance to it.[36]

'[A]s a "Nordic ballad" about a hero tragically overwhelmed while fighting the English', as Werner Habicht (2012: 29–30) has noted, *Macbeth* 'enjoyed Nazi favour to the very last'.[37] A typical production in Mainz in 1935 depicted Macbeth 'as the real hero and victor', while one functionary proposed, in 1940, that the play 'should be exploited for its propaganda value as an instrument for revealing the perfidy of the English' (Symington 2005: 253–4). Nazi defenders of Shakespeare had argued that Shakespeare 'advocated the submission of the individual person to higher public values (the state in the tragedies and histories, social structures in the comedies), and that many protagonists of his tragedies and histories were, indeed, Germanic heroes and epitomes of strong leadership, commanding and enforcing their subjects' allegiance' (Habicht 2012: 23). In the post-War period, Höfele notes, the perception of Shakespeare's tragedies reflected the Cold War division of the country: in the East, a focus 'on the dialectics of class struggle', while in the West, 'the timeless dilemmas of the human condition' (2016b: 722). Perhaps the ultimate dismantling of Shakespearean tragedy – Höfele calls it 'the zero point of tragedy' – is Müller's *Die*

Hamletmaschine. But his *Macbeth: nach Shakespeare* is nearly as powerful and disruptive.

Müller's 1972 adaptation of *Macbeth* proved indeed that 'One can say a lot of things about Stalin with a production of *Macbeth*' (Weber and Young 2012: 4). The play reflects his more general indebtedness to, and critique of, Brecht.[38] Müller had a career-long interest in Shakespeare, from an early translation of *As You Like It* to the later adaptation of *Titus Andronicus.* In April 1988 Müller gave a speech – 'Shakespeare A Difference' – to scholars at the Shakespeare Tage in Weimar, in which he commented on the contradictory stature of Shakespeare in the two Germanies at that moment in history, and in his own heritage: 'Shakespeare had no philosophy, no understanding of history: his Romans are of London.' He argued, more polemically, 'We haven't arrived at ourselves as long as Shakespeare is writing our plays' (Weber 1990: 33, 32).

While Müller takes the basic structure of *Macbeth* as a starting point, he strongly resisted Shakespeare's text and the entire tradition of the Authorized Version: '*Macbeth* was the Shakespeare play I liked least. Earlier I had translated *As You Like It* as faithfully as possible. In *Macbeth* I wanted to alter Shakespeare, line by line' (Cohn 1976: 88). Müller realized that the first scene of the play presented a significant problem: to keep it, 'I would have to fully accept this idea of predestination, that the chain of events is programmed by supernatural forces. Therefore I first eliminated that scene, and this resulted in an increasing number of changes' (Weber and Young 2012: 3). Still, Müller recognized another aspect of the witches that was crucial: 'In *Macbeth* there is an optimistic element of history, the witches. Every revolution needs a destructive element, and in my play that is the witches, they destroy without exception all those who possess power' (3). So the play begins with a version of 1.2, roughly following the Folio plot, with the prophecies roughly the same as well. But then there is the stage direction for scene 3 – '*Duncan, seated on corpses that have been stacked to create a throne*' (Weber 2012: 19) – and the play spirals into violence and abjection: peasants are introduced in order to be slain, Macduff cuts out a servant's tongue (36), the murderers cut off Banquo's penis (49), a Prisoner is flayed (64), and so on. Duncan, Malcolm, and Macduff, totally inverting the Authorized Version, are as cruel and murderous as Macbeth. When Macbeth's head is brought in on a spear, Rosse and Lenox greet Malcolm

> Hail Malcolm, King
> Of Scotland. See how high he once has climbed
> Who was it before you. Learn from his case,

to which Malcolm replies, 'Know, you can't fool around with the boy Malcolm. / For your head is a place here on my spear.' This stage direction follows: '*Malcolm laughs. Rosse and Lenox point at Macduff. Soldiers kill him*'. The play ends with an entrance of the witches, whose choric greeting – 'Hail Malcolm Hail King of Scotland Hail' (75) – is chilling enough even before one recognizes that in German the word is '*Heil*'. Müller's adaptation says something about Hitler as well as Stalin.

Müller also decentralizes character and agency. For his East Berlin production ten years later, Müller split Macbeth's character into three different actors to emphasize not the individual but systemic structures of power and corruption,[39] while the set 'represented

FIGURE 2 *Heiner Müller. Dieter Montag (o), Michael Gwisdeck (u.) in 'Macbeth' von William Shakespeare R.: Heiner Müller Volksbühne am Rosa-Luxemburg-Platz - 1982 (Photo by Wolfgang Falk/ullstein bild via Getty Images).*

the inner court of a typical Berlin working class apartment building, with a telephone booth ... and trash heaps' (Weber and Young 2012: 4) (**Figure 2**). Müller's adaptation received criticism from some East German reviewers for its 'pessimism' and anti-humanistic effect (Mahlke 1999: 40). As Thomas Sorge (1994: 72) wrote, 'The desired historical perspective ... (Duncan=feudalism; Macbeth=dissolution of feudalism/advent of early bourgeois egotism; Malcolm=socially relatively unspecified promise of an area [*sic*] of peace and prosperity), was efficiently deflated by the adaptation, especially with regard to Malcolm as a bearer of hopes for better times.' Müller's rewriting of *Macbeth* parallels other twentieth-century revisions in that Malcolm's supposed legitimate succession, a hallmark of the Authorized Version, is inverted: Müller couldn't stomach him (or any part of the play) as 'a bearer of hopes for better times'. When the Berliner Ensemble revived Müller's play in 2018, 'Blood dominated the production', contaminating 'all of the bodies onstage; passing from witch to mortal, from husband to wife, from man to man'. This production's Malcolm was 'a traumatized, lonely figure' who, when he 'finally got his hands on the crown, blood poured from his mouth as he raised his arms in triumph, a lunatic grin spreading across his face' (Rycroft 2020; see below for further versions of Malcolm). This production seems to have been true to, perhaps even outdoing, Müller's as 'a picture of the world flooded with blood' (in Kott's phrase).

Absurd Macbeth

Ionesco's darkly comic *Macbett* (1972, like Müller's play) also strongly resists the perceived traditional elements of the Folio: thus, Ionesco has no Lady Macbeth but a Lady Duncan, there are two not three witches, and so on. Like many before him, Ionesco critiqued Shakespeare for having placed Duncan's murder off-stage: 'You think that I, myself, I do not hesitate to put the slaying on the stage.'[40] Perry (2000: 95) observes that Ionesco 'ties up some of Shakespeare's loose ends' by revealing that Macol [=Malcolm] is really Banco's biological son – hence in effect redressing a common complaint about the failure of the witches' prophecy to come good. Brecht's influence is evident in such estranging techniques as the introduction of the Butterfly Hunter, the Lemonade Seller, and the *'life-size dolls [that] represent the other* GUESTS' in the final banquet (Ionesco 1973: 87sd).[41] Ionesco's debt to Alfred Jarry's *Ubu roi* is marked most specifically by Macbett's final word, 'Shit!' which in the French (*'Merde'*) echoes the first word of Jarry's play (*'Merdre'*).[42]

Ionesco's ideological reinterpretation of Shakespeare's text owed much to Kott: 'I got the idea from my friend Jan Kott, the author of "Shakespeare, Our Contemporary" .... There is a king, a tyrant, vicious and criminal. Then comes a young prince, handsome, brave and pure, who kills the tyrant and takes his place. He in turn becomes a tyrant. Another young prince – handsome, brave and pure – kills the tyrant and becomes king. And so on' (Hess 1972). Ionesco added, in a later interview, that Kott 'thought of Stalin' and inspired his own piece, in which he tried 'to show once more that every politician is paranoid and that all politics leads to crime'.[43] Describing his play as a 'mélange' (Bonnefoy 1966&1977: 162) of Shakespeare and Jarry, Ionesco offered that *Macbett* is still a comedy: 'I hope people will laugh' (Hess 1972) – though perhaps not at the *'forest of guillotines'* (Ionesco 1973: 31sd) that dispatches enemies of the state.

Ionesco's sardonic plot summary of the 'handsome' young prince who succeeds a tyrant and then turns into a tyrant himself ad infinitum darkly parodies the Folio's 'line of kings' in 4.1. It reorients Duncan and his supposed legitimacy from the weak king of Shakespeare's play, to the lecherous, vicious, and cowardly tyrant who stays so far away from the danger of battle that he can only see the front 'through my telescope' (23). In Ionesco's brilliant irony, Duncan's on-stage murder comes through the ritual most designed, historically, to illustrate the monarch's 'sovereign power' (71): the 'heavenly gift' (70) of the Royal Touch in 4.3. After the Monk (Banco in disguise) blesses the royal sceptre, Duncan begins to heal the sick (suffering from leprosy, scrofula, bodily agony) with divine invocations (73), only to be murdered by the unholy triumvirate of Banco, Macbett, and Lady Duncan. Ionesco may not have known of King James's scepticism about the ceremony he inherited from Queen Elizabeth, and his cynical embrace of the ritual as a technique of legitimating his reign, but Ionesco foregrounds and inverts this key element of Shakespeare's play. The result doesn't just undermine the ritual, but hollows it out altogether, as the 'divine' blessings are given by Banco, who '*strikes the first blow*' (77sd).

Like Müller, Ionesco also refuses to see Macbeth's as a tragedy of character or 'ambition'. Macbett's characterization, like others in the play, is flat and robotic, as indicated by the technique of parallels and exact verbal repetitions first with Banco, then with Duncan, and the unoriginality of his language; moreover, there is no 'tomorrow' speech or any of the Shakespearean soliloquies that produce such a profound illusion of interiority. Instead, there are repetitive cycles of violence, treason, and murder. Perry describes this cycle in Kottian terms: 'All who want the crown are conspirators; all conspirators want the crown because the crown is what is wanted' (Perry 2000: 93).

If Ionesco's Duncan is a tyrant and Banco a conspirator (as he was in the early chronicles), Ionesco's greatest act of reinterpretation comes in the figure of Macol. Macbett scoffs, after the witches' prophecy that he himself will become king: 'It's impossible. Duncan has a son, Macol, who's studying at Carthage. He is the natural and legitimate heir to the throne' (38). When Macol finally enters the play at the end, Lady Duncan announces, in a parody of romantic 'lost child' narratives, that he isn't her son, but was adopted by Duncan: 'Banco was his father, his mother was a gazelle that a witch transformed into a woman' (99). There's nothing magical about Macol's defeat of Macbett however: 'MACOL *stabs* MACBETT *in the back*. MACBETT *falls*' (101sd.). As the people herald Macol as their new king, he orders them: 'Quiet, I say. Don't all talk at once. I'm going to make an announcement. Nobody move. Nobody breathe. Now get this into your heads. Our country sank beneath the yoke, each day a new gash was added to her wounds. But I have trod upon the tyrant's head and now wear it on my sword' and a man then '*comes in with Macbett's head on the end of a pike*' (102sd.). As the people curse the head, the '*forest of guillotines*' reappears '*as in the First Scene*' (103sd.). At this point, Macol ends the play with an almost verbatim quotation of Malcolm's 'test' speech to Macduff in 4.3 of the Folio, only now it is no 'test' of Macduff but a chilling promise of future tyranny. Beginning 'In me I know / All the particulars of vice so grafted', Macol speaks for thirty-seven uninterrupted lines, while the crowd dissipates and at last the Bishop '*goes dejectedly out right*' (105sd.). The play ends with Macol pledging to 'Pour the sweet milk of concord into Hell, / Uproar the universal peace, confound / All unity on earth', and finally, 'First I'll make this Archduchy a kingdom – and me the king. An empire – and me the emperor. Super-highness, super-king, super-majesty, emperor of emperors' (105), after which '*He disappears in the mist*' (105sd.) and the Butterfly Hunter once more crosses the stage. We are a long way from the reading of Shakespeare's play as authorizing, in Malcolm's ascent to the throne, a lawful and 'righteous' renewal.

Irene R. Makaryk has described a landmark, but at the time virtually unknown, *Macbeth* production in Ukraine by Les Kurbas in 1920/24, which powerfully anticipated Ionesco's treatment of the ending, though there is no evidence that Ionesco knew of it, nor that it influenced other productions (Moschovakis 2008: 24–5). One of the actors proclaimed (the 1920 version) as 'a production that is in harmony with our times. Using the tools of the theater we fight against power-hungry tyrants and pretenders to the throne' (Makaryk 2006: 19–20). For the 1924 version, Kurbas offered a 'new, radical' version of the play, with the set in part alluding to contemporary political posters (Makaryk 2006: 23). The style of acting, as Makaryk describes it, anticipated Brechtian alienation effects: 'Every aspect of the production was placed in quotation marks' (25). The chief alteration, anticipating Kott's interpretation, was the introduction of three interludes by a Fool (based on the Porter), who appeared in one as the Grim Reaper; more significantly, he appeared at the end, dressed as a bishop 'in gold tiara and white cassock', and

> crowned Malcolm to the solemn music of an organ made ironic by the delicate sounds of the piccolo and the rougher harmonium. Just as he did so, a new pretender approached, killed the kneeling Malcolm, and took the crown. Without pause, the bishop once again intoned the same words, 'There is no power, but from God.' As the new king was about to rise, a new pretender murdered him, and the ritual was repeated once again. (28)

The power of this ending felt like 'an exploding bomb' (28) to one of the actors, and it has now become a familiar, cynical turn in modern productions. Kurbas's originality did not penetrate to western Europe until much later.

Scotland: David Greig's *Dunsinane*

No play, it is safe to say, is more 'Scottish' than *Macbeth*, and the Scottish playwright David Greig took it on in *Dunsinane* (2011).[44] Any casual reader of Greig's drama quickly recognizes the influence of Brecht (see Wallace 2013: 31–6). As Greig does not feel he himself has a 'Scottish voice' (Billingham 2007: 78), with the example of 'Brecht in particular ... it occurred to me that if I wrote a play as if it was in translation, it would allow two things: a certain sort of formal poetic language because it wouldn't be pretending to be naturalistic as it was obviously translated, and the freedom to write working-class characters as I required them to speak' (Whitney 2010). A few years before *Dunsinane*, Greig had warmed up by adapting Jarry's *King Ubu*, now set in an old people's home.

Dunsinane begins where *Macbeth* ends, with the defeat of Macbeth and the triumph of Malcolm, led to apparent victory by Siward and his invading force. But in a radical departure, Lady Macbeth has not perished after all – not only has she survived, but she now has a name (Gruach) and a son (Lulach),[45] neither of which Shakespeare had granted her. Greig's Macbeth never appears in the play. Most Scots, Greig claims, know that the real King Macbeth

> probably wasn't a tyrant, he was probably quite a good king. He ruled for about 15 years at a time in Scottish history when the turnover in kings was something like one in every six months, so he must have been doing something right... So the cheeky bit of me thought, 'What if the stories of Macbeth being a tyrant turned out to be propaganda, a bit like the weapons of mass destruction?' (Whitney 2010)

– i.e. a pretext for invading a country. Macduff provides a terse account of Macbeth's offstage death: 'I cut his throat. / His head's on a stick in the castle yard', to which Siward's 'It's over', is answered by Macduff: 'Yes' (25). But of course it's not over at all, it's only beginning. The English attempt to bring order to Scotland lurches into catastrophe.

The play follows a devastating arc, as the rational, 'enlightened' Siward becomes ever more confused by Scotland, and as a result ever more brutal in his methods; the Scots, Gruach in particular, remain a complete mystery to the invaders. Siward is, Greig has said, genuinely 'a good man who is trying to do the right thing. It's just that every single action he takes in pursuit of the right thing leads to more and more bloodshed' (Brown 2011). Siward's confidence is clear: 'We'll set a new king in Dunsinane and then summer will come and then a harvest and by next spring it'll be as if there never was a fight here. You'll be amazed how quickly a battle can disappear' (24). But then Siward meets Gruach and from that point on nothing that follows makes any sense to him. When he challenges what Malcolm had told him about the situation, Malcolm's reply invokes the Scots' very different understanding of language and truth: 'are you going to continue with this insistent literalness? "You said" – "He said" – you sound like a child' (29).

Siward is undaunted in the beginning, telling Gruach 'My job is to build a new kingdom – not to settle old grudges. So I have to clear away the past now. I have to uproot now and clear away all past claims and – That way there is a chance that we can establish a fair peace in Scotland in which every clan can flourish – including yours' (33), and he instructs his soldiers to conduct themselves morally with the Scots: that way, 'We will make them to trust us' (44). He refuses to kill a farmer Malcolm wants out of the way because 'I will not kill a man for doing a reasonable thing' (52), but after Siward leaves, Malcolm orders others to kill the man and his family. Eventually, Siward begins to order and commit increasingly violent acts himself. Even his chief aide Egham is taken aback when Siward orders the burning of a village and all the people in it: 'It's a bit Scandinavian, isn't it?', but Siward responds, 'If we make a threat we have to follow it through' (94). Even the sinister Malcolm asks Siward to hold back, but Siward replies: 'You don't restrain a dog when he's chasing a deer' (107). The link between Siward's rationality – 'I'm a soldier. I like clarity' (108) – and his violence becomes ever stronger, and he himself ultimately kills the Scottish Boy after an initial hesitation (123). As with most of Siward's actions, however, the result is the opposite of what was intended. Siward imagines that 'A knife is a knife, a neck is a neck. / He's dead', but Malcolm sees the Scottish reality: 'I think it's more likely that by killing this boy you have given him eternal life' (125), and in the final scene, Gruach confirms that Siward has brought upon himself and England an endless line of resistance: 'For as long as I reign I'll torment you and when I die I'll leave instructions in my

will to every Scottish Queen that comes after me to tell her King
to take up arms and torment England again and again and again
until the end of time' (136). Siward's defence resounds with irony:
'Everything I did, I did because I thought that doing it was for the
best' (132).

Greig never names 'Iraq' or 'Afghanistan' in the play, but at
some point audiences realize that the play is a temporal palimpsest,
that Siward's actions refract current political issues regarding the
extended occupation of these countries. Greig's 'starting point' for
the play, he said, was the question '"What happens after the dictator
falls?" Macbeth is a play about the toppling of a dictator; we would
see in it a mirror of Ceausescu or Gaddafi ... However, as we're
living in an Afghanistan/Iraq world ... [the play is] about an English
garrison trying to survive in hostile territory' (Brown 2011). The
parallels go beyond Siward's own actions to such incidents as the
Hen Girl, seemingly modelled on the idea of a suicide bomber –
after suffering abuse and humiliation from the English soldiers, she
stabs one of them, tries to free the prisoners, and then stabs herself.
Egham then comments: 'We have got to get out of this fucking
country' (119). Indeed, but somehow they can't.

Like Müller, Ionesco, and others before him in the modern
period, Greig inverts the traditional reading of Malcolm. The Stuart
triumphalism in which Malcolm is not only the 'rightful' successor
to Duncan but also a righteous man has given way to a depraved and
murderous sociopath. Not to be outdone by Ionesco's or Müller's
vicious Malcolms, Greig's Malcolm is without human feelings at all –
ordering the murder of innocent families, the burning of villages,
and worse. Promising 'total honesty', Malcolm tells his nation:

In that spirit I offer you the following. I will govern entirely in
the interests of me. In so far as I give consideration to you it will
be to calibrate exactly how much I can take from you before
you decide to attempt violence against me. I will periodically
and arbitrarily commit acts of violence against some or other
of you – in order that I can maintain a more general order in
the country. I will not dispose my mind to the improvement of
the country or to the conditions of its ordinary people. I will
not improve trade. I will maintain an army only in order to
submit you to my will. As far as foreign powers are concerned
I will submit to any humiliation in order to keep the friendship

of England .... And, most important of all, you need not waste
even a minute of your long cold nights wondering about whether
you are in or out of my favour. You are out of my favour. Now
and always. (80–1)

After this astonishing speech, the politics of the Scottish court,
usually so murky, clarify in a hopeless image of tyranny: not
Macbeth's tyranny, but that of the supposedly righteous successor,
Malcolm.

Political adaptations of *Macbeth* thus began immediately after
the Restoration, and continue to the present. As Greig said in an
interview, 'It's just the best play about power, governance and
tyranny that exists. It covers anything from Mafioso families to
Communist dictators .... There will never be a situation where the
overthrow of a tyrant is not germane to the day's politics' (Anon.
2016). These revisions described above add up to far more than
just tying 'up some of Shakespeare's loose ends', as one critic
said of Ionesco's version; rather, they constitute often radical re-
thinkings of the play's representations of sovereignty, succession
theory, regime change, and, especially, Malcolm's 'righteous' claim
to the throne, as well as the play's relation to the political worlds
around it.

Wartime Macbeth

Simply transposing the time of *Macbeth* from eleventh-century
Scotland to the present or recent past may lead to *au courant*
political interpretation, but it may also provide greater accessibility
for viewers by projecting a more familiar political situation.[46]
Many wartime updatings of *Macbeth* have been made in the last
twenty-five years.[47] Bogdanov's 1998 film, for example, opens
with the three witches as haggard women picking over the corpses
of a modern battlefield, when Macbeth and Banquo come riding
up on motorcycles. Duncan, back in the command tent, is in full
'contemporary' military gear with a sweeping leather overcoat. In
this severely cut version, the 'warlike army' in 4.3 is composed of
missiles and choppers, and, after a violent fight at the end, Macduff
grabs Macbeth's gun, shoots him, and drags his body in front of a

jeep. In the final scene, Macbeth's body is dumped by a front-end loader into the trash dump seen at the beginning, and the witches come to strip valuables from his body. There is little remarkable in these scenes of updating, but Bogdanov hints at a more cynical interpretation when his Malcolm smirks at the camera at 'Hail, King', and the circularity of first/last images suggests a cycle of violence that will not be resolved by Malcolm's ascent. The image of trash, moreover, indicts the waste of war in that society; although the witches have some supernatural powers (they disappear into the air in fragments in 1.3), they are primarily bag ladies, the poor detritus of the kingdom.

Bogdanov does not develop these political implications at much length, nor does Gregory Doran in his 2001 version. The video of this stage production translates the setting primarily through costumes, as most of the play takes place in a cavernous deserted warehouse: Macbeth and the other soldiers wear modern combat gear, their faces smeared with camouflage, carrying assault rifles, and so on. Duncan – unlike the powerful thane in Polanski's film – is a figure of holiness in a white gown and golden back-lighting. Malcolm is, contrary to his passivity in the plot, a strong soldier. This production wonderfully conveys Macbeth's increasing paranoia and desperation (the jerky movements of the camera are unsettling) even as it reinscribes the Authorized Version of the play: thus, in 4.3, Malcolm is seen with a crucifix looming over him, and at the end he is presented not with Macbeth's head but with the crown, and in his final speech there is no reference to the creation of 'earls' (an English, not Scottish title) or to the 'dead butcher'. In an image undermining the glorification of Malcolm, though, Doran (as many have done since Davenant; see **Chapter Three**) ends with an image of Fleance looking on, reminding the viewer that Malcolm's reign does not lead to a future succession of his line.

The adaptations described above are designed for a popular film or television audience; their ultimately conservative interpretations of the plays reconfirm traditional notions of *Macbeth*. The TR Warszawa *Macbeth: 2007* (directed by Grzegorz Jarzyna), however, unsettles its audience, through its two-level, multi-space setting (thus forcing a viewer to, as it were, multi-view and compare actions on one level with another), its war setting and brutality, and its alienating techniques of characterization, speech, and costuming. To say that this production was controversial is an understatement.

Charles Isherwood's review of the New York production perfectly reflects his assumption of the fallacy of fidelity:

> Jarzyna is putting Shakespeare to his own uses, repurposing the play as an allegory of the reckless abuse of power in the chaotic atmosphere of war: specifically the American-led war on terror. The problem with imposing a blunt contemporary interpretation on a classic text is that you risk vitiating the power of the material, stunting its theatrical potency.

Shakespeare's play, Isherwood asserts, 'really isn't a war play' and is just another example (cue the nationalistic note) of eurotrash (Isherwood 2008). Other reviewers were more sympathetic while still invoking a supposed original: 'the production [in Edinburgh in 2012] is most compelling when it's least Hollywood and most Shakespeare' (Gardner 2012). The production is 'repurposing the play', which is a (known) 'classic text', 'most Shakespeare', while the director 'is putting Shakespeare [the cultural icon, not so much the play] to his own uses': such comments can more easily be made from a privileged political position.

The setting of *Macbeth: 2007* suggested, at various moments, a castle, a war-ravaged village, a mosque, and a giant war machine. In the first scene, 'Major Macbeth' beheads an enemy combatant – it's the Middle East, though this time the victim is Muslim, as are the witches, who wear veils. Helicopters arrive with soldiers shimmying down ropes, video monitors dot different levels of the stage (Macduff's face appears on six screens during 4.3). The setting was the Western invasion of Iraq, but as Jarzyna said in an interview, he had broader interests as well:

> The reason we initially did this [allusions to US troops] was the war in Iraq. But I remember something Putin said after Chechnya, where the Russians killed thousands of people: 'We have a lot of things still to do'. It's the same mechanism, the same power .... Macbeth is a beast, but a reflective one. Putin is much simpler than that.
>
> (Dickson 2012)

Jarzyna said that the frenetic action of the production was quite deliberate: 'For me, the play is like a movie. It's very fast, the scenes are very brief. Macbeth doesn't have time to make proper decisions – he just has to act.' And he can really only do one thing, the thing that makes him feel alive: kill ('This is what you always dreamed of', Lady Macbeth tell him). At the end, Macduff beheads Macbeth, repeating the opening scene, and holds it up to Malcolm, who puts a helmet on it, with laughter. A programme note on the theatre company's website reproduced Jan Kott's interpretation of the play quoted earlier ('A production of Macbeth not evoking a picture of the world flooded with blood, would inevitably be false'). Jarzyna obviously did see *Macbeth* as a 'war play', and his analysis went beyond the (perhaps) facile contemporary parallels to something deeper, the ways in which war – masculine violence – corrupts and degrades all types of relationships: the sickening behaviour of the soldiers finds its parallel in the relation between Macbeth and Lady Macbeth.

Jarzyna's staging – with its inconsistencies, dislocations, multiple viewpoints, grotesque inventions (Lady Macbeth was electrocuted by a washing machine, and there was a man in a rabbit suit) – worked, in Brecht/Ionesco style, to prevent audience sympathy for any of the characters, forcing it to think about the horrors before them, not whether Macbeth's 'ambition' would be punished. In 2012, ironically (or not), the theatre company TR[48] Warszawa was itself quartered in a theatre 'that [had] doubled as a bunker during the second world war' (Dickson 2012).

Rupert Goold's 2010 film received the same kind of praise (though much more of it) and condemnation ('the director gimmicks everything up' instead of 'relying on *Shakespeare's* words', Mahon 2007: 81) as Jarzyna's production. But Goold's film reached a far broader audience (disseminated on public television in the United States), in part because of the known star power of its actors (Patrick Stewart and Kate Fleetwood), in part because while it is an updated version, it remains relatively close to the Folio, and uses Shakespeare's language, which Jarzyna did not. The film's setting is the Second World War and after, and Stewart's Macbeth alludes to Stalin. The visual resemblance is striking and compelling, but Goold extends the parallels in many ways: the Thane of Cawdor, for example, after being captured, sits strapped to a chair, his head hooded; a uniformed soldier marches briskly in and shoots him in the head. Goold also mixes in videotape and film footage of the Second World War battle scenes, Soviet troops marching with missiles through Red Square, and so on. An even more compelling insight develops in the banquet scene, when Macbeth forces his sycophantic followers to laugh when he laughs, stop when he stops, and then degrade themselves in a bout of musical chairs. This tyrannical behaviour reproduces the self-contradictions, banality, cruelty, and sheer idiocy of a Stalin or any other dictator. The more disturbing effects of Goold's film, as in Jarzyna's, stemmed from the relation between Macbeth and Lady Macbeth, the dearest partners of greatest collapsing into hatred and indifference (registered by Goold through their handfasting through the film).

Much of the military aspect of Goold's film is straightforward – generals, soldiers, cannons, tanks – but other aspects of his film (the 'gimmicks') produce genuine horrific effects, above all, the Witches (see **Figure 1**) – nurses, household servants, spectres, omni-present. I will not dwell on them here – they are probably the most-noted element of the film – except to note how Goold deployed them as just one of a range of shots and effects borrowed from slasher or horror films, such as the overhead lights that go on or off as one walks down the hallway, or the elevator to hell that, noir-like, casts bars across their faces as the Macbeths go up, then down. Goold's film illustrates well Lanier's observation that adapters deal not with an originary text but

> with a much more inchoate and complex web of intervening adaptations or, just as important, with the protocols – formal and ideological – of genres and media that have little to do with the Shakespearean text. (2014: 23)

Thus, one might argue, Goold finds contemporary equivalents to what we would imagine the early modern horror of regicide to be, or the fear of witches: the slaughter of Macduff's family registered by the forgotten doll left behind in the shower and the camera cut to a Bechstein piano at a high-culture song recital (4.2 to 4.3); the Witches' costumes suggesting both nurses and nuns, supposed figures of nurture and healing; the Porter as both skinhead and sexual pervert. If the supernatural has lost some of its hold over modern audiences, these other effects – 'gimmicks' or not – produce dread and horror of a related kind. Like Heiner Müller, Goold finds that 'One can say a lot of things about Stalin with a production of *Macbeth*', and even more about Stalinism and the effects of tyranny.

Müller and Goold take very different approaches to the play, but both see a terrible modernity in its politics. *Macbeth*'s depiction of war prompted an unexpected touring production in 2004, sponsored by the war machine *primus inter pares*, the US Department of Defence. The then-Chair of the National Endowment for the Arts, Dana Gioia, had approached the Pentagon to bankroll Shakespeare productions to tour at US military bases. The Alabama Shakespeare Festival's production, directed by Kent Thompson, staged the play in a set designed to invoke Stonehenge, 'to create a bold contrast between the sensual, passionate, and earthy world of medieval Scotland and the pristine, calculating world of Christian England', including costumes inspired 'by the appealing (if ahistorical) look of *Braveheart*' (Gioia 2004: 6). This adaptation seems to have been a 'normative MACBETH', in Fedderson and Richardson's term: the director commented that the play 'is a cautionary tale of the dangerous, intoxicating temptation of ultimate power' that reveals 'the troubling, dark soul of human evil' (6). Gioia must have concurred with this Authorized Version, because he 'insist[ed] that the choice of "Macbeth" reflects no underlying message; it is just a short well-known and portable play with a small ... cast' ('Let slip' 2004). The production may have had more troubling elements in it, in the form of a callous Duncan and a shifty Malcolm, according to one reviewer (Ford 2005: 171). If *Macbeth* can be used – as if it is *not* 'political' – to teach business leadership or just serve as neutral entertainment for the military, it can only be by disregarding over four hundred years of political adaptations and interpretations.

The very model of a modern major dictator

Contemporary adaptations, then, have become increasingly 'political', even if at times only in outward form. 'General Macbeth', as Mary McCarthy terms him in her essay, 'is not a monster' (1962: 234), not even much of a general ('pedestrian', 232), but 'the contemporary Macbeth', she writes, 'may breed monsters' (240), and modern adapters have linked Macbeth to the full range of contemporary monsters: Stalin, Hitler,[49] Idi Amin,[50] and others, as we've seen, from Ceaucescu to Salazar. Barbara Garson's 1967 play *MacBird!*, which refers to the 1963 assassination of John F. Kennedy, has lost much of its edge because of its too-specific allegorizing of characters and events, and perhaps also because of its broad scattershot of satiric targets. Garson borrows lines and ideas from several other Shakespeare plays (the Prologue borrows from *Henry V*'s prologue, for example), but its essential basis derives from *Macbeth*, as did the initial idea from her own slip of the tongue in a speech in which 'Lady Bird Johnson' came out as 'Lady MacBird Johnson' (Buhler 2008: 259). Its contemporary moment of success, however, was curtailed by the 1968 assassination of Robert F. Kennedy, a character in the play, after which productions of *MacBird!* were cancelled across the country. Garson's play was a controversial success, but the imprecision of its focus – was Lyndon Johnson really behind the assassination of JFK? Was JFK in the same position as Duncan, or perhaps more his opposite? – makes it less compelling today.

Finally, Seth Greenland's 1994 play *Jungle Rot* invoked *Macbeth* in its representation of the 1961 assassination of Patrice Lumumba (Buhler 2008). Greenland's Lady Macbeth is 'Patience Stillman' (a fraught name, to say the least), wife of a minor US diplomat in the Congo (now Zaire), who herself attempts to murder Lumumba with – shades of *The Revenger's Tragedy* – poison in her lipstick, an overdetermined plot point if there ever was one. But she cannot do it, so it falls not to her Macbeth-figure husband, but to a bland CIA agent, to do the deed.

* * *

Political adaptations of the play since 1664 reflect transformations in the interpretation of the character Macbeth, as we have seen; when a given Macbeth is linked with Stalin or Hitler, his victims receive even more sympathy than the play gives them, and his opponents are frequently made, if not saintly, then at least politically justified in his removal. Who would not have assassinated Hitler had they the opportunity? But the history of political adaptations also reveals some considerable revision and recalibration of the play's oppositional figures, Duncan, Malcolm, and Fleance, as we shall see in the next two chapters. They often turn out to be just new versions of the tyrant himself. The politics of the play have frequently been reversed since Davenant's time.

2

'The gracious Duncan' and 'our eldest, Malcolm'

The phrase 'the gracious Duncan' appears three times in the play – when Macbeth laments that he has murdered the king and defiled his mind only for Banquo's issue to succeed (3.1.65), and twice again when Lennox reports to the anonymous Lord (3.6.3, 10) on recent events in Scotland. In the first three centuries of Macbeth discourse that preceded Shakespeare's play, however, there are no references at all to Duncan's nature. In the first accounts in the chronicles,[1] Duncan is merely the king slain, not necessarily murdered, and little is said about him. By the sixteenth century, however, Scottish historians had developed two largely incompatible visions of Duncan, a contradiction that Shakespeare's play embraces but one which has forced modern adapters to make difficult, usually binary, representational choices. Duncan, then, is (1) Shakespeare's 'most ideal king', 'gracious and kindly' (Paul 1950: 197), 'adroit and very much in command … a perfect, courteous king' (Hall 1982: 234). The long-enduring Royalist reading of the play, as we saw in Chapter One, requires such a reading. But (2) Duncan is also a Weak King, with both personal and political failings, as evidenced by the chaos from which Scotland must be rescued as the play begins. Similar difficulties, as we will see, also attend representations of Malcolm.

As we saw in the Introduction, John Major in 1521 analysed Duncan's death by noting 'Now those kings showed a grave want of foresight, in that they found no way of union and friendship with the opposing faction […] for to gain a kingdom many a wicked act is done' (Major 1892: 120–1). Here is one of the first instances of Duncan as Weak King, which would soon be considerably surpassed in Boece's 1527 narrative, which offers a damning interpretation of Duncan. Boece described him as 'so merciful, that he appeared not able to punish the vices of his people'; Macbeth, by contrast, 'was given as much to cruelty as Duncan was given to piety'. While Duncan governed his realm 'in good peace and justice' at the beginning, thanks to the continuation of his father's counsellors, 'Yet the feeble mind of Duncan, when it was patent to the people, was not only cause of great sedition among the nobles, but occasion to Danes to attempt new wars against the Scots', and ultimately 'more able to govern an abbey of monks than to guide any band of warmen' (Boece 1821: 2.253). Holinshed related that Macbeth spoke 'much against the king's softness, and overmuch slackness in punishing offenders'; Duncan was a 'dull coward and slothful person' (1808: 5.265, 267). George Buchanan developed the narrative further, blaming, as others had done, the victim Duncan as well as his murderer Macbeth. Duncan was

> a Prince of great Courtesy, and of more Indulgence to his own Kindred, than became a King: For he was of a mild and Inclinable Disposition […] he administered Justice with great Equity … he would not suffer the Great men to oppress Them [the poor]. But, as these Virtues did endear him to the Good, so they lessened his Authority amongst the Lovers of Sedition, so that his Clemency to the Former occasioned the Rage of wicked men against him. (1690: 7.207)

Duncan was an 'effeminate [we shall return to this trope] and slothful King' (7.207), incapable of effective rule, and Macbeth 'had always a Disgust at the un-active Slothfulness of his Cousin' (7.210).

As a consequence of particular political or religious positions, the weak Duncan could also be represented as 'gracious' and saintly, his lack of worldly competence turned, through ideological pressure, into a virtue. For John Leslie – adviser to Mary Queen of Scots – Macbeth 'impiously murdered the saintly (*sanctissimum*) King Duncan' (Bullough 7.518). Duncan was

> a man in whom clearly nature had placed nothing of cruelty, no moroseness, no bitterness, so that he would not avenge the deepest injury done to him. Having such marvellous lenity of

mind, when the populace, like wild beasts loosed from all restraint, had impiously abused it with sinful license, because he could in no way lay aside his clemency, he handed over the cares of administering the kingdom to Macbeth, a man rather more inclined to severity than himself. (7.517)

Leslie's account verges on hagiography, the blame for Duncan's failure now the 'wild' and 'sinful' populace, not the politics of court faction.

The language of these earlier adaptations constructs Duncan as either weak, feeble, slothful, and 'effeminate', or as 'saintly' and too good for this world. In his report of a performance at the Globe in 1611, Simon Forman noted only that Duncan was 'king of Scots, and it was in the days of Edward the Confessor. And Duncan bad them both [Macbeth and Banquo] kindly welcome', without any further characterization (Chambers 2.337). Forman's association of Duncan with Edward the Confessor, to whose court Malcolm flees, however, is a further reflection of (though also contrast to) Duncan's holiness: Edward (in the play) can cure the sick of the King's Evil – 'at his touch, / Such sanctity hath heaven given his hand [...] a most miraculous work in this good king' (4.3.143-4, 147) – while Scottish kings have no such power. But 'Gracious' (190) Edward – the adjective linking the two kings – also provides the ten thousand English soldiers to invade Scotland and 'Lent us good Siward [...] An older and a better soldier, none / That Christendom gives out' (4.3.190-3). Edward thus provides an example of holiness *and* military strength to which Duncan might aspire.

In much of modern criticism, the Duncan of Shakespeare's play has enjoyed a surprisingly good press, following Paul's interpretation. Paul attempted to counter criticisms of Duncan's personal qualities by arguing that he was 'too old ... to fight personally in battle but nowise lacking in courage or firmness' (Paul 1950: 197). For Maynard Mack, Jr., Duncan is 'Loved, loving, trusting, generous, surrounded with images of fertility and divine grace too numerous to count[;] he is presented to us, in a brief glimpse, as the ideal king for an ideal world' (Mack 1973: 150). As Mack goes on to say, Duncan of course does not live in an 'ideal world'. The problems are thus not his, but those of the world. Adelman (1992: 132) notes, though, that this notion of Duncan as 'the single source from which all good can flow' is a nostalgic fantasy: 'Heavily idealized, this ideally protective father is nonetheless largely ineffectual: even while he is alive, he is unable to hold his kingdom together.' An even more sceptical account of Duncan's practical failures has been mounted by Berger 1980, and many others following him. Goldberg astutely observes that 'No one speaks about Duncan in these [idealized] terms before his death' (1987: 261n.5), though Macbeth worries that Duncan's virtues 'Will plead like angels' (1.7.19) against his murder. Still, Goldberg's point holds: Duncan is *remembered* in a way that differs from the pragmatics of his failing rule. His idealization follows his murder in a kind of recoil from the fact. The truth of Duncan's actual rule is that as the play opens, the kingdom is threatened and unstable: there is treason at large and foreign invasions; Duncan has initiated a new system of succession and named as his heir a son who also did not fight; and the play offers several occasions when the audience sees Duncan's failure to see beyond surfaces and faces. Can Duncan be both 'gracious' and a bad king?

Shakespeare's play represents both sides of Duncan inherited from the chronicles: the weak king and Leslie's '*sanctissimum Regem (qui illum tanto honore ornarat)*' (Leslie 1577: Ff3r). Duncan appears only in 1.2, 1.4, and 1.6, and is murdered between 2.1 and 2.2. He speaks relatively few lines, and seems both generous in his praise ('O valiant cousin, worthy gentleman', 1.2.24) and hopelessly naïve, particularly when he greets Macbeth after the battle –

> There's no art
> To find the mind's construction in the face:
> He [the Thane of Cawdor] was a gentleman on whom I built
>   An absolute trust.[2]
> *Enter* MACBETH, BANQUO, ROSS, *and* ANGUS
>   O worthiest cousin (1.4.11-14),

and when he arrives at Macbeth's castle: 'This castle hath a pleasant seat, the air / Nimbly and sweetly recommends itself / Unto our gentle senses' (1.6.1-3). The play's Duncan is also extremely passive, as numerous critics have pointed out: he is not shown engaging in battle himself (nor is Malcolm), instead rewarding those who kill in his name with titles and honours, the political currency of the play's Scotland.

The Duncan of the Folio, however, is accorded respect if not beatification throughout his brief life, in spite of his political failures. After his capture, Cawdor 'Implored [Duncan's] pardon, and set forth / A deep repentance' (1.4.6-7). And when reporting to Duncan in 1.4, Macbeth invokes, however obsequiously, the bonds of king/subject loyalty: 'Your highness' part / Is to receive our duties, and our duties / Are to your throne and state, children and servants, / Which do but what they should, by doing everything / Safe toward your love and honour' (1.4.23-7). When Macbeth begins to hesitate in killing the king, he reflects that 'this Duncan / Hath borne his faculties so meek, hath been / So clear in his great office, that his virtues / Will plead like angels, trumpet-tongued, against / The deep damnation of his taking-off; / And pity, like a naked new-born babe, / Striding the blast, or heaven's cherubin, horsed / Upon the sightless couriers of the air, / Shall blow the horrid deed in every eye, / That tears shall drown the wind' (1.7.16-25). Duncan's divinity – not his weakness – is emphasized after his death in Macduff's announcement of his murder: 'Most sacrilegious murder hath broke ope / The Lord's anointed temple, and stole thence / The life o'th'building' (2.3.67-9). One can hardly make a stronger association with the divine than with the Eucharist itself.

But the other side of Duncan, already evident in his political and military passivity, receives emphasis in the horror of his mutilated body, which Macduff also announces: 'Approach the chamber and destroy your sight / With a new Gorgon … look on death itself … see / The great doom's image' (2.3.71, 77-8). As Marjorie Garber (1987) and others note, the reference to the Gorgon (here, Medusa, the mortal of three sisters, who turned those who viewed her face into stone) effeminizes Duncan's body, as do the rape-allusions to his murder ('Tarquin's ravishing strides', 2.1.55; 'their daggers / Unmannerly breeched with gore', 2.3.116-7), the penetrative nature of the assault on a helpless victim in bed, and Macbeth's description of his wounds ('his gashed stabs looked like a breach in nature / For ruin's wasteful entrance' [2.3.114-5]).[3] Duncan's body is further reduced to a mere vessel ('Yet who would have thought the old man to have had so much blood in him?' [5.1.39-40]) of the fluids of lineage/death: 'The spring, the head, the fountain of your blood', Macbeth tells Malcolm and Donaldbain, 'Is stopped, the very source of it is stopped' (2.3.99-100). This bifurcated royal image – sacred body and leaky corpse – reflects something of the early modern concept of the King's Two Bodies, as Ernst Kantorowicz (1957) has taught us. The Body Politic and the Body Natural remain important concepts through which to view the early modern body.

Yet how can this body – unified in theory, divided in reality – be represented on the stage or in film, or, for that matter, in the court? King James I's enfeebled, at times slovenly, and, to some court observers, repulsive personal bodily habits contrasted enormously with his claims of sovereign power: 'Kings are justly called Gods, for that they exercise a manner or resemblance of Divine power upon earth', he lectured Parliament in 1610, 'For if you will consider the Attributes to God, you shall see how they agree in the person of a King' (McIlwain 1918: 307).[4] James at least had the power of the kingship to enforce, to the extent he could, his own self-image, but adapters, especially those who work in film or the stage, confined by the tenets of pseudo-realism, have a more difficult task. Their choices for Duncan's physique, clothing, speech, and actions reflect both sides of Duncan, but rarely at the same time. If the issue in Shakespeare's time was the King's body politic or body natural, for later adapters the issue became whether Duncan was indeed a 'gracious' figure, or one who actually deserved his fate, who brought it upon himself, as some chroniclers suggested. In theory, Duncan should have been sacred and untouchable, but the changing political contexts of the play have led, increasingly, to ambivalent or even hostile representations. Perhaps the most complete reduction of Duncan to non-royal status appeared in Alan Cumming's 2012 one-man performance of all the roles: Duncan became a childish fop, and when Cumming sought something in the room to represent Malcolm, he found a baby doll in the corner (see **Epilogue**).

Bad Duncan

The first adapters followed the Royalist line in representing Duncan as gracious, even holy, and depicting his murder in apocalyptic terms; the nature of the victim was not in doubt, so the focus was primarily on the perpetrators. Duncan continued inviolate in many adaptations, but a counter, more sceptical or negative view of Duncan has emerged in more contemporary works. Ionesco, as we saw in **Chapter One**, turned the play's values inside out. He understood that the vision of Duncan as 'generosity incarnate ....

He is virtue itself .... He's incorruptible' (8-9) was a mirage. His cowardly Duncan sought refuge far behind the battle lines ('Safety first, I always say', 20), where he will watch the action 'through my telescope' (23). Even the witches critique his cowardice: 'He doesn't know how to hold an ax .... He can't fight himself – he sends other out to do it for him .... He'd be too frightened' (50). Ionesco's mordant irony parodies Duncan's Folio speech of gratitude in 1.4: 'Thank you all again, dead or alive, for having defended my throne ... which, of course, is also yours. When you return home, whether it be to your humble villages, your lowly hearths, or your simple but glorious tombs, you will be an example to generations to come, now and in the future and, better still, in the past' (28). Banco and Macbett pivot easily from the idealization of Duncan as divine ruler to the complaint that he is 'A real autocrat! Nowadays autocracy isn't always the best way to govern' (66), and then demonize him with the same enthusiasm with which they had praised him earlier:

Banco.   The blood we've shed for him.
Macbett. The dangers we've undergone.
Banco.   Ten thousand chickens, ten thousand horses, ten thousand recruits. What does he do with them? He can't eat them all. The rest just goes bad.
Macbett. And a thousand young girls.
Banco.   We know what he does with them. (68)

In their novelization of the play, Hartley and Hewson likewise turned Duncan into a paedophile (see **Chapter Five**). Heiner Müller simplifies Duncan's indebtedness to others for his safety and his unacceptable privilege with a curt stage direction opening scene 3: *'Duncan, seated on corpses that have been stacked to create a throne'*. He then proceeds to hold up the executed Cawdor's head and *'Boxes the ears of the head'*, eventually letting it drop to the floor (Weber 2012: 19).

Adapters produce a 'bad' Duncan through a combination of his flaws: his violation of Celtic norms; his cowardice/weakness; his immorality. Susan Fraser King's historically based novel (see **Chapter Six**) describes Duncan as 'not the warrior' that Macbeth and Banquo are (King 2008: 138), though not a coward; his strategies in politics and battle are deeply flawed, and lead to his unsteady claim to power. Aware of Macbeth's threat, Duncan attempts to poison Macbeth (249), but he survives. Duncan is ultimately killed, as he was in the early historical records, in a one-on-one combat with Macbeth: 'It was brutal and fast. Duncan was powerful, bullish, and persistent. But Macbeth had greater skill, and his sword was swift and sure; a taller man, he had the longer reach' (266). Duncan wounds Macbeth, but is eventually vanquished – yet Macbeth resists administering a coup-de-grace over the prostrate king, thrusting his sword into the ground and walking away (267). Following a code of honour, the Macbeths aid in helping deal with Duncan's wounds, but he dies nevertheless (269). A worthy but dangerous opponent, King's Duncan just couldn't handle Macbeth.

In Lisa Klein's young adult novel, *Lady Macbeth's Daughter* (see **Chapter Six**), Lady Macbeth (or 'Albia') resents Duncan ('that imposter, undeserving and untested, placed on a throne of ease by his grandfather Malcolm!' [Klein 2009: 15]), well aware of her own royal bloodline. When the King visits Macbeth's castle, Duncan is further revealed as degenerate – 'The king is drunk .... his eyes barely able to focus' (49) – who seals his own fate by naming the ineffective Malcolm his successor: 'How dare Duncan', she says to herself, 'whose grandfather shut my kin out of the succession – now try to extend his rule to the next generation! The injustice of it brings my blood to the boiling point' (50), and he is murdered that night. John Passfield's *Lord and Lady Macbeth: Full of Scorpions Is My Mind* represents Duncan in similar terms: his 'foolish strategy' (Passfield 2019: 20) reinforces Macbeth's sense of his own superiority ('Either Duncan must be deposed or I shall not serve', 20), and his violation of the system of succession (36-7) is the last straw. At the very least, Duncan is frequently depicted as taking the credit for Macbeth and Banquo's accomplishments, as he is in Marc Brozel's 2005 *Shakespeare ReTold* film, where the real stars of Duncan Docherty's three-star Michelin restaurant are the subordinate chefs Joe Macbeth and Billy Banquo. Going several steps further, however, Richter and Andrade's *Marqués – a narco-Macbeth* displays Duncan as a violent drug cartel war-lord who has the bleeding messenger at the beginning shot in the head (2016: 12), and, in a drugged state, engages in a violent struggle with Macbeth (Marqués), 'mule-kicks Doña Marqués in the stomach', fires a pistol which inadvertently 'hit Lillia [his wife] in the chest', and then is stabbed repeatedly by Marqués until he succumbs.

Similarly, the Duncan of the 2001 film *Rave Macbeth* is a drug lord – working ultimately for Hecate – who runs the 'Club' where E and other drugs are sold. The Duncans in *noir* adaptations (see **Chapter Four**) are invariably made men who have murdered their own way to the top, and in most cases fully deserve their violent deaths. Thus, Duncan is often not represented as *sanctissimum* but as *maxime malevolos*, from Ionesco's tyrant to contemporary gang leaders.

Duncan on screen

Modern filmmakers have tended to show one side or the other of Duncan, but rarely have managed to suggest both. Orson Welles (1948) showed a fleshy, solid Duncan, dressed in kilt with thick accent, but Welles also interpolated a scene in which the assembled Scots knelt in Christian prayer, held candles, and renounced the Devil. Almond's BBC television version (1983) showed a powerful chieftain with walrus moustache, leading his troops without fear. Probably the most powerful Duncan ever shown on screen was Roman Polanski's brute (1971), effortlessly riding horseback at the head of his troops, personally lifting the chain of office from the neck of the Thane of Cawdor, and greeting Macbeth in a shot surely meant to call to mind King James himself (**Figure 3**) – with the essential difference that Polanski's warrior holds a sword rather than the traditional orb and sceptre of peace. Bogdanov's film (1998), set in a modern period of war, showed Duncan as a highly capable and charismatic military leader, out among his troops on the heath, while Goold's film (2010) offered a similarly modernized war setting with Duncan as a strong and cunning military figure in a shiny leather military coat. Wright's 2006 film, set in modern-day Australia's underworld, makes Duncan a *capo di tutt'i capi* with expensive suits, a rasping voice, 4 o'clock stubble, and a $250 haircut. Daniel Coll's 2012 film showed a strong Duncan, powerfully built, wearing what were supposed to be fur and ermine but looked more like a shag rug or beach towel. Finally, the 2015 Kurzel film showed Duncan as strong, independent, wearing a vaguely druidical costume, powerfully drawing bow and arrow, and fully the equal of Macbeth.

FIGURE 3 *Duncan. Macbeth directed by Roman Polanski © Playboy Productions, Caliban Films 1971. All rights reserved. Screen grab.*

Images of a powerful, even militarized Duncan such as these beg a difficult question: how could such a skilled warrior as Kurzel's archer or a hardened survivor like Wright's Godfather – such 'masculine' men – be so incompetent in managing their kingdoms, so blind to the treachery of their erstwhile supporters? Only a few directors have represented Duncan in his weakness, rather than his power. The Casson film (1979), for example, shows a white-bearded, white-garbed Duncan with a large gold crucifix hanging from his neck, his expression often sad, even pain-wracked, hardly able to stand on his own without Malcolm's assistance (**Figure 4**), and actually carried in to Macbeth's castle in 1.6. Taking Duncan's holiness even further, the Doran film shows Duncan entering in a blaze of golden light through an open door, holding a sceptre with cross, as the assembled court sings a *Te deum*. These are holy kings, but they are virtually begging to be murdered. Casson's Duncan is particularly pathetic when he arrives at Macbeth's castle, his bodily infirmity figuring his political weakness.

FIGURE 4 *Malcolm and Duncan.* Macbeth *directed by Philip Casson* © A&E Home Video 1979. All rights reserved. Screen grab.

The powerful Duncans make equally confident, impressive entrances to Macbeth's castle in 1.6: Polanski's Duncan dances with Lady Macbeth, while Goold's enters through the kitchen (not noticing the murderous witches chopping up meat), where he is fed a morsel by Lady Macbeth. Bogdanov's Duncan has changed into a sleek white Nehru suit as he enters with confidence; he is, Lehmann has noted (2003: 237), 'a portrait of senile capitalism in its worst incarnation ... a noir father'. Wright's smooth gangster Duncan, also changed into leisure wear, actually flirts with Lady Macbeth at the party. These powerful Duncans are men of the world, at home in the salon as well as the battlefield. Their patriarchal corruption is suggested by their indifference to and ignorance of others: in many ways, they deserve to be murdered. The 'divine' Duncans, by contrast, virtually serve themselves up to be devoured.

Duncan's body

Thus most films of *Macbeth* have not quite succeeded in representing the *idea* of the King with two bodies, but many films and stage productions have, perhaps in recompense, resorted to graphic visions of the King's third body – his dead one – as a huge contrast to the formerly powerful king. Shakespeare famously did not show the murder scene, but that has not prevented adapters from describing or displaying the primal scene, that which would turn the viewer to stone, in various levels of bloody detail. Welles apparently began the practice in film, with a quick view of the murdered king in his bed, and while Polanski gave us the first film view of the murder itself, in exceptionally gory detail, he also added the twist of Duncan awaking just as Macbeth is about to pull away, breathing the word 'Macbeth' which launches a murderous attack; Polanski's camera then lingers on the king's mutilated body. Bogdanov also provides a shot of the bloat king's body in striped pajamas, while Coll shows the murder itself discreetly from behind the bed. Wright copies Polanski in several ways, showing Duncan asleep in bed, then waking to recognize Macbeth, then his bloodied body after the attack. Kurzel follows this tradition in showing the king asleep, waking to recognize Macbeth, and bloodied in death, with Macbeth lingering on the floor beside Duncan's body.

The scene that Shakespeare withholds from his on-stage audience has almost become *de rigeur* at the cineplex. And just in case the audience hasn't seen enough, Kurzel offers a final, full frontal view of Duncan's ruined body. Many of the recent print adaptations of the play similar feature lengthy descriptions of the carnage, often with the Duncan-figure opening his eyes, recognizing Macbeth (as in Polanski), and even fighting back. The video of Branagh's 2013 production shows Duncan in bed at the end of a long shot, and Macbeth crawling onto the bed to stab him repeatedly. As Susan Zimmerman points out, depictions of Duncan's body rather miss the point:

> The withholding of the dead Duncan from view reinforces Macduff's description of the King's body: it is a 'new Gorgon' (2.3.73), a reincarnation of the female Medusa ... the prohibition of the Medusa foregrounds the danger of apprehending that which exists outside any symbolic frame of reference ... To view the Medusa is to discover the indeterminacy of originary being and to lose one's 'self' as a consequence. (Zimmerman 2005: 173)

The exposure or description of the murder and the display of the King's body, generally not (perhaps ever) done before the twentieth century, reflects the necessity for adapters to find for contemporary audiences the equivalent horror of what regicide may have meant to an early modern audience, especially in secularized societies. Branagh's 2013 production took place in a deconsecrated Victorian church, deploying formerly holy ground to produce an effect of sacrilege in the regicide. Passfield (2019a: 45) offers a straight-forward adapter's logic behind his showing of the scene in a different aesthetic medium: 'It is interesting that Shakespeare has Gloucester's eyes cut out on stage and yet has Duncan murdered off-stage. I felt free to alter the scenes of the play, to add scenes to those of the play or to omit scenes of the play as the novel required them.'

Although the Folio withholds the sight of such carnage, it does continue to invoke the result of it: Duncan's third, dead body after his murder, from Lady Macbeth's 'Had he not resembled / My father as he slept, I had done't' (2.2.12-13) and Macbeth's wish that the knocking at the gate would 'Wake Duncan' (2.2.77). The king's body never seems quite at rest. We have already quoted the lines about 'The Lord's anointed temple' and the 'new Gorgon' – "death itself [...] The great doom's image', according to Macduff. Macbeth betrays his anxiety in describing the scene: 'Here lay Duncan, / His silver skin laced with his golden blood / And his gashed stabs looked like a breach in nature, / For ruin's wasteful entrance' (2.3.104-7), the unreality of the silver/gold allusion pointing to both Duncan's royal nature and Macbeth's royal designs. Later, after Macbeth's departure to Scone to be invested with the kingship, Ross wonders 'Where is Duncan's body?' – a question that resonates throughout the play. In this case the answer is straightforward: 'Carried to Colmkill, / The sacred storehouse of his predecessors / And guardian of their bones' (2.4.33-5). But Duncan is far from forgotten: Macbeth laments that he has murdered 'the gracious Duncan' for Banquo's descendants (3.1.67), and describes to his wife how he remains haunted by the dead king in 'terrible dreams / That shake us nightly':

> Better be with the dead
> Whom we, to gain our peace, have sent to peace,
> Than on the torture of the mind to lie
> In restless ecstasy. Duncan is in his grave,
> After life's fitful fever, he sleeps well. (3.2.18-23)

Duncan's figurative sleep – his passivity, his blindness – led to his murder, but now his sleep is a good thing. The ghost of Banquo is only, Lady Macbeth says, 'the air-drawn dagger which you said / Led you to Duncan' but Macbeth fears 'If charnel-houses and our graves must send / Those that we bury back, our monuments / Shall be the maws of kites' (3.4.62-3, 71-3). Worst of all, 'The time has been / That when the brains were out, the man would die, / And there an end. But now they rise again' (3.4.78-80). Macbeth is speaking of Banquo's ghost here, but he is no less haunted by Duncan. Macbeth's nemesis Malcolm, for example, is identified simply as 'The son of Duncan' (3.6.18, 24), and Macduff reemphasizes Duncan's spirituality in describing him to Malcolm: 'Thy royal father / Was a most sainted king' (4.3.108-9). Lady Macbeth, on the other hand, has fallen into a permanent coma/ memory of 'the old man' who 'had so much blood in him', so much that 'Here's the smell of the blood still; all the perfumes of Arabia will not sweeten this little hand' (5.1.33-4, 42-3). Duncan's memory

– simultaneously the 'sainted king' and just an 'old man' – at last vanishes in the play's final bloodbath. Or does it?

Duncan's ghost

Given Duncan's importance in the play, and prominence even after his death, it is somewhat surprising that Shakespeare showed Macbeth haunted by Banquo's ghost, rather than Duncan's (as Brutus was by Julius Caesar's ghost, or Richard III by his many victims; Claudius is an outlier). But Davenant remedied that omission in his adaptation, when his Lady Macbeth tells her husband '*Duncan* is dead. [...] And yet to Me he Lives. / His fatal Ghost is now my shadow, and pursues me / Where e're I go'. Macbeth tells her it is just her 'Fears [...] there's nothing', in a reversal of the banquet scene, but Duncan's ghost reappears right on cue: 'As King', she tells Macbeth, 'your Crown sits heavy on your Head, / But heavier on my Heart: I have had too much / Of Kings already. See the Ghost again. [*Ghost appears*', but it won't speak to her (Davenant 1674: 53). As we saw in **Chapter One**, Ducis followed suit by producing Duncan's ghost for the 1784 coronation scene, in which Macbeth 'sees the spectre or shadow of King Duncan ... standing and bloody before the door and on the level of the chamber where this Sovereign and the Prince Glamis have been massacred' (Golder 1992: 212). Milton had imagined a work in which 'the matter of Duncan may be express't by the appearing of his ghost' (Milton 1938: 245), and Duncan's ghost, or corpse, has a habit of returning at the end of productions of Verdi's opera (see **Chapter Eight**). The author I.W.C. argued in an 1825 essay that in the banquet scene not one but 'two ghosts are seen, Duncan's first, and afterwards, that of Banquo; for what new terror ... is to be produced by the re-appearance of the same object in the same scene? ... which [ghost] had the superior claim, or what was the more likely to harrow the remorseless bosom of Macbeth?' (I.W.C 1825: 334). Answering his own question and reading the scene in excruciating detail, I.W.C. concludes that 'The ghost of Duncan having performed his office, and departed, Macbeth is at leisure to ruminate on the prodigy' (335).

Few other adapters followed Davenant or accepted I.W.C.'s logic, but in nineteenth-century burlesque adaptations, Duncan often lived on. In the 1838 *Macbeth Modernised* (Wells 1978: 2.152), the undead Duncan pops into the battle between Macduff and Macbeth, hides behind a screen to observe Lady Macbeth, who, when she sees him, says 'Ha! the King not dead! then a Queen I ain't; / But think not I am going to scream or faint!' (153). Duncan spares Banquo (also alive) and Macbeth, but pronounces this misogynist shrew-punishment on Lady Macbeth: 'a sentence worse / Than death itself. Lady, you don't converse ... for one whole week' (155), but even that punishment is reprieved and the play ends with all singing 'a health to our guests all around' (156). Not to be outdone, Francis Talfourd, in his 1849 *Macbeth, Somewhat Removed from the Text of Shakespeare*, waited until Macbeth was (apparently) slain before his Duncan reentered the play: '*Duncan* enters, comes between them [Malcolm and Macduff], nods and winks at them, takes the crown, and places it on his own head. They fall back in astonishment' (Wells 1978: 3.42). Macbeth, too, rises alive, saying to Duncan, 'I tender, Sir, of course, my resignation' (43) and, joined by the revived Banquo and Lady Macbeth, this adaptation, too, ends with a group song to 'our kind friends here to-night' (44). In a far bleaker adaptation, Tom Magill's 2007 film *Mickey B* (see **Chapter Four**), Duncan's ghost sits with Banquo's ghost, hovering spectrally in an empty prison cell. 'Th'unguarded Duncan' (1.7.70) may be dead but his dead body has risen again in some adaptations, his bloodied third body or his ghost at times overwhelming his other bodily representations.

'Our eldest, Malcolm'

As the Royalist interpretation of the play has pivoted, in many modern adaptations, some adapters have, as they did with Duncan, totally transformed Malcolm from the righteous, 'almost saintly figure' (McLuskie 2009: 47) who has 'legally inherited' the throne from his father to a murderous tyrant: as we saw in **Chapter One**, Müller, Ionesco, Greig, and many others see the new regime as no better than Macbeth's rule, indeed, as part of an endless cycle of political tyranny. The crowning of Malcolm at the end of the Folio has, for adaptations still adhering to the Authorized Version, been a celebration of legitimacy and peace, culminating in the new 'honors' granted to the survivors of the 'dead butcher and his fiendlike queen'. The presentation of the sword rather than Macbeth's head (in Davenant and Ducis) indicates a ritual of healing and justice, while in some contemporary adaptations, by contrast, a sinister Malcolm instigates a new wave of violence on the spot.

Malcolm has been characterized in these negative ways at the end of the story through staging, rearranging of his lines, costuming, or a wholesale revision of the stage directions, as in Müller's cascade of 'Heil's or Rupert Goold's blood-soaked Malcolm holding Macbeth's severed head up in what he thinks is triumph. The Folio does suggest a circularity, in the account of the traitor Macdonwald's severed head, 'fixed ... upon our battlements' (1.2.23), matched by 'Th' usurper's cursed head', Macbeth, brought in by Macduff. Aside from a well-earned distrust of the instruments of regime change, adapters have also had to deal with the scene that contains most of Malcolm's lines in the play, 4.3, the 'test' of Macduff while Malcolm is in the English court of the off-stage Edward the Confessor.

For film and stage productions especially, 4.3 has often been critiqued as too long, too boring, too confusing (what exactly is Ross doing in withholding, the first time around, his dreadful news?), too undramatic. Major cuts are the norm. The interlude in the middle of the scene – the account of Edward the Confessor's healing of the sick through the Royal Touch – is rarely if ever performed. Ionesco had ironically used the idea of the scene, though with Banco rather than Macol disguised as the Monk, as a vehicle for murder rather than healing. In his encyclopaedic summary of productions through about 1977, Marvin Rosenberg described the scene as a whole in detail, noting the symbolic importance of the Doctor interlude, yet apparently could not find a single production of it to mention (1978: 550–2). John Wilders's survey notes that it was cut altogether by Garrick, Phelps, Kean, and Forbes-Robertson (among others he does not mention), while the promptbook of a 1976 production indicates that Trevor Nunn 'cut the Doctor and gave his speech to Malcolm' (2004: 187).

I have already alluded, in the Introduction, to Gary Taylor's suggested rewriting of the scene to accord with notions of Shakespeare's and Middleton's presumed religious positions, but Taylor is not alone in re-imagining the problematic scene. Nevil Coghill anticipated Taylor in suggesting that the scene *should* have shown an interview between Macduff and Edward, as (presumably) anticipated by the unnamed Lord at 3.6.29-31 ('Macduff / Is gone [to England], to pray the holy king upon his aid / To wake Northumberland and warlike Siward etc') rather than the Doctor of the Folio. 'In the scene that seems to have been lost', Coghill speculates,

> I would suppose there to have been the solemn procession of the holy King, under a canopy, borne perhaps by monks, with a ceremonial bell before it, and, behind, a troupe of scrofulous wretches; then a solicitation of Heaven, during which all would kneel; and the bestowal of a golden stamp on each would follow, with the ensuing miracle of a cure, so easily effected on the stage by the concealed removal of an ulcerous mask; and after that some notes of a *Gloria* or a *Te Deum*, and finally a prophecy of victory to Malcolm and a blessing on Scotland pronounced by the Saint. (Coghill 1975: 232)

The scene would thus triumphantly celebrate the sacred nature of kingship *per se*, and provide a view of Malcolm himself as saint-like, hailed to crush the satanic enemy. Coghill scripts a stage direction that anticipates Taylor's (both borrowing from Clowes's account of Elizabeth's ritual of the royal touch):

> *Enter a Dumb-Show of St. Edward the Confessor with monks and a troupe of scrofulous wretches. All kneel. The King touches the sufferers and hangs a golden chain about their necks and they arise healed. A* Gloria *is sung. The King blesses Malcolm at a distance, and exit.* (Coghill 1975: 232)

In this version the blessing is actually on Malcolm, rather than 'Scotland', yet '*at a distance*', for some reason. The only version of the play I have found that has incorporated this 'missing' scene is J. C. Cross's opera/ballet mashup of 1809, in which Edward not only appears, but speaks to Malcolm and Macduff: 'Heaven with zeal my bosom warms, / Brave Siward, with ten thousand men in arms / Shall aid you. The English feel blest, / In granting succor to the brave opprest' (Cross 1809: 20).

Many mainstream adaptations continue to give us a righteous, legitimate, and even holy Malcolm – in Casson's 1979 film, Roger Rees wore a white cable-knit turtleneck sweater under a blazer that made him look like he rowed crew for Oxford [see **Figure 4**]. In Rebecca Reisert's young adult novel, Malcolm is a teen heart-throb as seen by the narrator/daughter:

> A young nobleman stands in the doorway to the scullery shed. He is the most handsome young man I have ever seen. He is tall and slender and dressed in silken clothes of deep green and gold. His hair, too, is silken, the color of a roasted chestnut. His beautiful head is large for his body, but it has a finely drawn face with heavy-lidded eyes and a rosy mouth. It is a face that would not look amiss on the neck of Saint John in an illuminated gospel. I suddenly long to run my fingers across those heavy eyelids, to stroke that soft mouth. What would it be like to kiss that mouth? With a start, I jerk my thoughts back to the moment. (Reisert 2001: 158)

Later, as the new king, this Malcolm proposes marriage to the narrator, who declines. Contrast Reisert's Malcolm with Ionesco's tyrant Macol or Greig's sociopath addressing his people: 'I will govern entirely in the interests of me .... You are out of my favour. Now and always' (Greig 2010: 80–1). Something similar happened with the transformation of Fortinbras in adaptations of and writings about *Hamlet*. For both plays, regime change at the hands of a foreign invader has become, after the twentieth century, not something to celebrate. The reversal of moral polarities in representations of Duncan and Malcolm reflects strong political reinterpretations of the play, as well as the representation of Fleance.

3

The return of Fleance

Fleance speaks only one and a half nondescript lines, a total of
fifteen words in the Folio[1]; he is referred to in 3.1, when Macbeth
interrogates Banquo about his plans, and he is present (but silent) in
3.3, when the dying Banquo calls out to him: 'Fly, good Fleance, fly,
fly, fly! / Thou mayst revenge' (3.3.16-17). Yet Fleance's character
carries a symbolic and dramaturgical importance far beyond this
minimalist appearance, particularly in terms of an adaptation's
political concepts. While many adaptations have, historically,
included key characters in more scenes than the text allows them –
such as Witches – it's unusual to find so much made of so little, in
Fleance's case.

Fleance's political-genealogical importance is signalled in the first
set of prophecies (Banquo 'shalt get kings, though thou be none',
1.3.67), and confirmed in 4.1, in a manner devastating to Macbeth,
when he returns to the witches for the second set of prophecies. Few
stage or film directors have resisted the spectacular effects of the
cauldron, its disgusting contents, or the spectral images of the three
apparitions: 'an armed head' (4.1.67sd), 'a bloody child' (4.1.75sd),
'a child crowned, with a tree in his hand' (4.1.84sd). Yet in purely
historical terms, the crucial final vision in 4.1 – the Show of Kings,
when Macbeth sees the 'show of eight kings, the last with a glass in
his hand; and Banquo' (4.1.110sd)[2] – is far more important. This
key moment in the play brings together questions of sovereignty and
succession, and it seemingly refers to King James himself, perhaps
sitting in the audience in 1606,[3] said to be the lineal descendent of
Banquo and his son, Fleance. Since all the images are 'like the first'
(4.1.113), that is, 'like the spirit of Banquo' (111), they are also
presumably like Fleance as well, who had escaped. Fleance's place

in the politics of the Jacobean succession was therefore absolutely crucial.

Who was Fleance historically? Among James's most important claims to the throne of England in 1603 was the descent of the house of Stuart in the aftermath of the reign of Macbeth, King of Scotland. **Figure 5** shows the genealogy as represented by John Leslie, a Catholic supporter of Mary. This famous image represents the origin of the Stuarts. At the very top of the flourishing tree is 'Jacobus', our James, and next his mother Mary Queen of Scots. We move down from James through the line of Stuart monarchs, and then through others to 'Fleanchus', or Fleance, and at the very foundation, solid as a rock, is 'Banquo', the Banquo of Shakespeare's play. Thus, the link is established from Banquo, in the reign of Macbeth, who was 85th king of Scotland, to James VI, the 106th king of Scotland.

As chroniclers told the tale, when Macbeth's men murdered Banquo, Fleance fled to Wales, where he eventually impregnated the Welsh princess; the furious father 'conceived such hatefull displeasure towards Fleance' that he killed him. The daughter delivered a bastard and now fatherless son, Walter. When he was a young man, Walter was taunted 'that he was a bastard, and begotten in unlawfull bed', and in anger, he killed his tormentor, fled Wales for Scotland, achieved honor and reputation there, and so was made 'lord steward of Scotland' (Holinshed [1587] 1808: 5.272), hence the family name Steward/Stuart. Several generations later, one of the Stuart descendants married Marjorie Bruce, daughter of Robert Bruce, and their offspring became Robert II, and the rest followed in more or less orderly fashion, leading finally to James.

One wonders why this genealogy would have been a comforting narrative of origin for James, as it involves a possible rape, or at best illegitimacy, murder, and a kind of rags-to-riches story that hardly reflects ancient nobility. But this founding myth of the Stuart dynasty was a product of the imagination, not historical fact. Banquo and Fleance were invented by the Scottish historian, Hector Boece in 1527 (see the **Introduction**); prior to his work, no such persons had ever appeared in chronicles, court records, or any other document (Aitchison 1999: 117–8). Boece's creation of Banquo and Fleance solidified the line of Stuart succession, producing a direct derivation from the Welsh, hence English, line for the Stuarts, as well as connecting the Stuarts to the long Scottish line back to Noah. Within a few decades, the historical fantasy of the

FIGURE 5 *Stuart genealogy. John Leslie,* De origine moribus, et rebus gestis scotorum libri decem, *Rome, 1578. Folger Shakespeare Library DA775 L4 1578 cage copy 1. Public Domain. https://creativecommons. org/licenses/by-sa/4.0/. All rights reserved.*

Banquo-Fleance myth had congealed into accepted historical fact, except for cautious remarks by a few sceptical historians.

Shakespeare proves to be an outlier to this genealogy by his conspicuous omission of any reference to Fleance at the end, thus leaving the play's final – and for the Jacobean regime most historically significant – prophecy unfulfilled. Many readers and directors have also seen this omission as an aesthetic failure, and Brecht, as we saw in Chapter One, had noted the issue of Fleance's absence in the play when he ventriloquized the complaint of his 'friend' that the audience 'has every right to expect Banquo's son to become King before the curtain falls …. [but] he never appears again. It can only be assumed that the playwright forgot about him or that the actor who took the part wasn't good enough to be included in the final curtain call.' This complaint, which Brecht mocks, had been registered centuries before. The significance of Fleance's presence/absence in the play derives above all from his genealogical importance, but Brecht also identified a formal or structural issue that is separate from the concerns of Stuart history. Both threads – political and formal – will lead to similar kinds of adaptation.

I argue here that Shakespeare's omission of Fleance at the end was both a political choice – a resistance to a particular genealogical narrative about power – and a choice about dramatic form. Bringing Fleance back at the end of adaptations produces a 'closed frame' that suits certain aesthetic assumptions and theories, from the neo-classical demands of the seventeenth century to contemporary expectations of coherence, whereas there are other examples, in Shakespeare, of the 'open frame' ending, such as *Hamlet* (the Ghost does not reappear at the end, as he does in *The Spanish Tragedy*), or *Love's Labour's Lost*, with its deferred marriages. In political terms, ironically, Fleance's return in many recent adaptations undermines the legitimacy of Malcolm's coronation, even as it obscures or reverses the play's succession politics. Fleance's return, which has no textual or historical authority, has in effect become the default ending in modern adaptations, especially film, stage, and operatic productions.

The revision of Fleance began, however, with Davenant's adaptation of *Macbeth* in 1663–4. Among his 'improvements' to the Folio, Davenant brings both Fleance and Donalbain (who would, in the chronicles, ultimately usurp the throne after his brother's death) back in the fifth act, to confront Macbeth. Donaldbain says, 'Hearing of aid sent by the English King, / To check the Tirants Insolence; I am come / From Ireland', while Fleance has come not from Wales,

but 'I from France, we are but newly met' (Davenant 1674: 57).
Fleance has just this single line in Davenant, and Macduff still kills
Macbeth, but Fleance is present in the battle scenes and joins in the
general 'joyful Acclamation' to Malcolm's reign (66). The effect, as
Simon Williams has argued, is to enhance 'the illusion that social
and political retribution is the sole cause of Macbeth's downfall'
(Williams 2004: 57). Davenant elides the sharp irony of bringing
these two figures into the general chorus that acclaims Malcolm's
crowning, instead emphasizing the healing goodness of the general
weal against the single erring individual who has brought his ruin
upon himself. An edition of the play published in 1731, 'Written
by Mr. Shakespear, with Alterations by Mr. [Nahum] Tate', copied
the Donaldbain-Fleance material exactly. While none of the major
scholarly editions of the plays from 1709 Rowe through 1767 Capell
incorporated these additions, stage productions frequently did.
Fleance began to appear, silent, in scenes such as 1.6 – in Macready
and Nunn, for example, where the 'temple-haunting martlet' speech
was a 'paternal lesson' for Fleance (Wilders 2004: 104-5n.) and 3.1
as well as the fifth act battle scenes. Fleance's innocence was further
enhanced in J. C. Cross's 1809 opera/ballet in an invented scene,
after he has escaped the murderers: a stage direction reads: 'Fleance
enters and laments the death of his father, and prays to Heaven
for protection, and goes off – the Murderers pass, seemingly in
search of Fleance' (Cross 1809: 15); thus Heaven intervened. In
3.1, Kemble, Macready, and Phelps all introduced stage business
with Fleance (Macready 'stroked the boy's hair, a gesture to which'
one critic objected that it inferred 'a cat-like propensity to play with
his victim, very foreign from Macbeth's nature', while Helen Faucit
as Lady Macbeth did the stroking: a 'representation of smooth
treachery in the tender playing of her fingers about the head of the
child Fleance' (Wilders 2004: 137n.). Modern and contemporary
adaptations have likewise frequently amplified Fleance's presence.

The modern Fleance

Many adapters rightly assume that modern audiences would not
know the chronicle history of Fleance (or themselves were unaware
of it) and instead have provided a 'closed frame' that establishes
both formal symmetry and a new political valence – in some cases,

we might term it conservative, as it follows a Royalist interpretation (so Fleance joins with Malcolm, as in Davenant and others), but in other versions, there is an almost Kottian charge (as Fleance, even occasionally Donaldbain, will threaten Malcolm).

One of the earliest versions, the final scene of Orson Welles's 1948 film, supplements the Folio's ending with a forward look into Scottish history[4]: when Macbeth's head is severed, his crown falls to the ground, and the camera shows the legs of a figure as the crown rolls next to him. Macduff shouts 'Hail, Malcolm, King of Scotland', but Malcolm's final platitudinous speech is deleted, and the camera pans over the crowd of warriors shouting in approval. But then we see a three-second shot of the figure who has picked up the crown: Fleance. While the Folio says nothing about what happened to Fleance except that he 'is scaped' (3.4.18), Welles not only brings him back at the end (as he does the witches), but indicates, with the crown in his hand and his determined look, that he will someday wear the crown as well as hold it, and that Malcolm's reign is already under threat (as the return of the witches also implies). In these implications, Welles clarifies where Shakespeare's text is ambiguous: the Folio simply ends (though with foreboding repetitions of the first few scenes) with Malcolm's final speech, inviting all 'to see us crowned at Scone' (5.9.41). Shakespeare ends his play with Fleance somewhere in exile, his fate uncertain, while Welles invents a scene in which Fleance witnesses Malcolm's ascent, implying Fleance's ultimate triumph, not that of his descendants, as he himself picks up the fallen crown. Most films, as well as other productions, now offer similar stagings.

The 1983 BBC film also brings Fleance back in 5.2; when Lennox refers to 'many unrough youths, that even now / Protest their first of manhood' (5.2.10-11), he places his hand on Fleance's shoulder, marking him as being like Siward's son. At the end, after Malcolm invites his men 'to see us crowned at Scone', this Fleance walks towards the throne where Macbeth's lifeless (but not, in this production, headless) body lies, and turns a cold stare at Malcolm, whose sense of triumph fades and his hands lower the crown he had just raised. The implication is clear: Malcolm's just-announced reign is already under threat, and he and the entire court recognize it; in both the Welles and BBC versions, the youthful Fleance's gaze represents a future that undermines the triumphant present moment.

Some recent versions of Verdi's opera have also brought Fleance back, in ironic endings that undercut the great resounding final chorus of 'Victory' and Malcolm's declaration 'Scotland, trust in

FIGURE 6 *Fleance. Zurich Opera production of Verdi's* Macbeth *directed by Franz Welser-Most © RM Arts/ZDF, La Sept, and Image Entertainment 2002. All rights reserved. Screen grab.*

me. / The tyrant is dead. / I shall make everlasting / The joy of such a victory'.[5] The 2001 production at the Opernhaus Zürich, however, showed Fleance remaining after the others had left the stage and raising the crown above his own head (see **Figure 6**). A 2011 Boston production was far more disturbing in its return of Fleance, crowned by the blood-stained ghosts of all of Macbeth's victims – Duncan, Lady Macduff, Banquo, and Lady Macbeth, thereby obscuring (in the background) Malcolm's triumph and undermining both the music and the new regime's claims to legitimacy. The 2007 Metropolitan Opera Production, directed by Adrian Noble, showed the victorious Malcolm being hailed by all his countrymen when Fleance, easily identified by his long red scarf, enters stage left, takes off his cap, and he and Malcolm look at one another.

Threatening Fleance

Many recent adaptations of *Macbeth* offer two distinct though related versions of Fleance: as an innocent, even a child, who nevertheless comes to claim, or project, his destiny; or as a young adult revenger, every bit as ruthless as the man who had his father killed. In the chronicle narratives, Fleance was not only *never* king, he was himself murdered by the father of the Welsh princess. By the time of Malcolm's ascent, the Fleance of the chronicles was probably already a ghost himself (doubly so, since he never existed). Like Welles's film, William Reilly's 1990 *Men of Respect*, a gangster adaptation, follows the play's plot fairly closely. Here, a dysfunctional family of father, wife, and son – fortune tellers – takes the place of the three witches; in the equivalent to the play's 4.1, the wife offers Battaglia three prophecies, but there is no show of kings to follow. Rather, the film cuts to a scene of Macduff's son playing cards, and to the family's slaughter. The end of this film also brings Philly/Fleance back from exile; he has escaped the shooting of his father as he leaves a butcher shop. The final scene shows Philly/Fleance at the center of a noir-inflected mafia ceremony that marks him as 'a man of respect' – the same ceremony that inducted Battaglia/Macbeth earlier in the film – while Mal/Malcolm looks on with approval.[6] The early modern politics of succession are, again, scrambled here. This film's Fleance was not a man of the streets at all, but an accountant/money man: 'MBA Baruch', his father proudly tells everyone, as he and his son wash vegetables and cook Italian food. But Philly's steely gaze at the end heralds his transformation into a made man. Another gang version of the play, the 1996 film *Macbeth on the Estate*, includes a comparable scene, when the young, scarred skinhead Fleance forms a gun with his fingers and 'shoots' Malcolm, who has brushed past him, in the back of the head, at which point a gunshot is heard and the screen goes white; the Fleance-figure has pointed directly at the viewer, and the cycle of violence, it is implied, continues through the next generation.

The significance of Banquo's son in these adaptations derives directly from the Macbeths' lack of a son, as it does in the Folio. As we will see in **Chapter Five**, Lady Macbeth's childlessness has been a long-standing critical problem, yet it is also Macbeth's problem. He laments, once he is king, that he grips 'a barren sceptre', which will be 'wrenched with an unlineal hand, / No son of mine succeeding. If't be so, / For Banquo's issue have I filed my mind [...] [made] the seeds of Banquo kings' (3.1.61-9), and Macduff exclaims that he cannot take proper revenge on Macbeth because 'He has no children' (4.3.219).[7] Banquo, by contrast, has demonstrated the potency of his 'seed', and he and Fleance serve as inversions of

Macbeth's failure to enact the patriarchal obligation to produce a new generation of males. In many modern adaptations, the Macbeths' lack of issue becomes as well a uniquely feminine tragedy for Lady Macbeth, as much as or even more than it is a patrilineal tragedy for Macbeth. In Holinshed, however, Lady Macbeth in fact *did* have a son by her previous marriage, Lulach (or Lugtake), who was briefly put on the throne after Macbeth's death, only to be overthrown by Malcolm. Shakespeare also carefully erases this other son from the play as well.

The 2006 Wright film, set in a modern gang underworld, constructed Fleance as Revenger. Sharing a room with his father in Macbeth's mansion, Fleance is at first shown ogling a guard nuzzling a woman in the hallway, then holding a book: an innocent. Escaping the ambush in the forest, he reappears in what is left of the Show of Kings in 4.1 as an older, hardened figure – a nightmare suffered by Macbeth. Hailed by his henchmen as King, Fleance pulls a gun and shoots directly into the camera (i.e. into Macbeth). A moment later, Macbeth looks up to find the entire vision gone. There is no 'line' of successors. Later in the film, as Macbeth is being assaulted, Fleance – now the teenage youngster again – joins in, hiding on the truck (sign on the side: 'Birnam Timber') that bursts into the compound. In Wright's film, even Malcolm – who in the Folio does nothing in battle – joins in the assault. Young Fleance enters the scene powerfully, taking a gun off a dead combatant, walking into the bedroom where Macbeth has died embracing Lady Macbeth's corpse, and, wheeling around, shooting the waiting woman who has unluckily entered the room. After Fleance and Macduff leave the room, the camera focuses on Malcolm: he spits on Macbeth's corpse, and his face slides into a creepy grin. The film ends as Macduff and Fleance walk out together into the night mist, as the 'Tomorrow' speech is read voiceover (leaving out the 'sound and fury' lines). Fade to black. While Malcolm seems certain that he will take over, his creepy smile indicating his satisfaction, the alliance between Macduff and Fleance (now like father and son) indicates (along with Macbeth's 4.1 vision of Fleance being hailed as King) that Fleance's reign will come just as soon as he gets out of his teenage years.

Brozel's 2005 film also reinterprets key issues of maternity and succession. The prophecy that the sons of Billy Banquo will take over Duncan's kingdom – in this modernized culinary version, a three-star Michelin restaurant – isn't enough in itself to spur Macbeth to kill him, but Brozel's Banquo tells Macbeth that 'we're having another baby [...] all boys so far, so another boy'd be good', and that he and Freddy/Fleance are taking a ride on their trail bikes the next morning because it's 'a father and son thing' and 'sometimes, afterwards, I actually sleep properly'. (It would seem difficult to overdetermine Banquo's murder, but Brozel manages it.) Macbeth, of course, is not sleeping at all, and his wife Ella delivers a long soliloquy in which Lady Macbeth's reference to having given suck is hugely amplified, painfully conveying the story of their son's death (see **Chapter Five**). Brozel's Macduff has no son, however, just two daughters, and their murders are distanced, indicated only by bloodstains on a blanket.

Billy Banquo's murder – so inevitable after Ella's soliloquy – is not shown; rather, Freddy/Fleance turns a corner in the woodland bike path to find his father's mountain bike knocked over, the deed obviously done. The end of this film depicts Malcolm – previously, a feckless kitchen assistant with no discernible skills (who for a while was even a *vegetarian*, the lowest form of life in this gourmet kitchen) – in charge of his father's restaurant, and taking over the TV cooking show ('Dining at Docherty'). As he steps into the alley for a smoke, he sees the three witches again (in this version, three bin-men who ride a garbage truck) who say nothing, only staring at him. But when the truck turns off, the figure of Freddy, on his trail bike, is revealed staring at Malcolm. Fleance isn't particularly threatening here, but his mere presence unnerves Malcolm, again heralding a future destiny that seems, like other of Fleance's final-scene appearances, a repetition of the past.

The 2003 Doran film also brings Fleance back to the final scene. In an interview, Doran reflected on the Fleance problem, in terms nearly identical to Brecht's, when one of the actors raised the question,

'What happens to Fleance?' The Witches' apparitions tell Macbeth that Banquo's offspring will be kings. But in the last scene, Malcolm has reclaimed his rightful position as Duncan's nominated successor. Other productions have had Donalbain hovering in the wings, in sinister anticipation of his turn, but surely Fleance, once he escaped the murderous thugs who dispatch his father, might have been alerted to his destiny by the

Weird Sisters? As Malcolm gave his maiden speech as Scotland's new ruler, we had Fleance appear, watching quietly. Perhaps all this is going to happen again?

(Doran 2006: 19)

Doran's comment typically elides the genealogical and historical issues, rationalizing the revision on aesthetic grounds. In asserting that Malcolm 'reclaimed' [sic] his 'rightful' position as Duncan's nominated successor, Doran then begs the question that the play declines to answer: whether Fleance's 'destiny' is to inherit the throne himself. Historically, of course, he does not.

In the film, as Macduff kneels with the crown to hail Malcolm, a figure in the foreground appears, rattling a totemic charm against his leg; the next camera shot reveals it to be Fleance, still the child of 3.3, but with an ominous expression on his face. This talisman was originally created by the witches, and worn by one of them on her army jacket, as a kind of parody of the military epaulets worn by the men, and of the medallion signifying the title of Thane of Cawdor given to Macbeth by Duncan. The talisman had been torn off the witch's uniform by Banquo in a flurry of action in 1.3. The chain of transmission – from the witches to Banquo to Fleance – makes Fleance's appearance at the end even more ominous, and while there is a link between the demonic prophecies and the line of Banquo, the link between them here suggests a contamination that was certainly never part of the genealogy that James traced.

The problem for adapters who create a 'return' for Fleance, then, is whether he is a reassuring figure of order who reconfirms Malcolm's legitimacy (as in Davenant), a naïf who is like the 'child crowned' in the second prophecy of 4.1, or whether Fleance is a threatening figure of menace, his return signalling a cyclical continuation of violence and subversion. At the same time, though, a 'return' of Fleance also has the contradictory effect of moving the play's resolution to the plane of the personal and familial, so that the violence (past, present, and future) is retributive and individual rather than systemic. Granted that the individual and the systemic are closely related, nevertheless in his return Fleance represents the revenging son of a murdered father, a Hamlet – or rather, Fortinbras – figure who has somehow entered the wrong play. Recent directors have taken Banquo's dying words to his son ('Fly, good Fleance, fly, fly fly. / Thou mayst revenge –') to be virtually a stage direction for a 'revenge' scenario at the very end. Fleance 'mayst' revenge, but in some adaptations it is a certainty. Even those adaptations that do not bring Fleance back at the end frequently represent some circularity, the end reflecting the beginning, as the cycle of violence seems to start again, as seen in the more radical interpretations of Kott, Ionesco, and Müller. Polanski's 1971 film ends with Donalbain returning and descending into the witches' lair, an ending slightly more consonant with the early chronicle histories than those adaptations that bring Fleance back.

The nature of Fleance's return also depends on how these versions have depicted Malcolm and the rule he represents. If he is a Machiavellian schemer – he has, after all, equivocated in lying to Macduff, then taking it back – then Fleance's return represents a correction or, in many cases, a threat from the future (as in *Macbeth on the Estate* or the Wright film, where Malcolm smirks to the camera). In Kurzel's 2015 film, the final scenes depict an apocalyptic conflagration, with Macbeth's dead body still semi-upright as the red-tinted smoke and haze surround him and burning embers fall from the sky. Fleance returns, finds him, and takes his sword. Kurzel then intercuts images with Malcolm and Fleance, establishing their similarity: thus the view of Fleance with the sword jumps to a shot of Malcolm's sword, and after we see Fleance running with the sword and disappearing into the smoke, the camera cuts to Malcolm at his throne, who then thinks of something, and also is seen running with his sword out of the castle. The implication is that he must take care of Fleance, who has fallen back into the catastrophic natural world, and that this end-of-world setting will be replayed.

In contrast, the 1978 Casson film follows the Folio more closely, by bringing on neither Fleance nor Donalbain. Instead, Casson shows Macduff's entrance after killing Macbeth as a repetition of Macbeth's entrance after killing Duncan: instead of Macbeth's head, Macduff holds two bloody daggers, and the film's final shot places the bloody hands and dagger next to the crown. Malcolm's period of rule, it is suggested, will be unfortunately like his father's, and so Casson achieves the same effect without Fleance. Even an innocent Malcolm, like the feckless student-type (Roger Rees) wearing a crew-neck sweater in Casson's film (see **Plate XX**), who does not face a Fleance at the end, is tainted by the implication of a renewed cycle of murderous violence inextricably linked to the kingship.

Fleance's return signals an inherent instability in Malcolm's new regime that ironically repeats the initial instability in Duncan's at the beginning of the play. In suggesting such a cycle, these adaptations are reproducing, consciously or not, Jan Kott's 'Grand Mechanism', which is 'the image of history itself [...] Every successive chapter, every great Shakespearean act is merely a repetition' (Kott 1964: 10). It is precisely this vision of the play that led one unsympathetic, state-supporting reviewer of a 1977 Bulgarian production to condemn the idea of a 'return' while explicitly linking such a vision to a particular conception of Shakespeare as author. The terms of this critique, worth quoting at length, openly acknowledge the ideology at work:

> [In this production] this conflict [between Macbeth and his opponents] is entirely abandoned and replaced with the idea of the absolute power of violence in the world and its endless repetition through time and generations. It would be a great pity if the authors of the production thought that in this way they had modernized the 'old' Shakespeare. Taking away the splendid triumph of retribution in Macbeth is tantamount to denying Shakespeare's humanist pathos. And this is exactly what the production tries to convince us of when Macduff fights Macbeth not as a legitimate revenger but rather as a common weak dueller; when Malcolm amidst a corpse-strewn wilderness receives a crown and a sword from the hands of murderers who are Macbeth's former tools; and when, at the end, a flock of youngsters fly onto the stage and seize the weapons of their massacred fathers in order to start a new scuffle.
>
> (Shurbanov and Sokolova 1996: 109)

The 'splendid triumph of retribution' should be, according to this critic, untainted by ambiguity, scepticism, or cynicism, then – the very qualities, one might say, of the Shakespearean text itself at this point.

All politics is local, however, and many adaptations continue to offer similarly unironic, almost utopian endings. Clearly, how one views the end of the play impacts (as well as it is determined by) one's own political moment, just as it impacts one's conception of Shakespeare as either a celebrator of the restoration of order with a 'humanist pathos' or as a sceptic undermining the claims of power.

Fleance 2.0

The adaptations I discuss below have different target audiences, and each certainly differs from the now high-culture model of Shakespeare, while also appropriating some of the cultural capital of 'Shakespeare'. And while these versions have many different threads and ideas, each not only brings Fleance back, but in some cases elevates him into a fully developed, significant character.

Hartley and Hewson's 2012 *Macbeth: A Novel* runs roughly parallel to the Folio's plot. The authors recognize and enhance Fleance's genealogical significance, and in effect redress the complaint of Brecht's 'friend'. In this novel, Fleance knows himself to be a clear succession threat to both Macbeth and Malcolm. His father Banquo actually proposes to Macbeth that he take Fleance as his heir: 'My own son ... Fleance. Take him as your own .... Adopt him into your line' (179); he 'is a decent, honorable boy. Intelligent and loyal' (183). The Macbeths had lost their only son six years earlier, and Macbeth is affronted by Banquo's suggestion: 'I will not suffer such extortion' (183). The novel thus overdetermines the threat posed by Fleance that had appeared in the witches' prophecy. Later, we learn how little the revenger this Fleance is at first: 'He had that brooding, dreamy look his father hated. Sometimes he hummed to himself or mouthed silent words, lost in a world only he could see .... Banquo's frustration built' because Fleance would rather read in his room than practise with his sword (189). Just fifteen years old when his father is slain, he fled south under pursuit, sleeping rough: 'Fleance ... was now invisible, dead to all who sought him. And seek him they did' (229). Rather like Edgar becoming Poor Tom in *King Lear*, Fleance disappears in order to preserve himself. He is saved by the Three Sisters (his 'Guardian angels', they say, 231), makes his way to Macduff's castle, and together they flee to King Edward's court in England. In the meantime, Donaldbain – who has also returned – loses Malcolm's confidence, and Malcolm, as in so many modern adaptations, begins to turn negative, and eventually into a petty tyrant figure: 'Malcolm took a bit of his mealy apple and scowled. It was so difficult to get decent food away from the palace. *When this is over*, he thought, watching Dunsinane burn, *I will spend a month in Forres doing nothing but take my idle leisure*. The battle was won. The peace, such as it was, would be his to relish' (297).

Fleance has joined the battle with Macduff, Malcolm, and Donaldbain, but afterwards, as seen by one of the weird sisters, he is described as 'a skinny, trembling figure, with wispy beard and shabby armor, bloodstains upon it. His face is set in angry fright, and his sword quivers before him' (305). He has enough force to remind her that she had 'promised me ... A throne. Some elevation', and so he is mockingly greeted 'All hail, Fleance ... Hail monarch of the piss pot. King of the kitchen hearth'. His future cannot be in Scotland, they tell him: 'Malcolm loathes you, and MacDuff, though decent, sees his dead wife and bairns each time he sets his eyes upon your bony frame. There's nothing here for Banquo's son but death and misery' (307). And then they instruct him to follow the path (though a sanitized one, sans rape) that Holinshed had described:

> Go south and west, boy. To Wales and the court of a prince called Gruffydd ap Llywelyn. There, marry his daughter and take the name Steward, for that is what, in truth, you'll be .... And die a lowly, insignificant death, knowing none of those who follow you to greatness will remember the cowardly boy who sired them from a distance. (307)

Fleance is banished in humiliation, and the novel ends with the three sisters; when they see the haughty Malcolm, one of them, threatens, 'I never met a man I liked called Malcolm' (309).

If Hartley and Hewson's novel adheres fairly closely to the plot, Lisa Klein's 2009 *Lady Macbeth's Daughter* does not, as the title alone indicates.[8] The hitherto unknown daughter, Albia, was born to Macbeth and Grelach (=Gruoch) but, because she was a girl, she was rejected and taken away by Grelach's nurse to be raised by Banquo and his family. The novel proceeds from Albia's point of view, and the reader can see her maturing and (since knowledge of the basic story is assumed) can anticipate the discoveries she will make. Albia has the Second Sight, but does not know her true identity until she is a teenager (94-6); the discovery horrifies her. Meanwhile, her step-brother Luoch (=Lulach) still lives with the Macbeths. Albia describes Luoch, age fifteen: 'his face is becoming square and manly, his shoulders wide' while Fleance 'is a fine-looking boy, blue-eyed, sturdy and quick' (48). Albia and Fleance fall for one another, but Albia is ultimately frustrated as Fleance reveals his own desires for greatness: 'that same ambition that drove Macbeth to his cursed crimes' (196). In the final scenes, Albia even tries to fight Macbeth herself, but he spares her. Just as Macbeth is surrendering to Albia, however, Macduff appears and slays him. When Fleance returns, there is an erotic embrace with Albia, and he tries to head off Malcolm's offer of marriage to Albia. She asks Fleance to come away with her but when he hesitates, she demands to know whom he would choose to rule Scotland. Albia realizes that Fleance still hopes to become king himself, and that marriage to her would provide a 'stronger claim' through her 'family's [royal] lineage' (231), a trope often seen in feminist adaptations. Albia comes to a proto-feminist conclusion: 'now I see that men still clamor for revenge and power over each other' (231), so they go their own ways. Albia flees Dunsinane to avoid marriage to Malcolm, and she reunites with, and ultimately forgives, her mother Grelach (and incidentally, through magical powers, heals her mother's wounds). This being a young adult novel, however, the romantic plot with Fleance is not abandoned: 'One day, Fleance will find me. But not yet' (237). Rebecca Reisert's young adult novel *The Third Witch* similarly elevates Fleance to a potential love interest for the narrator, who has in fact saved Fleance (she was the Third Murderer) when he and Banquo were attacked. This Fleance is neither much of a soldier (he tells his father 'I wish to be a scholar, sir' [Reisert 2001: 87]), nor a successful lover, as his offer to take Gilly away is declined at the end.

No author, it would seem, has taken the revision of the play's ending and the return of Fleance as far as Noah Lukeman, in his 2008 play, *The Tragedy of Macbeth, Part II: The Seed of Banquo*. I have already quoted Lukeman's remarks in the **Introduction** to the effect that Shakespeare could not have been so 'careless' as to leave these elements unfulfilled; given Shakespeare's other multi-part plays, could he also have intended a second part of *Macbeth*? Lukeman's play parallels some of Shakespeare's *Macbeth* in its structure: it begins with three witches, they utter three prophecies to Malcolm (who has been on the throne for ten years), there is a banquet scene, a sleep-walking scene, and a coronation scene at the end. However, Malcolm now fills the Macbeth-slot: starting out as a good king, he descends into murder, madness, and sees ghosts (even that of Macbeth himself) and has hallucinations, until he is killed by Cawdor (son of the Cawdor in Shakespeare's play) at the end. The prophecies work in a contrary chronological order: 'Hail to thee, King of Scotland!', 'Hail to thee, Thane of Cawdor', 'Hail to thee, master of Macbeth' (2008: 16) (the latter turns out to be the hitherto-unknown daughter of Macbeth and Lady Macbeth). In the second set of prophecies, 'Fleance will attack. / But you shall find him first', 'Norway shall invade, but will not win. You shall / be greater than she, yet lesser', and 'Your [marriage] union shall not last. / Torn asunder it shall be, by man of no woman born' (74-5).

The daughter of the Macbeths turns out, to the surprise of all and suspicion of some, to be a saintly figure, dispensing justice to the poor and caring nothing for her own self. Malcolm convinces her to marry, in a wooing scene borrowed in part from Richard and Lady Anne's in *Richard III* (43-5) and she becomes Lady Malcolm. Opposition within the court appears in the form of Seyton (who schemes to marry his own daughter Syna to Malcolm), a devious and deceitful Nurse, and others. At one point, Donaldbain returns to aid his brother against Norway's invasion, but Malcolm, blinded by fear and the pressure of unscrupulous court factions, kills his own brother. From that point on, Malcolm's guilt consumes him, he becomes more murderous and tyrannical, and is even turned against his wife, with the result that Lady Malcolm is hung in public as Malcolm watches from a window (120-1). In the meantime, Fleance (whose beloved Fiona has been murdered) has returned, and sees pretty much the same Show of Kings that Macbeth saw ('The last holds a glass .... The seed of Banquo stirs', 122); Cawdor's son joins Fleance's forces, and they kill Malcolm. The Three Murderers (of Fiona, and before that, Banquo) are brought before Fleance and Lukeman provides a structurally formal but morally ambiguous ending to his play:

Fleance stabs and kills all three. The crowd cheers.
ALL. Hail, Fleance ! All hail the boy king!   *Exeunt.* (135)

Lukeman has both repeated and changed many elements of Shakespeare's play, and his adaptation seemed to have been heading towards a wholly positive final scene of Fleance's crowning, but it is considerably undermined by his murderous revenge on the Three Murderers (not that they don't deserve it), and by his being hailed as a 'boy king', suggesting yet another cycle, in which an unprepared king begins his reign with murder. Lukeman's ending provides a small reminder of the ending of Ionesco's version.

* * *

Why, to return to the original question, have so many adapters brought Fleance back in the final scene, either as childlike icon of the future, soldier-in-waiting, mafia inductee, outright avenger, or newly crowned king? It is of course unreasonable to expect any modern audience to know that King James traced his lineage back to Banquo's descendants, though surely some members of Shakespeare's audience knew this supposed genealogy. Fleance's return fulfils, as Brecht noted, an ideological need for a 'closed' aesthetic form, in which *all* the prophecies will be fulfilled before our eyes. Indeed, Fleance's threatening posture – his look at Malcolm with the crown in his hand, in Welles's version, or his rattling the witches' talisman in Doran's, or his appearance as king in Macbeth's dream in the Wright film – suggests his own not-too-distant seizure of the throne rather than, historically, his *son*'s return to Scotland, then his *descendant*'s marriage into the Bruce family, and so on. In other words, what is historically inaccurate in these films is produced for the sake of formal aesthetic coherence: making Fleance himself the figure of return. In doing so, some of these adaptations ironically articulate a conservative politics, just where Shakespeare's Folio, I believe, is most subversive. Fleance's return signifies a restoration of order on a personal level – a 'splendid triumph of retribution' expressive of a 'humanist pathos', as the Bulgarian reviewer put it. Such an ending may even suggest the rule of the innocent (as in the Brozel film), as well as a coming (or imminent) revenge that will be visited on all those (Malcolm included) who have been responsible.

Yet the man responsible for the death of Fleance's father Banquo is no one but Macbeth, and he is himself dead, as the returning Fleances invariably witness. So who, or what, can Fleance be revenging? Productions in which Fleance turns against Malcolm or Macduff turn the play into a revenge melodrama, reducing it to the level of the personal and the individual, as in Michael Starks' 2006 film, in which Fleance himself shoots Macbeth. Perhaps this effect is inevitable, given most films' focus on character, but the playtext, as we have seen, declines to close its narrative frame. Both its politics and its form are 'open'.

The Folio, then, not only does not particularly 'flatter' King James in representing his ancestor, as so much earlier criticism asserted (see **Introduction**); rather, the Folio constructs a final scene that seems to valorize Malcolm's ascent as a restoration of the principle of patrilineal inheritance that Duncan initiated, but at the same time, in suppressing all reference to Fleance at the end, quite specifically declines to look forward to the 'line of kings', even with James himself (perhaps) present. In the Folio, Fleance's fate is outside the scope of the play. What is suppressed inevitably returns, however, even centuries later.

4

Noir Macbeth

When the Hogarth Press announced in 2013 that its new series would see Shakespeare's works retold by acclaimed and bestselling contemporary novelists, there was both high interest and some scepticism about the very idea of the project. Adam Gopnik's *New Yorker* review ('Why Rewrite Shakespeare?') of the first three novels was subtitled 'When psychological novelists adapt the Bard's plays, they impose a value system that he didn't share' – a sentiment frequently invoked against *any* kind of adaptation into a different medium. Gopnik argued that 'The novelistic, psychological work of explaining why evil people are evil gets very little energy from him [Shakespeare]. His villains are the products not of trauma and history but of nature and destiny. ... Our novelists aim at modernizing Shakespeare by adding history or a greater sense of justice or more compassion to plays that seem to lack them' (Gopnik 2016; not all readers, needless to say, would agree with Gopnik's notion of Shakespeare).[1] The novelists wrote narratives inspired by the plays, rather than simply trying to prose-ify them. For *Macbeth*, the writer was the Norwegian crime novelist Jo Nesbø. The dust-jacket blurb offers a quick summary:

> Set in the 1970s in a run-down, rainy industrial town, Jo Nesbø's *Macbeth* centers around a police force struggling to shed an incessant drug problem. Duncan, chief of police, is idealistic and visionary, a dream to the townspeople but a nightmare for criminals. The drug trade is ruled by two drug lords, one of whom – a master of manipulation named Hecate – has connections with the highest in power, and plans to use them to get his way.
>
> (Nesbø 2018)

Inspector Macbeth is the head of SWAT 'and a man already susceptible to violent and paranoid tendencies', and the reader is promised a story that explores 'the darkest corners of human nature, and the aspirations of the criminal mind'.

Nesbø himself chose *Macbeth*, he said in an interview ('it's my favorite Shakespeare play') and set his story in a bleak, depressed, drug-ridden 1970s Scottish city – i.e. Glasgow.[2] Nesbø captures the grit and danger of his semi-imaginary city well. The novel's setting and contemporary action turn the reader towards issues of social critique and modern political corruption, as a more approachable substitution for the no longer contemporary relevance of the Folio's takes on tanistry and divine right. Nesbø reinterprets the play's supernatural elements – Hecate is a drug lord (the drug is called 'Brew') – while also providing a considerable amount of backstory for each character: Macbeth spent part of his childhood in an orphanage, and Caithness (a woman here) and Duff are having an affair. Nesbø includes plenty of violence in his novel's 446 pages, described in the kind of elaborate detail that only a novel can. At the end, a one-eyed boy (about to lose his other eye), asks, 'Do you think Macbeth's successors will be any better, fairer or more compassionate? Is there any reason to think they will be?' (442) – a line that aptly echoes Macbeth's dying line in Heiner Müller's play, 'My death won't make your world a better place' (Weber 2012: 75). Indeed, Nesbø's novel ends with the promise of a new dominant drug lord, who promises the city: 'I owe it hell on earth' (446). Inspired by the play, this adaptation reinterprets it in a contemporary setting, rather than following along, scene by scene, as some novelizations do.

I will consider, in this chapter, a number of adaptations that, like Nesbø's, resituate the play into some form of gangster or crime milieu; I will also explore the rich history of aligning the play's politics and themes with what are seen as correlative social models of masculine hierarchies, homosocial bonding, class, and violence in the 'mean streets' of Dunsinane. For representations of Duncan as a crime boss, *capo di tutt'i capi*, see **Chapter Two**. Here I will look at some of the generic elements and representations typical of the crime/mystery genres.

From 'The Curse' to Thurber and Brecht

Although it was chance that allowed Nesbø to choose *Macbeth*, it came as no surprise that the play was interpreted through the trope of crime. On one level, the play has served crime writers/ adapters well simply for its associations with murder and violence, as in the Nicolas Freeling novel, *Lady Macbeth* (see **Chapter Five**), but particularly for the spurious legend of the play's unnatural and dangerous theatrical history[3] – that even in the opening production, Shakespeare was supposedly forced to take the part of Lady Macbeth, that many actors over the years have died while acting one of the parts, that productions invariably fail, or that even uttering the name of the play produces bad luck. In Brozel's 2005 film, set in a restaurant, when the name of the infamous real-life cook Gordon Ramsay is mentioned, the shocked kitchen staff reminds the offender never to utter the name of 'the Scottish chef' ('we don't use that name in this kitchen') – an intertextual joke connecting the play's production history, the play's supposed curse, and present-day popular culture 'reality' cooking shows. The play's 'curse' has provided the grounding for a great many crime-inflected works, such as Marvin Kaye's *Bullets for Macbeth* ('A murder during the production of Macbeth in New York triggers an investigation into this murder and the third murder [*sic*] of Banquo in the play. The investigation leads to the Folger Library in Washington' (Kaye 2012). The well-known mystery writer Ngaio Marsh, in one of her last books, *Light Thickens* (1982), offered, as one reviewer summed up, 'Four murders. Three witches. A fiendish lady. A homicidal husband. A ghost. ... the new London production of "the Scottish play" promises to be a smash until gruesome pranks begin plaguing rehearsals. ... the last act ends in real-life tragedy ... murderous jealousy' (Goodreads 2014). Dozens of other plays, novels, and children's books turning on the play's 'curse' could be noted. Stephen Philip Jones's 2001 novel *King of Harlem* doubles the stakes with its setting during the rehearsal and production of Orson Welles's so-called 'Voodoo' production in 1936 (see **Chapter Seven**), when one of Welles's actors is arrested for murder and two detectives are brought in to solve the case so that, yes, the show can go on.

James Thurber's 'The Macbeth Murder Mystery' (1942) set the
comic standard for analysing the Folio's disconcerting omissions
and inconsistencies. Thurber's narrator encounters an American
Woman touring England at his hotel in the Lake District. Thinking
she had found a new murder mystery to read at night, she is
bitterly disappointed to discover its true nature ('You can imagine
how mad I was when I found it was Shakespeare' [Thurber 1942:
33]). Still, trained on the novels of Agatha Christie, especially
the insights of Hercule Poirot, the Lady soon discovers, to the
narrator's astonishment, that neither Macbeth nor Lady Macbeth
was involved in Duncan's murder: 'You suspect them the most, of
course, but those are the ones that are never guilty – or shouldn't
be, anyway' (34). Working around plot difficulties in her theory –
'There wasn't any ghost' (36); 'She wasn't asleep at all' (37) in the
sleepwalking scene – the Lady concludes that Macduff was the real
villain. The narrator returns to the play himself, and claims that
the murderer was actually Lady Macbeth's father, who was also
the Third Murderer and the Old Man with Ross in 2.4, as well
as, inevitably, '*one of the weird sisters in disguise!*' (39). Thurber's
narrator and the American Lady perfectly embody the kind of
reader who takes the play as a riddle with secret meanings – the
impossibly close reader, some of whom elsewhere find Bacon's name
in acrostics throughout the First Folio. Thurber's parody pivots
on elements of the play that not only distinguish it – violent acts,
dismemberments, secret murders – but also invite scrutiny, like the
mystery of the Third Murderer, apparently sent by Macbeth out of
'mistrust' (3.3.2) of the first two. The Third Murderer has proven to
be a handy character who turns out to be Seyton, Ross, the Servant
who brought in the two murderers to Macbeth in 3.2, one of the
three weird sisters, Hecate, the Porter, Lady Macbeth's 'daughter',
or even Macbeth himself in various adaptations.[4]

Even a more 'serious' writer, Bertolt Brecht, was drawn to
the crime elements of the play. In his 1940s stint in Hollywood,
following his departure from Europe, Brecht generated many ideas
for films, some of them Shakespearean adaptations (such as *Der
Hamlet der Weizenbörse* ['The Hamlet of the Wheat Exchange'],
and *Desdemona*) (Brecht 1969).[5] Brecht developed one film project
into a more elaborate script, however, written in English, with
Ferdinand Reyher and Peter Lorre listed as co-authors.[6] Brecht had,
in September 1945, written in his journal that the three authors

had made a copy 'for the film', and went on to note that 'the great
Shakespeare motif, the fallibility of instinct (the indistinctness
of the inner voice), cannot be renewed. I am singling out [or
"emphasizing"] the defenselessness of the little people against
the dominant moral code, the limit of their capacity for criminal
potential' (Brecht 1995: 232).

In the Foreword (I quote throughout from the third, latest
version, printed in Brecht 1997: 143–62), Brecht says they have
adapted *Macbeth* 'into a modern equivalent' because

> It is a good crime story ... It is a good acting story, its leading
> roles, especially that of Lady Macbeth, offering much to fine
> actors ... It is a good love story, of a couple not divided but
> welded in a bondship of murder ... [and] It is a good story not of
> far away and long ago but recurring again and again in common
> life without losing its profound appeal.
>
> (143)

The Foreword also notes that the authors had 'purposely used
a dry police-report style ... and understated the dark richness of
the material, even the great love story, in order to set down simply
the basic line of picture which should be as powerful as the urge
in men and women to hurry along their luck with some ill-starred
assistance from themselves' (143). Like the Hamlet of the 'Wheat
Exchange', the 'Lady Macbeth of the Yards'[7] brings the royals down
many pegs, to the common everyday life of the would-be bourgeois
worker.

'John Machacek' is a 31-year-old 'steer cutter' who finds
a message from a fortune cookie that has blown from a nearby
restaurant; it reads: '*Be bold in your undertakings and fortune is
yours*' (144). Later that day, a 'big well-dressed drunk', a 'cattle-
dealer named Duncan', falls into a cattle pen, is nearly trampled to
death, and is saved by Machacek. Duncan promises to reward him,
and Machacek excitedly tells his wife, 'We got a market!' (144).
But Duncan apparently does not come through with his promise,
tries to kiss Mrs. Machacek after he declines to pay Machacek's
medical bill (a knee injury suffered when he saved Duncan), and
then invites the Machaceks to his country home in 'Duncanville'.
After more insults and disappointments, Mrs. Machacek produces
a meat cleaver taken from the meat packing plant, Machacek kills

Duncan, and they dump his body into his car, forcing it into a river. At this point, we learn that Mrs. Machacek's first name is 'Bess', in one of Brecht's finer ironies.

After the murder, Machacek begins to win at every gambling event he attempts at a local amusement park, and Eddie Bancroft (=Banquo) starts to become suspicious. The amusement park features a 'Singing Witch' with a 'cauldron' (151), who offers three prophecies, the key one being that Machacek will 'meet a chilly end'. The next day, Duncan's lawyer sends them a title to the market, just as Duncan had promised. Eventually Eddie Bancroft begins to take advantage of them, Machacek has 'bad dreams' (153), and 'Police Inspector Duffy' takes on the case searching for the missing Duncan. After resisting Bess's sexual overtures (in her attempt to find out what he knows), Eddie is locked into the meat locker by Bess and freezes to death. Machacek hallucinates seeing him, and Bess sleepwalks 'holding a flashlight' (159). Inspector Duffy suspects the couple, and proves his case by producing Machacek's hat, which he had lost at Duncan's house during the murder. Bess confesses, and Machacek – now being trampled by a herd of cattle (as Duncan was at the beginning) – clutches his hat 'and an almost happy grin comes over his face. The thunder of the herd passes on and the dust settles' (162).

While Brecht follows the Folio's main plotlines and consistently transforms the play's motifs and scenes into modern equivalents, the film script feels leaden and pedestrian in many ways. Brecht certainly demonstrated 'the defenselessness of the little people against the dominant moral code' and 'the great Shakespeare motif, the fallibility of instinct', as his journal entry asserted, but in transforming the story into one of 'common life', Brecht more than a little 'understated the dark richness of the material'. Heiner Müller once remarked that what he found 'boring' in Brecht, compared to Shakespeare, 'is that he diminishes figures'.[8] The narrative point of view, within but above the characters' minds, also subjugates them; it's not known how this might have been represented in a film (a voiceover is often used). Brecht's film script reflects his long-standing interest in the devastating consequences of what he called the 'new ambition' – in this case, not for a royal title, but for the (bourgeois) title to a market. Macbeth's ambition, like Hamlet's 'new thinking' or Brutus's 'new drive for freedom' (Brecht 1995: 263), represented for Brecht one of the pivotal points in which the 'feudal' values of the ruling classes are challenged by those of the new rising classes, with tragic results. In transferring the play's actions from Shakespeare's imaginary Scotland to the American Midwest, Brecht could easily shift the status of the principal characters to something much lower, and place social class under capitalism under interrogation. Moreover, the idea of 'Chicago' has considerable importance in Brecht's drama: the city is 'the core of Brecht's American imagination and experience, ideologically as well as geographically', as Reinhold Grimm (1989: 232) notes, and clearly a trope for the excesses and alienation of capitalism. Though Brecht apparently 'never stayed in Chicago, even overnight' (225), he would have seen the stockyards when he passed through the city. The change in Macbeth's name, finally, suggests as well the status of an eastern European immigrant.

Brecht's concern in this script for the kind of tragedy 'recurring again and again in common life' clearly reflects 'the defenselessness of the little people against the dominant moral code', but he found no success in attempting to sell it. In July 1946, he wrote Reyher that Lorre had not been able to place it, and in a 23 March 1947 letter Reyher wrote Brecht asking if he knew that Columbia Pictures was 'offering a pretty fair sum for the Lady Macbeth, which was turned down by Lorre's agent because of additional stipulations which made it too expensive' (Lyon 1980: 80). In the end, the proposed project failed, perhaps, Brecht speculated to Reyher, because Lorre was 'probably having difficulties getting the starring role' (Lyon 1980: 80). Given Lorre's previous career – especially as the murderer in Fritz Lang's *M* (1931) and as Raskolnikov in Josef von Sternberg's *Crime and Punishment* (1935) – he had considerable credentials as a villain.

The mob

Brecht wrote his 'good crime story' in the heyday of *film noir* and it was inevitable that a classic *noir* version would eventually appear, as it did in Ken Hughes's 1955 film *Joe MacBeth* (**Figure 7**). Here the New York crime boss 'Duke' rewards Joe with a lake-side mansion for killing his enemies,

FIGURE 7 'Joe Macbeth'. Columbia Pictures presents Paul Douglas, Ruth Roman [in] Joe Macbeth, c. 1955. Folger Shakespeare Library ART Vol. f119. Public Domain. https://creativecommons.org/licenses/by-sa/4.0/. All rights reserved.

but, goaded on by his ambitious wife Lily and the prophecy of a nightclub fortune-teller, Joe eventually murders Duke. He begins to suffer from nightmares and visions. One night, he believes his house has been entered by his enemies, and he uses a submachine gun to spray the moving curtains, unintentionally killing his wife, and soon meets a similar end himself. The tropes of *noir* are invoked throughout: tough-guy talk, black-and-white palette, shadows barring and imprisoning the characters, and lots of fog and smoke. As one of the advertising posters put it, 'A man lusting for power ... A woman hot with ambition ... and not a moral between them! ... Scarface ... Dillinger ... and now ... Joe MacBeth'. Hughes's film is perhaps the earliest *noir* version seen by a popular audience, and it inaugurates (for *Macbeth*) what Douglas Lanier has termed 'the corporate *noir* genre', which addresses 'the contradictory loyalties and paranoia of the upwardly mobile organization man of the '50s' (2002a: 170).

William Reilly's 1990 film *Men of Respect* updates the gangster element by making it clearly the Mafia; appearing the same year as Coppola's *The Godfather, Part III*, Reilly hired actors already associated with crime and violence, some of whom had worked for Coppola.[9] As in *Joe MacBeth*, there is a fortuneteller rather than witches, who tells him 'you will be *capo d'regime*', and 'will be called *padrino Battaglia*'. Macbeth/Battaglia is inducted into 'our thing' in an initiation ceremony, thus becoming a 'made man' or 'man of respect'. Reilly adapts the play's language to his cultural moment with some sharp *noir* dialogue ('All of these guys is of woman born. They can't do shit to me'; 'He's history. Tomorrow, he'll be geography') and the expected violence. Since the crime family is so blatantly Italian, Reilly invokes the usual stereotype and makes food visually important. The mob always likes to eat well, from *The Godfather* to *The Sopranos*. Reilly's film begins with a mob assassination in a restaurant, a little girl's birthday cake one of the victims, the cheap claret and tomato sauce mingling with quite a lot of blood. Macbeth calls his wife from the kitchen of the eponymously named 'Diner', and the Macbeths welcome the godfather/Duncan to their restaurant, where the guards' coffee is spiked and Duncan is stabbed (while sleeping in a room in the back, post-hooker) during one of the film's many thunderstorms. Macbeth dreams that Banquo and Fleance stab him at a cookout, and when he awakens he calls them while they are preparing a dad/ son dinner. Macbeth asks Banquo to pick up a 'couple pounds of provalone' at the 'Porcelli Bros.' butcher shop, where a hit man takes out Banquo. The banquet scene takes place on the patio of the restaurant. In the film's equivalent of 4.1, the witch-figures are watching a French cooking show on TV, as the TV chef, preparing *capo pecore*, splits a sheep's head and helpfully explains, 'Be careful not to lose the brain', and to place both sides on a well-greased baking sheet, 'eyeball side down', which seems always a good idea.

Reilly makes three important changes that reflect the choices of other adapters through the centuries. First, as we will see in **Chapter Five**, Ruthie, his Lady Macbeth, has had an abortion so as not to interfere with Macbeth's career; second, he shows Ruthie's suicide (she cuts her throat over the bathtub she had been scrubbing of imaginary blood); and third, as we saw in **Chapter Three**, he brings Fleance back at the end, in a Mafia initiation ceremony that parallels Macbeth's. Reilly's film begins with a radio announcer's voice reading the news, and as he tells of a murder 'gangland style', Reilly places a written epigraph on the screen: 'There is nothing but what has a violent end or violent beginnings ... ' – which is, somewhat surprisingly, from Hazlitt's 1845 *Characters of Shakspeare's Plays*.[10] The epigraph shot then fades into Battaglia entering a restaurant to gun down three mobsters. Reilly develops, at greater length and in greater detail than Hughes's *Joe MacBeth*, the analogies between the violent warrior hierarchy in Shakespeare's play and the violent mobster hierarchy in the Mafia (American version). Both cultures are masculinist, and in both women are expected to sacrifice or be sacrificed. Each culture is vertically organized, with a single king/*capo* at the top.[11] To achieve that position is both the desire and the destruction of those below who attempt to take it over.

Geoffrey Wright's 2006 Australian mob film also features much ingesting of food and wine and (by Lady Macbeth) cocaine. Duncan's arrival at Macbeth's home is preceded by a shot of a maid carving a roast (and then the inevitable thunderstorm). Lady Macbeth spikes a bottle of Hermitage Bin 15 for Duncan's guards. The banquet scene displays a lavish spread (roast chicken, potatoes), and another Australian red, while Macduff kills Macbeth in a well-equipped wine cellar, but only after Macbeth smashes a fine claret (vintage unknown) against his head. These food/wine gestures invoke familiar modern indices of wealth, display, and corruption, but Wright's version of the 4.1 cauldron scene moves to another level entirely. Wright's witches are three young teenage girls, who are, in 4.1, nude and strangely tattooed. Macbeth finds them in the well- appointed modern kitchen. The ingredients of the cauldron bubbling on the stove are a mix of the previous night's banquet and the Folio's gruesome ingredients. The camera lingers over eyeballs, organ meat, etc. All three witches, then Macbeth, drink from the cauldron, and the effect on him is immediate; the prophecies then take place during a hallucinogenic orgy. Wright's version of 4.1 insists on showing, in gruesome detail, a vision of perversion on multiple levels: the central room of the home, the essence of nurture, the faux-innocent physical attractiveness of the witches contrasted by the physical disgust invoked by the meats, worms, and eyeballs of the cauldron: no doubt, the scene shows, *their* sexuality is depraved, their organs no less horrible than those they handle in the kitchen.

Wright's film includes tropes of the contemporary action film – bloody shootouts, car chases – and this mob barely nods at the Mafia's deep sense of 'honor'; instead, drugs, the essential business of this underworld, are everywhere, from the drugs that Macbeth and Banquo ingest, to the line of coke Lady Macbeth takes in 1.5, the drugged wine for the guards, and the injection the doctor gives her in the sleepwalking scene equivalent. This Lady Macbeth, as we will see in **Chapter Five**, is empty inside from the beginning, sexually unresponsive to Macbeth, clearly mourning a dead child (she looks with a troubled face at an empty child's swing during the 'unsex me' voiceover), and she is found, a suicide, in a bathtub full of blood. Wright struck an original, disturbing note with his conception of the witches as schoolgirls, dressed in identical school uniforms, introduced while engaged in a wilding during which they desecrate a cemetery by scratching out the eyes of a memorial statue and uttering animal-like screeches. Their initial appearance is, for a few seconds, coded as innocent and virginal, so that their abrupt transformation into something demonic is shocking. At the end, Wright has also brought Fleance back as a figure of revenge (see **Chapter Three**), suggesting the inevitable circularity of this culture's violence, though Wright seems to have little interest in investigating the systemic sources of this violence, or the origin of drugs (aside from Lady Macbeth's despair), whereas Nesbø offers a much wider view, in terms of class and poverty, of the society he depicts and its need for drugs. For Nesbø, the collapse of his novel's Glasgow stems in large part from the collapse (or perhaps the triumph) of a virulent form of capitalism; Wright's underworld, by contrast, is more hermetically isolated.

Billy Morrissette's 2001 film *Scotland, PA* blends (to use a food metaphor) *noir* and food tropes in a darkly comic 1970s world of murder and fast food. Pat and Joe 'Mac' McBeth work at a sad restaurant, Duncan's Cafe in Scotland, Pennsylvania, presided over by Norman Duncan. The usual plot ensues: Joe and (especially) Pat chafe at their low-class positions, Joe is passed over for promotion to manage the restaurant, but then Pat and Joe receive a brilliant idea prophesied by the three witches (here, three stoned hippies): drive-through. After other machinations, they murder Norm by dunking his head in a deep fat fryer. A drop of burning-hot grease flies onto Pat's hands, and she tries various ointments to salve her (increasingly imaginary) wound; by the end, she thinks her hand is falling off. Duncan's eldest son Malcolm has sold the restaurant to the McBeths, and business booms. But then enter Lieutenant McDuff to investigate. Eventually, Joe is killed in a fight with McDuff. Pat cuts off her hand with a meat cleaver and bleeds to death, and – with Malcolm no longer around – McDuff takes over and renames the restaurant 'McDuff's', which is now vegetarian (!): the 'Home of the Garden Burger'.

The film has been attacked as 'an incoherent adolescent rant' (Fedderson and Richardson 2008: 313) but also superbly analysed (along with the Brozel film) by Calbi (2013) in terms of the film's exploration of 'meat', incorporation, and Duncan's murder as 'an act of symbolic anthropophagy' (28). Lehmann (2003: 245) has placed the film in a 'Western *noir*' genre as a 'literal tragedy of appetite'. The film also establishes a conflict between the 'American' desire to better oneself and move up in the world, with the realities of power and hierarchy. The allusion to the mega-chain McDonald's and its global spoliation of the environment and human health subverts the fantasies of capitalist triumph that Joe and Pat have. The film's final image is of McDuff, in a chef's hat, eating a carrot. He has no customers, because 'meat' rules this world, as a figure for multiple appetites, and there is no Fleance or Malcolm come to redeem the world. Joe's death comes, ironically, when he falls and is impaled on the steer horns – perhaps a steer that was served up with fries – that function as his car's hood ornament.

Moving to a very different kind of *noir*, Vishal Bhardwaj's Bollywood film *Maqbool* (2003) sets the story in the Mumbai underworld, mixing the genre of masala and *noir* tropes with the plot of *Macbeth*. Bhardwaj focuses more attention on the relationship between Maqbool (=Macbeth) and Nimmi (=Lady Macbeth); she is, for example, the mistress of Abbazi (=Duncan), and rather than renouncing her 'sex', Nimmi weaponizes it in order to manipulate Maqbool into the murder (made all the more necessary when Nimmi is displaced by Abbazi's new mistress). Nimmi even pulls Maqbool's own gun on him, in a scene finely balanced between the threat of violence and eroticism, compelling Maqbool to speak his love for her. The murder is shown – the crime/mob genre really demands it – as Maqbool shoots Duncan as he sleeps; the blood spatters on Nimmi, who shoots the guard when he comes in. Maqbool's motivation is thus far more personalized and sexualized than in most adaptations. When Maqbool is 'crowned', Nimmi sees Kaka (=Banquo) brought in dead and Maqbool hallucinates seeing him open his eyes. While Maqbool does ascend to take over the mob, the film focuses more intently on the development and collapse of his relationship with Nimmi. She becomes pregnant (as so many Lady Macbeths do; see **Chapter Five**), but the father's identity remains uncertain. The pregnancy is difficult: Nimmi can't sleep and claims the foetus 'won't sleep', it 'wails all the time'; Maqbool replies 'we killed its father'. The child is born, however, as – in one of the most overdetermined symbols imaginable – a solar eclipse is about to begin. Both Maqbool and Nimmi hallucinate and experience night terrors of guilt and remorse. After Nimmi dies, Maqbool goes to the hospital where her child has been taken up by Guddu (=Fleance), and as Maqbool tries to leave, he is shot dead. Bhardwaj's powerful film leaves its songs and dances, in the middle of the film, far behind with Maqbool's and Nimmi's deaths. The film suggests how this mob underworld reflects its corrupt society; the witches, for example, become here two corrupt policemen, who make prophecies as well as cover for the mob.

Penny Woolcock's 1996 film *Macbeth on the Estate* downshifts the story in terms of social class and mob coherence, setting the play in a contemporary English public housing development, the Ladywood Estate in Birmingham, England. The opening scenes offer a bleak, despairing landscape of burned-out cars, torn-up lots, huge rats, broken windows, and a group of inhabitants reduced to little more than a desire for drugs and alcohol. Presiding over the local gang – many of the actors actual residents of Ladywood – is one of the most dissolute and threatening Duncans ever seen, played by traditional hard man Ray Winstone. Woolcock locates the play's considerable violence in the even more violent world of the underclass, feeding on the scraps that capitalism lets drop and destroying themselves; none of the film's violence reaches beyond the estate, but what is beyond the estate has produced it in the first place. As Woolcock noted, this is a world in which 'Whole communities [are] being criminalised or semi-criminalised where the alternatives were less than minimum wage jobs' (Woolcock).

Woolcock had made a television documentary about Ladywood, *Shakespeare on the Estate* (1994), in which Michael Bogdanov (director of the 1998 film *Macbeth*) led locals through various scenes from the canon. A few years later, she felt she needed to return to Ladywood as she was 'still obsessed with finding a way of telling the real story about what I was seeing'. For Woolcock, 'If Shakespeare is kept traditional, then it's just for the tourists and the dead'. She placed this Macbeth on an estate because of 'this idea of feudal warlords slugging it out over money and territory. It's a place where politics has failed' (Rampton 1997). She learned from her documentary that 'Instead of imagining a post-industrial vacuum populated by victims I started piecing together a picture of a thriving marginal economy with an alternative system for keeping order' (Woolcock).

On top of this radically different setting, Woolcock made another radical choice: the characters only speak, more or less, lines from the play, with the result a fascinating disconnect between the richness of the language (though now in thick lower-class accents[12]) and the modernity on show. The effect is similar to Baz Luhrmann's in his *Romeo + Juliet*, though Luhrmann reveled in highly saturated colours and operatic staging as a high-flying counterpart to the language, while Woolcock offers only a persistent glare and gloom, and the chief musical scene features headbanging music called up by Duncan. The archaic language at some times hardly even registers: 'Here the actors in modern dress are delivering lines in Elizabethan English, and it sounds like the way they speak now', Woolcock noted (Rampton 1997). There are inspired moments of linguistic and social convergence: Banquo's 'insane root' (1.3.85) line is delivered as he offers Macbeth a joint, and Macbeth's line 'restless ecstasy' (3.2.23) is delivered as a bag of cocaine is brought out.

Woolcock's reinterpretation turns the witches into three teen-age urchins of the estate, the 'weird children', and the cast list includes both the unusual ('Crackhead's Sidekick') and the invented ('Duncan's Widow' and 'Duncan's Girlfriend'). Perhaps the most unusual aspect of the casting, however, is that the actors are racially diverse to an unusual degree – and unusual because the social world that Woolcock depicts seems not to be racist in the slightest. Black and white and brown skins mix together in relative harmony, and there are mixed-race marriages (Duncan and his wife) with mixed-race children (Malcolm and Donalbain), and a black Macduff. No racial insults are heard. Macbeth's motivation for going through with the murder derives from a highly eroticized Lady Macbeth. In the film's equivalent of 1.7, he throws her on their bed, him on top, but when he asks 'if we should fail?', she flips him over, climbs on top (figuratively as well as literally) and says 'We fail?'

Woolcock employed several of the themes we have seen in other adaptations. She shows the murder of Duncan – when Duncan opens his eyes, Macbeth puts a pillow across his face and slashes his throat; Woolcock also shows Lady Macbeth's suicide, as she walks off a rooftop to fall to her death, her body splayed on the grungy pavement as the estate's onlookers look on. Lady Macbeth has given birth (see **Chapter Five**), the child has died, and in the equivalent of the sleep-walking scene, Lady Macbeth walks into the bedroom (a boy's, judging by the blue paint and Aston Villa football jersey), and delivers her 'unsex me here' speech. Woolcock also brings Fleance back at the end, providing a closed-frame ending. Macduff had begun the film, standing in a wasteland between estate buildings, with an invented speech in faux-Elizabethan setting the story ('I tell of a time not long past, with Duncan, the King ... he was a man of war ... but in time Duncan grew fat, slack, and many miserable men took occasion thereof to trouble the peace, in seditious commotion'). At the film's end, we see Macduff in the same place, looking directly at the camera; Woolcock's final, biting social comment has Macduff speaking Ross's line from 4.3.164-5: 'Alas, poor country, almost afraid to know itself'. In the Folio, Ross had responded to Macduff's 'Stands Scotland where it did?', but Woolcock's framing of the line opens it out to include the whole wasteland of a contemporary world.

If there is a bleaker world of crime and poverty than the Ladywood estate, it is probably a *favela* in Brazil, which is the setting for Quentin Lewis's 2019 film *Macbeth O Rei Do Morro* (the English title is *Macbeth King of the Favela*). Lewis reduced the play to 106 minutes, with four acts of approximately the same length, each filmed in a single long take; various scenes, characters, and speeches are cut, though most of the iconic soliloquies are present in some form. The result is rather like the First Quarto of *Hamlet*: the play is there in skeletal form, and the deletions and abbreviations lead to a greater emphasis on pure action, particularly with the camera's long continuous takes. As in Woolcock's film, Lewis's characters speak the play's language (as far as I could tell via subtitles), with only a few additions; thus the (two) witches, in the equivalent of 1.3, say of Duncan (as if they've been reading Buchanan's *History*), 'He is more a tyrant than a king. Filling his pockets by selling drugs. It is time for a new king', and after the murder, Lady Macbeth declares 'The Kingdom is ours' – sentiments evident but unspoken in the Folio. Lewis updates the setting as one would expect: cell phones, guns, cocaine. The stripped-down action creates even more lacunae than the Folio has, as one scene flows quickly into the next. Lewis's film offers a powerful combination of erotic display and terrifying power in the two witches, but even more so in his Lady Macbeth. With so much of the plot stripped away, the actress Mariana Lewis dominates the screen and certainly dominates her Macbeth. Her suicide, if that is what it is, stems from the pills given to her by one of the witches. When she scorns 'Infirm of purpose' (2.2.53) when Macbeth won't take the daggers back to the murder scene, her voice and face are full of contempt while also plying Macbeth with a seductive smile. She is truly one of the terrifying Lady Macbeths. Lewis also shows the murder of Duncan: Macbeth puts his hands over Duncan's face, stabs him, and blood spatters onto the camera lens for the rest of the scene. At the end, we only see Macduff shooting down at where Macbeth should be, then spitting on his body, and declaring 'Hail King, for so thou art. Hail King of the favela', though Macbeth is not visible. At the very end, Lewis provides an overhead shot of Macbeth's body sprawled next to one of the buildings, and the camera pulls up to show the roofs of a small clump of buildings with a nearby road. The image does *not* show the massive sprawl of the favelas often seen in news and documentaries, with hundreds of thousands of houses, dirt roads, and feral animals roaming the slum. Instead, the final image suggests just how small the world of the gang is, how claustrophobic the surroundings are (made more so by the moving camera and long takes that swirl around the buildings). Lewis doesn't probe what is outside the favela or what has created it, or what its relation to the (presumably) nearby 'normal' city is. There is nothing in Lewis's film like the final line and image of Woolcock's Macduff: 'Alas, poor country, almost afraid to know itself'. There is, instead, a different, more localized kind of despair in the hot sun and saturated colours of the favela.

The 2001 film by Klaus Knoesel, *Rave Macbeth* (a German-made film with dialogue entirely in English), also shifts the play into a drug culture – criminal, if not quite Mafia. The rave dance scene is presided over by 'Dean', who notes that the wild scene has nothing to do with the disk jockeys and everything to do with 'E' or ecstasy, but he says at various points that he wants to run a 'clean' operation, which in this context means rampant drugs (but not for the staff) to a level of intoxication short of vomiting or (at the least) death. Marcus (Macbeth) and Troy (Banquo) are made Dean's new 'seconds' moments after they receive the prophecies (Marcus will become 'King of the Rave') from three spectral 'witches'/party girls. Unlike almost every adapter of the play, Knoesel makes extensive use of Hecate, who here is the male metrosexual (and ghostly[13]) head of the operation, to whom Dean reports. Hecate has a very long voiceover at the beginning of the film, setting the story in history ('At a time when people didn't dare to doubt the magic power of wizards and witches, Shakespeare immortalized the story of Macbeth. A man who let himself be seduced by such forces etc.') and preparing the turn to the present ('Since then, countless generations have gone by but stories repeat themselves. Today, we witches and warlocks still exist, but people don't notice us much, perhaps due to the changes in the tools of our trade'). The new 'tools' are shown in a video collage during the speech: beatings, shootings, the full criminal toolbox. Rather than the magic of the past, 'we use chemicals instead, which are far more potent and effective, such as E, ecstasy'. Knoesel's opening few minutes display humans as totally controlled by both E and by the surveillance-manipulation of Hecate; driving home the point, the film at many points has a 'human' character speaking a line which is at the same time echoed in Hecate's voice, and eventually becomes his voice entirely, while the 'human' figures regress into a pixelated background screen. This film denies Marcus/Macbeth's free will more than almost any other adaptation.

Although a puppet of Hecate, Marcus strikes one note of independence in relation to Lidia (Lady Macbeth). The film represents them as, at first, a real couple, with one extended sex scene at the club, fuelled by E, making clear their mutual desire. And Knoesel further emphasizes their bond when he shows Marcus becoming jealous of Troy (Banquo), who kisses her on the dance floor and, according to Lidia, says he wants her. Thus, the murder of the Banquo figure here has little to do with reproduction, lineage, or succession, and everything to do with erotic desire. When Dean tells Marcus to forget about Lidia and 'love', Knoesel gives Marcus a surprisingly sentimental (in this context) speech: 'I know what love is, and it doesn't come in a pill. ... Love is love, man, no artificial chemical can duplicate what love feels like.' But at this moment, Lidia – who has visually become harder and more demonic as the film progresses – is in another room at the club murdering Elena (Troy/Banquo's girlfriend), who has seen too much (i.e. Troy murdered by Marcus). And Lidia increasingly dominates and controls Marcus. One of the witches says in voiceover as Marcus and Lidia are initiating sex, 'Behind every good man there is a great woman' and another says 'It's a shame: all brawn, no brains' as she caresses (in a ghostly way) Marcus. That the power has shifted to Lidia becomes even clearer when Lidia tries to tamp down Marcus's growing hysteria, and wash the blood from his hands ('it's my turn to take care of you'), at which point she briefly hallucinates a crown on her own head. She never becomes as weak as the traditional Lady Macbeths, though both she and Marcus have hallucinations (whether from guilt or E is hard to determine), and it is she who orders Marcus to 'shoot him' when Macduff comes for them. In Knoesel's film, the murder of Troy/Banquo carries far more significance than the murder of Dean/Duncan (Dean pulls a gun on Marcus, then lets him go, and Marcus then stabs him). At the end, after they die, Marcus and Lidia stand up, and Marcus's voiceover wonders 'Had it all been a bad dream? ... Somehow we replaced everything [good] with hate. It really is too bad it had to end the way it did. I just hope sometime, somewhere, Lidia and I can get a chance to dance. Dance forever.' They are then joined by Dean, Troy, and Helena as the strobe lights continue and techno-music beats on.

Knoesel deploys an intense if narrow range of special effects in his translation of eleventh-century Scotland to the contemporary rave culture. The film's equivalent to 'magic' in the play is drugs in youth culture. Like Nesbø in his novel, Knoesel elevates Hecate – so often omitted in productions over the past decades, in part because of doubt whether the Hecate scenes are by Shakespeare (rather than Middleton)[14] – to a prominent role. Knoesel's Hecate is a puppet-master, coolly watching the humans make their mistakes, foreknowing what they will say and do. While the criminality of the drug culture is emphasized in the opening collage of current 'tools' of the trade, the focus eventually shifts more to super-heated young male machismo, jealousy, and desire. *Noir* adaptations transform the stakes for Macbeth, shifting from issues of royalty and succession to criminal gangs, and Knoesel's film changes them yet again, into becoming 'King of the Rave' and wanting to dance forever.

The 2016 play *Marqués – a Narco Macbeth*, by Stephen Richter and Mónica Andrade, transferred the play to contemporary Mexico and the hyper-violent drug cartels. The play follows Shakespeare's action closely, but with some provocative and disturbing innovations. Like so many adaptations, the Macbeths (Eduardo Marqués and Doña Marqués) have lost a child, but this version actually opens with Doña Marqués 'in labor' (9), the couple rushing to an emergency room with indifferent staff; it is too late, and the dead infant is carried out by a 'skull-faced nurse' (apparently a *Bruja*, one of the witches, 10).[15] After murdering David Ibarra (Duncan), the couple takes in one of his children, Donalbino, his 'eleven year old daughter' (33).[16] David's son Manuel (Malcolm) is a coked-up coward who is having an affair with Ibarra's '22 year old wife Lilia' (32); Manuel and the trophy wife are framed for Ibarra's murder. The families around the Marquéses are degenerate but their progeny mostly survive at the end. Richter and Andrade give Doña Marqués an additional family-related motive: Ibarra had murdered her father ('Do you have any idea what that man has done to my life?!' [32], she asks her husband). Moreover, David is an extremely cruel Duncan, who orders the equivalent to the Captain in 1.2 shot, and then orders, after the execution of the Cawdor figure: 'Put the video on the net' (14); said execution involves 'Three men in ski masks … One holds a machete, the other a chain-saw, the third holds a baseball bat' (16). Fortunately, the stage goes dark as the 'chain-saw roars to life' and the traitor's scream is heard (17).

Marqués, it turns out, is anything but a warrior at the beginning of the play; rather 'I'm an architect, not a criminal. But if I offend'

Ibarra, the witches have prophesied, 'I am dead. Everyone I care about will be dead' (24). Doña Marqués complements her husband's reticence with a dangerous intensity. When Marqués stabs David in the back but cannot finish the job and begins to struggle with him, Doña Marqués 'runs to the bar, grabs another knife, and cranks up the music to cover their deed …. [she] plunges her knife into David's back'; after a long fight, Marqués 'stabs him and stabs him without ceasing' (43). After Marqués becomes 'king and head of the largest cartel en [sic] Mexico' (19), as the witches had prophesied, he rapidly takes to his power and the violence he can wield, and, given the modern setting, establishes an elaborate surveillance system (like Hecate's in *Rave Macbeth*) in 'a dark control room with a massive grid of video screens, overhead' (60). The contemporary updating of the setting includes Marqués's equivalent of Macbeth's castle ('the magnificent white villa … pillars, archways, infinity pool, and the endless expanses of the Sea of Cortez', 29), the witches' lair ('a luxurious nightclub' in which male strippers 'strut and dance on stage', 80): medieval Scotland as Cabo San Lucas. In perhaps the most striking move, Siward becomes 'Major Burns' – a female U.S. Marine corps officer who leads the foreign invasion to place Manuel in charge, though she kills the Macduff figure herself (she 'unloads her entire magazine into Mendez', 102); it is difficult to think of a more appropriate corollary to the Scots being invaded by the English. Before she choppers out her crew, Burns presides over a selfie photo-op in one of the most cynical and negative endings any adaptation has mounted: Donalbino is brought in by a soldier, and 'stands with a traumatized look on his face next to Manuel. [Other characters] squeeze in. Everyone is holding their weapons. Marqués' head is at their feet', as the Puerto Rican Reggaeton song 'La despedida ["The Farewell"] plays' (104). Then, 'LIGHTS FADE'.

If the *noir* genre adaptations of *Macbeth* invoke gangs, violence, drugs, the mafia, and rigid masculinist hierarchies, what could be more *noir* than a cast of actual prison inmates? Such is the case with Tom Magill's compelling 2007 film *Mickey B*, with prisoner actors filmed in the Maghaberry Prison in Northern Ireland and set in a fictional 'Burnam Private Prison, Graveyard of the Forgotten'.[17] It is a *very* tough-looking place – lots of barbed wire, armed guards, snarling guard dogs, ominous music, corrupt prison officials – but there's one piece of unexpected literacy, when Peeper (the Porter) quotes Dante: 'Abandon hope all ye who enter here'. Magill reshapes the Folio plot essentially through cutting scenes and dialogue, but some of his adaptive choices will be familiar. He generally transforms the language into the prisoners' argot, but every once in a while employs Shakespeare's language (e.g. the oft-repeated 'What done cannot be undone') or cleverly revises it. The character equivalences are straightforward – Macbeth is Mickey B, Banquo is Banknote, Macduff is Duffer – with the exception of Lady Macbeth, who is a transvestite named 'Ladyboy'. 'She' (as the film refers to the male actor) has stereotypical feminine characteristics (long flowing hair, wears dresses, puts on lipstick) and the film probes gender identities carefully (see Bickley and Stevens 2020). But Ladyboy also invokes Satan in a mirror scene, and is the demonic pressure behind Mickey B – indeed, Ladyboy (like Kurosawa's Lady Macbeth, **Chapter Five**) directly calls for Banknote's murder. In the final confrontation, Mickey B is trapped behind bedsprings in his cell, murdered by a host of prisoners, not just Duffer. The film is replete with *noir* tropes, and offers no hope at the end, just a repetition of the beginning's 'We're all doing life. We're all doing time', while Malcolm plays chess with the prison officers, colluding with the enemy.[18] The film's final moment repeats a line from the beginning (also written in blood on the sheets of the dead Ladyboy): 'What's done cannot be undone'. The ending is as bleak as that in *Macbeth on the Estate*.

This dead butcher

The crime/mystery/gang adaptations of the play – when they are not simply invoking the play's title or major characters as a linguistic shorthand – overlap with what I have termed 'political' adaptations in several ways, from the fraught murder of the charismatic king/boss and the systemic instantiation of ambition in a rigidly hierarchical social world, to the deeply ingrained misogyny of a violent masculinist ideology. Many of the adaptations considered here, however, do not attempt to reach much beyond their own borders; *Macbeth on the Estate*, however, offers a horrifying vision of irremediable social dystopia, as does Nesbø's novel. Many crime adaptations, especially those set in modern urban gang settings,

show that the 'dead butcher' Macbeth deserves his ignoble end –
Brecht's 'John Machacek' actually *is* a butcher – and tend to level
out the moral plane of the characters, so that Fleance, for example,
becomes a made man and may even kill Macbeth himself in an act
both of vengeance and of hierarchical ascent. The result is often a
Kott-like view of the historical process: 'The new king will be the
man who has killed a king' (Kott 1964: 87).

5

Recuperating Lady Macbeth

Recent feminist scholars have recast the witches in a more positive light, as demonized projections of patriarchal anxieties, but Lady Macbeth has proven to be a harder case to rehabilitate (as witness Kate Fleetwood in Goold 2010, **Figure 8**). Her place in critical history, Cristina Alfar has observed, 'is one of almost peerless malevolence' (2003: 112). The Italian actress Adelaide Ristori, for example, described the character in her journal as a 'monster in human likeness' with 'inhuman power' over Macbeth: 'She becomes the Satanic spirit of the body of Macbeth. He has a hard struggle between the "wishing and not wish," that woman, that serpent, becomes absolute mistress of this man, entwines him in her grasp, and no human power can ever tear him from it' (Carlson 1985: 38). In the nineteenth century, as Georgianna Ziegler has shown (1999: 137), 'two images of Lady Macbeth – as barbaric and passionate or domesticated and caring – figure the conflicted notions about women's roles' in the Victorian period. Ziegler shows how Mrs. Siddons's overpowering portrayal influenced the view of Lady Macbeth throughout the century. In contrast to Lady Macbeth's frequent demonization, another actress, Ellen Terry, wrote that 'It seems strange to me that anyone can think of Lady Macbeth as a sort of monster, abnormally hard, abnormally cruel, or visualize her as a woman of powerful physique, with the muscles of a prize fighter! ... I conceive Lady Macbeth as a small, slight woman of acute nervous sensibility ... on the terms of equals [with her husband]' (Ziegler 1999: 128). No, Terry wrote in a letter to a male supporter, 'she was not good, but not much worse than many women you know – me for instance' (Auerbach 1987: 258).[1] Writing in 1884, Madeline Leigh-Noel saw Lady Macbeth as 'a

FIGURE 8 *Lady Macbeth*. Macbeth *directed by Rupert Goold* © *PBS Home Video/WNET.org 2010. All rights reserved. Screen grab.*

lonely woman, deprived of the love of a child and often solitary, lacking the companionship of her lord' (Ziegler 1999: 135). Other writers in this period saw Lady Macbeth as not a lonely housewife, but the amoral/immoral product of some distant barbarous age; as Anna Jameson wrote, 'Lady Macbeth is placed in a dark, ignorant, iron age; her powerful intellect is slightly tinged with its credulity and superstition, but she has no religious feeling to restrain the force of will' (Jameson 1901: 374); hence, she is not really connected to the Victorian concept of 'woman' at all. Such attempts to 'understand' Lady Macbeth anticipate more recent adaptations in significant ways.

After 1606, the name 'Lady Macbeth' essentially became 'a byword for any ambitious or cold-blooded woman' (Lanier 2006: 26), so much so that in most of nineteenth- and twentieth-century performances, Katherine Rowe argues, 'Americans especially resist a kinder, gentler, Lady Macbeth' (Rowe 2004: 127). Lady Macbeth may not kill Duncan in the Folio, but in his play, Charles Marowitz's Lady '*appears, takes hold of* MACBETH's *hands and drives the daggers into* DUNCAN's *heart*' (1978: 100). William Oldroyd's 2016 film *Lady Macbeth* is set in the nineteenth century, with the central figure Katherine in a loveless marriage to an older man, trapped in his house with her husband's tyrannical father; Katherine commits adultery and multiple murders, and is alone at the end with her unborn child. The film is indebted to Nikolai Leskov's 1865 novella *Lady Macbeth of Mtsensk* (as is Shostakovich's 1934 opera of the same name). In each case, 'Lady Macbeth' is a murdering wife. In Nicolas Freeling's 1988 crime novel, *Lady Macbeth*, the lady (at first thought to be a murder victim herself) is frequently compared 'with Lady Macbeth' because of her 'ambition ... force and tenacity ... she became over-dominant' (Freeling 1993: 211), which her husband came to resent. He hits her during an argument, she disappears to lead a more bohemian life, becoming ultimately an 'amateur terrorist' (234), planting a bomb on a bridge, and blowing herself up in the process (254). Near the end, Freeling's narrator observes that 'Macbeth and his wife destroyed one another. There is the tragedy. Strength and weakness hand in hand. What matter whether the kingdom be the size of Scotland, or that over-tidy four-room apartment of Elena's? What matter gun, knife, or bomb? It's a carnivorous world. We devour one another. Hate is love' (255). The novel concludes with an allusion to the play, while the narrator describes a simple picture called 'Eternity in Rotterdam': 'Fair enough, I thought. Little glimmer from that box of stupid Pandora's. Brief, and feeble, as a candle. But must keep lighting candles, no?' (256). Perhaps the most insidious allusion in the past few decades was a conservative critic's description of Hillary Clinton, then helping her husband run for President, as 'The Lady Macbeth of Little Rock': 'The image of Mrs. Clinton that has crystallized in the public consciousness is, of course, that of Lady Macbeth: consuming ambition, inflexibility of purpose, domination of a pliable husband, and an unsettling lack of tender human feeling, along with the affluent feminist's contempt for traditional female roles' (Wattenberg 1992).[2]

Yet in many recent adaptations, especially those inflected by feminist theory, a very different picture of the 'fiend-like queen' has emerged. These representations move far away from earlier adaptations in which 'Lady Macbeth' is either an ambitious, murderous woman, or a dessicated housewife. The works I will examine below instead seek an explanation or rationale for her behaviour through various strategies: by reference to her earlier marriage and son by that marriage (in Holinshed's *Chronicles* but suppressed in Shakespeare's play); to her situation as a woman in a culture of Celtic masculinity; and even to a supposed daughter with whom Lady Macbeth is ultimately reunited. The result is a repentant, heroic, even innocent – and above all, a maternal – Lady Macbeth.

Certainly the essential first step in recuperating Lady Macbeth into a potential figure of agency and self-empowerment, if not virtue, was to provide her with an actual *name*.[3] Although she is not named in Boece or Holinshed, the historical Lady Macbeth did have a name: in a contemporary document she is '*Gruoch filia Bodhe … regina Scottorum*' – Gruoch daughter of Bodhe … queen of Scots (Aitchison 1999: 48). Aitchison notes that Gruoch 'not only belonged to the royal kin group but was also directly descended from a previous King of Scots' (49). In adaptations that do use her historical name, it is variously spelled Gruoch, Gruach, Gruadth, Grelach, etc. I will use the spelling given in each version, reserving 'Lady Macbeth' for Shakespeare's character. The First Folio speech prefix is simply 'Lady' and in the stage direction of 1.5 she is noted as married: '*Enter Macbeths Wife alone with a Letter*'. Most editions of the play have named her as 'Lady Macbeth' (New Cambridge, Pelican, New Folger, Arden Two), or 'Lady M' (Riverside Two), but now also, following the First Folio, 'Lady' (Arden Three). The New Cambridge editor, in his 'List of Characters', even provides titles that the play declines to specify: 'Lady Macbeth, *Countess of Glamis, later Countess of Cawdor, later Queen of Scotland*' (100), while also providing 'Gruoch' in a footnote (101n.). The first reference to her historical name in a scholarly edition seems to have been in the Boswell/Malone edition, where there is a footnote saying 'Her name was Gruach, filia Bodhe' (Boswell 1821: 9). Giving her a name, her historical name, is a first step in detaching her from her nominal subordination as Macbeth's wife.

I argue here that these recent recuperations of Lady Macbeth, while feminist in intention if not always in outcome, participate in the larger cultural movement of adaptation that seeks to normalize the dramatic text as a whole. As we have seen with the return of Fleance in **Chapter Three**, these adaptations attempt to fill in gaps, resolve plot-lines, expand on characters' 'inner lives', and provide coherent psychological motives as part of a considered feminist response to patriarchal representations of female characters – and at times what Martha Tuck Rozett (1994) has termed 'talking back' to Shakespeare through adaptation.

Nineteenth-century literary heritage

In the Lambs' *Tales from Shakespeare* (1807), to take a highly influential example (written by Charles, not Mary), Lady Macbeth is simply a 'bad, ambitious woman' (Lamb 1909: 137), 'a woman not easily shaken from her evil purpose' (139), though – somewhat oddly – her 'manners were in the highest degree affable and royal', and she could play 'the hostess with a gracefulness and attention which conciliated every one present' (142); she dies 'unable to bear the remorse of guilt, and public hate' (145), though where the 'public hate' appears in Shakespeare's play, other than in Malcolm's final description of her, is unclear. Rejecting 'the commonplace idea of Lady Macbeth, though endowed with the rarest powers, the loftiest energies, and the profoundest affections, [as] nothing but a fierce, cruel woman, brandishing a couple of daggers, and inciting her husband to butcher a poor old king' (Jameson 1901: 356), Anna Jameson (1832) went on not to defend or rationalize Lady Macbeth's actions, but to explicate the character's dramatic power: 'She is a terrible impersonation of evil passions and mighty powers, never so far removed from our own nature as to be cast beyond the pale of our sympathies; for the woman herself remains a woman to the last – still linked with her sex and with humanity' (361).[4]

The Scottish novelist John Galt's 1812 play, *Lady Macbeth*, is one of the first to address the absence of Lady Macbeth in the Folio from 3.4, the banquet scene, to her sleep-walking in 5.1 and off-stage death. Galt begins his play after the murder of Banquo, with Macbeth seeing a 'gliding apparition' (1812: 116), the 'wraith' (117) of Lady twice, and is told that if it comes a third (what else?) time, 'The same day's sun that sees the queen a corpse, / O mighty king! shall never set to thee' (117). Lady herself suffers from her own hallucinations and Gothic-inflected nightmares,[5] hearing

The churm and chirruping of busy reptiles,
At hideous banquet on the royal dead.
Full soon, me-thought, the loathsome epicures,
Came thick on me, and underneath my shrowd,
I felt the many-foot and beetle creep;
And on my breast, the cold worm coil and crawl.
When all that was corporeal had resumed

Its elemental essence, I became
Lost in vacuity and silent gloom;
A strange oblivion of sense, space, and time. (120-1)

This Lady Macbeth possesses, Macbeth says, 'Spirit of valour, more
than masculine, / Whom nor disease, nor circumstance can daunt,
/ But still when heaviest prest springs into strength, /And with its
native royalty dilates / Still mightier than before' (135). The change
in her nature has been tremendous, from 'its high imperial arrogance
/ Into this weak and timid phantasy' (119). She is possessed now by
'the cancer of remorse' (131), yet even as she slowly fades away, she
still has the force to rally, even bully, Macbeth into rousing from his
own torpor to defend his kingdom. She rejects his reliance on the
prophecies for safety: 'Fye; be a man, and leave such idle search / To
cred'lous girls and boys professionless' (133), and later rejects the
'fatal sadness, that unmans you so', because it would 'better suit the
weak of my disease' (142).

Galt is among the earliest adapters whose Lady Macbeth – many
more would follow – has given birth, but Galt gives her the barest
sense of loss, and does not make her unexplained loss any kind of
motive. Rather,

Though I have felt
The pangs of birth, a mother's sleepless cares,
And watch'd my infant's couch with throbbing heart;
Sweet was that watching, and those cares were gentle,
And slight the pains [compared] to those I suffer now. (129)

Still, that maternal note reflects the softening of character that Galt
had aimed for. In the Preface to his collection of plays, Galt said, 'I
thought the almost satanic character of the Lady, possessed traits of
grandeur which might be so represented as to excite compassion'
(v). Galt provides Lady many speeches of grandeur and horror, but
she dies in a fever, in a 'deadly thirst' and hallucination of guilt:
'Ha! Wretch – 'tis blood! – ' (156), and only the servant Baudron
(the name refers to a type of Scottish cat, so possibly a demonic
figure) remains to pronounce a grisly epitaph: 'dreadful doom! to
die alone. – / Hither ye pale appall'd. This mighty dame, / Is now as
harmless as the sludge, that's cast / From the brief trenchment of a
baby's grave' (156-7). Galt quotes, alludes to, or inverts many lines

from the play to notable if melodramatic effect, none more ironic
than Macbeth's reference to her as 'My dearest partner of unhappy
greatness!' (122) and her attempt to reassure him that 'I will wear
boldly what I've dearly won: / What is done, is' (123). The play ends
with Macbeth going to his final battle and death: 'I go to meet her,
though it be in Hell!' (158).

Mary Cowden Clarke (1853), however, imagined a more complex
woman than Galt or the Lambs, and is one of the earliest adapters
to provide the character's historical name, which is offered without
comment: 'The lady Gruoch, descended of one of the noblest
Scottish houses, by orphanhood in her minority, became a ward
of the crown' (1887: 98).[6] In providing explanations and filling in
perceived lacunae in the play's narrative, Clarke makes Lady partly
the product of inheritance, as her own mother had 'pride of blood,
the daring aspiration of her nature ... [and] ambition', while also
scorning 'such qualities as she discovered in her husband' (99). In
Clarke's prequel, the infant Gruoch appeared to her father as 'this
tender blossom, this human bud awaiting with yet half-closed petals
its future development' (102). Yet her mother remained aloof, and
so 'the babe sucked bitterness, perverted feeling, unholy regret, and
vain aspiration, with every milky draught imbibed' (104). Soon, the
contaminating effects of the mother began to manifest themselves,
as the infant's hand 'clenched angrily, and struck and buffeted at the
golden rays [of the sun] they could not seize', though soon enough
she catches a silvery moth, and 'the next instant, the little fingers were
unclosed; to one of them stuck the mangled insect, crushed even by
so slight a touch' (107). Years later, she will destroy a bird's nest –
a martlet, not yet temple-haunting (126) – sending all the young
to their death without a further thought. The path from crushing
moths and killing birds to regicide seems inevitable. Early on, 'the
indulgence of her will, the right of command, the custom of seeing
herself obeyed in all things, became habitual to her ... She could
scarcely speak, ere her voice assumed the tone of authority' (109).
As a woman, Gruoch never hesitates to use her 'surpassing beauty ...
[evidenced] by the brilliancy of her complexion, by the lustre of her
golden hair, and above all, by the magic of a commanding presence'
(139) to wield influence over others, including, of course, Macbeth:
'their mutual looks and discourse grow more and more animated,
and reveal more and more how each is struck and enchanted with
the other' (140). Their marriage soon bears a fruit neither the play

nor the historical record ever imagines, a son 'Cormac' (164), who dies in infancy – at which point, more or less, Shakespeare's play begins. Clarke's account offers a far greater understanding, if not exactly sympathy, of the character, describing an evolutionary process – malevolent maternal influence, bad milk, and an overly indulgent father, in addition to some evil seed – where Lamb simply saw a bad woman. Clarke's introduction of the themes of milk, the maternal, and Lady Macbeth's child would be taken up by later adapters.

In her paper 'Gruach (Lady Macbeth)' read to the New Shakspere Society in 1875, Annette Handcock defended Lady Macbeth; she invoked Gervinus (who said that she had been made into 'a figure of virtue' in Germany), and then argued that 'Many good qualities, when carried to excess, topple over and become faults' (Handcock 1875: 133). Among these good qualities was that 'Gruach had evidently loved her father', since she could not kill Duncan (he 'resembled / My father as he slept' [2.2.13-14]), and 'She had been a tender mother'. In any event, 'the essence of her being, was devoted to her husband. ... She sees, feels, acts, but for him. Remember the age in which she lived.' The Countess even describes a portrait of Lady Macbeth, no longer extant, which she had heard about: 'It was the portrait of a small fair woman, with blue eyes, rather red (weak-looking?) about the lids' (134). F. J. Furnivall's response was dismissive: 'The notion that Lady Macbeth ... [acted] to gratify his [Macbeth's] ambition only, and not her own too', flies in the face of Holinshed's account and is 'flatly contradictory to Shakspere's plain revelation of Lady Macbeth's tigrish nature' (134).

Later adaptations

George William Gerwig's brief 1929 account of *Shakespeare's Lady Macbeth, A Study in Ambition* is one of a baker's dozen of such lives; all the others are virtuous ('Cordelia – A Loyal, Dauntless Daughter'), even Volumnia ('A Noble Roman Mother'), while Lady Macbeth is 'Temptation'. These lives were bound and could be purchased separately or together as *Shakespeare's Ideals of Womanhood*, a mid-American moralizing version of Clarke's work in the previous century. Each biographical essay begins with the assumption that 'The fundamental characteristics which go to make up Anglo-Saxon womanhood, the qualities of faith, of loyalty, or purity in its broadest and deepest sense, of sympathetic inspiration, have been as potent factors in the world's progress as have the corresponding ones of courage or chivalry or daring'. Moreover, Gerwig continued, 'The Heroines of Shakespeare present the particular types of heart and soul ideals which have made first the Anglo-Saxon, then the English, and lastly the American woman the embodiment of all that is good and true and wholesome' (Gerwig 1929: Foreword). Given this starting point, it is remarkable that Lady Macbeth should find a place in this virtuous group at all. Gerwig's account attributes her motives to traditional 'female' desires: like any good wife, 'She wants this kingdom, not in any sense for herself, but for her husband. She has set her heart supremely upon this, thinking that she has counted the cost, but, woman-like, really seeing nothing between her wish and its fulfillment' (15). This Lady Macbeth has given birth to a child, now dead: 'Had their child lived it [their misfortune] might have been different' (20). For Gerwig, the most shocking moment in the play is Lady Macbeth's 'I have given suck' speech and the horrible imagery attached to it: 'Their babe is dead – yet she can say this! Her resources, and the relentless way in which she employs them, are simply appalling, unless we bear constantly in mind that it is not for herself, but for her husband that she is striving so hard' (21). Gerwig's Lady exemplifies a kind of perfect housewife, whose ambition was not her own, and whose childlessness produced scarcely a ripple of motivation, and not a trace of hysteria.

Ruby Cohn once wondered 'Perhaps today's Lady Macbeth needs Women's Liberation' (1976: 101): her call has not gone unanswered, though many adapters have continued to assume a traditional characterization of Lady Macbeth, either as simply a demonized murderous woman, pushing her husband to murder, or as a passive subject, even a perfect housewife, withering away – as a woman supposedly would – under the pressure of guilt. One of the moments in the Folio that best exemplifies the dualistic interpretations of Lady Macbeth comes in an interpolated stage direction at 2.3.120. Davenant changed the Folio's 'Help me hence, ho' (2.3.119) to a more female-appropriate 'Oh, oh, oh. [*Faints*' (Davenant 1674: 23). Rowe's edition interpolated two stage directions that indicated female weakness and perhaps cunning

(*Seeming to faint* and *Lady Macbeth is carried out* [1709: 2323]),
which Pope (1723), Theobald (1733), Warburton (1747), Johnson
(1765), Capell (1767), and many other editors duplicated. Bell's
Acting Edition (1774) went even further, simply eliminating
Lady Macbeth from the scene altogether. Some modern editions
still have her faint, but most now have no stage direction and/
or a reference to Bradley's 'Note DD': 'Did Lady Macbeth Really
Faint?' (Bradley [1904] 1968: 418–20). Hard Lady Macbeths don't
faint, but distract weak husbands, as Macbeth seems about to give
away their secret.

By contrast to the sentimental self-denying housewife, Gordon
Bottomley's play *Gruach* (1921) offers a sympathetic, even proto-
feminist view of Lady Macbeth, signalled in part by his use of
her historical name as his title, though little in the play has any
historical basis. Bottomley's play occurs the night before the
planned wedding between Gruach and Conan, Thane of Fortingall.
Set in the small castle owned by Morag (Conan's mother), the place,
we are told more than once, is a 'threatening prison' (Bottomley
1921: 33), with Gruach a restless but subjugated prisoner whose
wedding gown is 'as heavy as fetters' (16). That night, the King's
messenger, Macbeth, arrives, and he and Gruach instantly connect
so powerfully that she will leave with him that same night; she plans
their escape, telling him that she will go first and that he should
'step then upon my footprints' (56). For Bottomley, Gruach must
escape her confinement to Conan, and the claustrophobic life he
represents, if she is to survive. Her escape represents a commitment
to nothing less than life itself:

> This is my hour of fate, this is the time
> When I must break the blind restricted seed
> That I am now, move with the winds of life
> And yield my mental issue to them again,
> Or in this present burial rot and change. (45)

In a note left to Morag, Gruach simply says 'I would live, so I leave
you' (55). Like a romantic maiden of the previous century, she says
to herself, 'O, let me dream anew, and in a dream / Of uttered scorn
sting vivid life to spring / Back to my sinking heart' (55).

But in addition to Gruach's quest for life at any price, Bottomley
also reaches back into the chronicles to invoke her royal

blood – a move now common in contemporary adaptations. As Morag says,

Her father was of dead King Kenneth's breed,
And though her line is dispossessed, she is yet
Royal in some men's minds, heiress of peril
But also of great chance. (11)

The unwitting Conan, coming down to an empty room on his wedding day, admits that 'I would not wed her if she had no land' (66). Gruach herself puts Macbeth straight: 'I am of a more ancient house of kings / Than you' (47).

Bonnie Copeland's romance, *Lady of Moray*, is parallel to but quite different from Clarke's *Girlhood* formula. On the very first page, the young Gruoch seeks out the witch Agne and with her help summons no less than Satan ('a face with bright burning eyes, a beak-like nose' [1979: 3]) to help 'Make me queen of Scotland' (4). No need here for the lost maternal motive, the witches' prophecies to Macbeth, or the resentment against Duncan's naming of his son as successor: this Lady is herself demonic from the start, signing a pact with Satan to pursue both her desire to be Queen and to take revenge against Malcolm II, who 'slaughtered my grandfather, Kenneth, to snatch the crown' (5). Copeland pursues, on the one hand, something of the historical record (thus, Gruoch marries Gillcomgain) while at the same time deploying the tropes of romance fiction ('Her hair fell loose and full and, catching the sunlight, shone as burnished gold. Her face was round, her lips full and strikingly red' [13]) mixed with anticipations of the Macbeth narrative to come. This assertive Gruoch enacts her own agency, but in cruel and selfish ways (of her marriage to Gillcomgain: 'To make him love her was to take possession of him, to dominate him, and she was certain of her powers in this' [95]). After numerous battles, betrayals, murders, and emotional upheavals, the novel ends with Gruoch, now a widow, and her son Lulach on the road to find Macbeth, who would surely harbour as great a resentment against Malcolm II as she did: 'Contrary to the laws of the land, Malcolm had named Duncan heir, though the dexter [i.e. right] line of succession should have been served. Macbeth stood foremost in that line' (309), and she goes, in the novel's final words, to 'walk a glittering pathway to her destiny as Queen of Scotland' (313).

Twenty-first-century adaptations

Several recent representations of Lady Macbeth leverage her royal blood, as Bottomley did, to explain, indeed justify, her actions in Shakespeare's play. Like Fleance, her genealogical significance is considerable, though his is articulated in the play text while hers is invisible in the play. In Susan Fraser King's novel *Lady Macbeth* (2008), though it is primarily a prequel to the play, Gruadh begins the narrative writing from her fortified castle, six months after the death of Macbeth, sending her defiance to Malcolm. Her lineage is everything – 'I am granddaughter to a king and daughter to a prince, a wife twice over, a queen as well' (King 2008: 2) – and in King's account this explains Gruadh's first marriage at thirteen, her pride, and her later actions; her second marriage, to Macbeth, came about because the victor in a combat often married the widow of his victim. King's more historically informed story rests with little ambiguity on the early modern succession politics that Shakespeare had so thoroughly mystified in his play, where there is no hint of Lady Macbeth's royal past.[7] Here, by contrast, is a conversation between Gruadh and her father, Bodhe:

> Bodhe narrowed his eyes. 'Old Malcolm [i.e., Malcolm II, not the Malcolm Canmore of the play] wants to keep the kingship in his bloodline. Duncan will name his own son as his tanist, and so it goes. We dispute that.'
>
> I nodded. 'Straight descent is not the Celtic way'.[8]
> 'Exactly. Our branch, not theirs, must rightfully supply the next king of Scots.' (2008: 60)

Gruadh will join forces with Macbeth, in part, because she has been denied her lineal rights. After Duncan's murder, Macbeth tells her 'Your ancient bloodline holds the key in this …. Because of your blood, you will not be called consort, but full queen, and crowned as such' (273). Pushing sympathy even further, King also makes Duncan responsible for the murder of Gruadh's father. By providing Gruadh motives for murdering Duncan, then, King rationalizes her character, transforming her actions into a rough form of restored justice.

Moreover, King (like Klein, below) will retrieve from the historical record of Lady Macbeth's only surviving child, from her first marriage to Gilcomgan: her son Lulach. Shakespeare erased the historical reality of this male heir in the royal line; the only trace remains, perhaps, in Lady Macbeth's infamous line, 'I have given suck and know / How tender 'tis to love the babe that milks me' (1.7.54-5). Gruadh therefore fights not only for her own right and her lineage, but also for her son's future, while Duncan – not the weak king (see **Chapter Two**) – becomes a killer, and his son Malcolm no better. Indeed, King will transform the murder of Duncan into a patriotic act, intended to free Scotland both from his treachery and from his weakness and inability to deal with Danish invasions and other subversions of his kingdom.

In line with this conception of a 'patriot' Macbeth, Gruadh is also newly imagined as a medieval eco-friendly preserver of traditional Scots folkways. It's not just that 'Straight descent is not the Celtic way', as Gruadh agrees with her father, but only in the North, where they rule, do the traditions of the 'Celtic way' survive, beneath a veneer of Christianity. Here there is respect for the land, a protective (if paternalistic) concern for the local populace, not to mention hints of magic and mystical powers. As in many modern adaptations, Gruadh herself has 'the Sight', the Celtic ability to see into the future. Duncan, by contrast, is an outlier, unable to conquer without foreign assistance and insensitive to the old ways. 'So long as we stay Celts', Gruadh says, 'and do not become Roman, or English, or Viking instead. I fear that the Scottish Celts will lose the old wildness, the old ways, for there is much that is good and beautiful in that' (191). Gruadh links herself as well to the Celts' 'long, proud history of warrior women' (62), and takes up the sword more than once.

These mitigations – revenge, lineal right, patriotism, cultural preservation – offer to explain the later Lady Macbeth of the play, but no historical-textual invention has been as powerful, or as prevalent, as the sympathy-inducing accounts of Lady Macbeth's often-multiple miscarriages. In King's novel, Gruadh gives birth to Lulach just after her forced marriage to Macbeth. After a long period of coldness, Gruadh comes to desire Macbeth ('I long to invite him to my bed', [148]), and soon is pregnant; however, 'One night I went to bed with indigestion and an aching back, and by the next day no longer carried a child.' Her reaction is to be 'Cold as stone ... bearing the devastation in silence' (182), but miscarriage after miscarriage follows ('my tiny hatchling slipped out of me on a slide of blood', 212), and she is no longer cold but heartbroken ('My heart still ached for a child', 217). Indeed, her maternal instincts become even stronger in protecting Lulach, who after the death of Macbeth (ambushed by a treacherous Malcolm) is crowned King of Scots, marries, and has a daughter. King ends her novel with Gruadh most definitely alive, concerned about Lulach's fate, secure for the time being, and defiantly rejecting suggestions from Malcolm that she marry him: 'I am done with sorrow and intend to seek a little peace and magic. For now' (330).

Lisa Klein's *Lady Macbeth's Daughter* (2009) takes the maternal theme even deeper into fantasy. Although also claiming to offer a narrative based on some part of the historical record, Klein nevertheless invents, as her title indicates, a daughter. Grelach gives birth to Albia at the beginning of the novel; the child, though, is deformed, with a 'crippled leg' (Klein 2009: 1), and is taken by her servant Geillis to raise as her own. Grelach is led to believe the child is dead, since Macbeth had ordered that the 'spawn of evil' be taken to the heath and left 'for the wolves' (8). The motif of the abandoned child, lame but healed by the good country folk, is pursued through the expected revelations at the end. Albia – who also picks up the sword, following the ways of strong Celtic women warriors, and who also has the Sight (99) – is horrified when she eventually learns her parentage years later, rejects all that her father Macbeth has done, and only at the last minute forgives Grelach. Along the way, Klein invokes tropes from the romance/adventure genres of *The Hunger Games*, *Twilight*, and Disney's *Brave* (including the red hair). Some of Klein's inventions go far beyond even the highly implausible, such as Albia's love for Fleance (who, according to the chronicles, must already be dead; see **Chapter Three**).

Klein's novel focuses primarily on Albia, but also provides an expiatory version of Grelach, through roughly alternating chapters of first-person narration. Grelach too suffers multiple miscarriages ('Like a wounded animal, I cry out as I feel the child slip from my womb ... a baby boy, perfectly formed but still and silent as Death' [20-1]). Even worse, she doesn't love Luoch (=Lulach), who entered the world when the midwife 'pulled from me a black-haired boy covered in wax and blood' (3), nor does Macbeth consider Luoch his heir. Grelach cannot love Macbeth, though she joins forces with him through the usual pride in her lineage: 'How dare Duncan – whose grandfather shut my kin out of the succession – now try to extend his rule to the next generation! The injustice of it brings my blood to the boiling point' (50). Like Gruadh in King's novel, Grelach does not die a suicide but survives Macbeth's death, is spirited away by one of her ladies, and is then brought to a difficult but (could it be otherwise?) tearful reconciliation with her daughter (Grelach has only recently learned that her daughter survived). As Grelach asks forgiveness, 'tears begin to course down her cheeks' (240), and the novel ends when Albia silently takes 'both [of] her [mother's] wounded hands in my own. The creases around her eyes and mouth, like so many rivers inked on Scotland's map, seem to relax, softening her expression. I glimpse my mother when she was my age. With my fingertips, I stroke the skin of her hands until the bloody spots begin to fade, then disappear' (242). The key sentence permitting this reunion, and the culmination of the entire mother-daughter narrative, is Grelach's assertion of maternal love, loss, and necessity: '"All that I did", she says, letting the tears roll down her cheeks unstopped, "was born from my despair ... at losing you, Albia"' (241).

In Hartley and Hewson's *Macbeth: A Novel*, the maternal theme is struck with Skena[9] giving birth, six years earlier, to 'a boy, the only child they'd ever had, the only one they ever would, a sickly babe who barely opened his eyes in his short life'; afterwards, 'Skena's womb was judged torn and fruitless' (2012: 53). Hence, there is no string of miscarriages, and no Lulach. Still, Skena blames Duncan's forcing them to move to Inverness for the miscarriage (68), and vows, 'Since Duncan's cruelty stole from me my child, I will be nothing but a vessel of hatred for him' (81). Duncan is further demonized by his boundless lechery: he not only makes a pass at Skena, but is seen, in some detail, forcing a kitchen girl to fellate him: 'The older he gets', one guard says, 'the younger he likes them' (115-16). So this Duncan *really* deserves to be murdered. Hartley and Hewson even have Lady Macbeth herself finish off Duncan, who, as in standard horror movies, isn't *quite* dead when she enters the room to place the daggers: 'Duncan's long, bony fingers rose and clawed at her throat ... the daggers in her hand found life, stabbed at him, his neck and face, his scrawny arm ... at last, she tore his talons free and fell back, staggering, crying, panting' (135). This account goes as far as absolving Skena – herself now the actual regicide – as one can imagine, from paedophile Duncan's vampire-like resurrection to the personifications and passive verbs ('the daggers ... found life, stabbed at him') that displace her agency.

Worse for Skena, the kitchen boy Ewan, who has become a surrogate child to her, dies when he accidentally drinks the poison procured for Duncan's guards, and Skena tearfully prepares his body for burial (146-52). As if to rub it in, Banquo brazenly attempts to blackmail Macbeth into naming Fleance as his heir – 'Take him as your own' (179) – hence providing justification for his own murder. At the end, urged on by the witches, who have reappeared to her when she flees Dunsinane, Skena slits her wrists: 'after the brief, exquisite agony, [she] lay back in the scented heather, wondering at the beauty of the stars and sky', free at last (281).

David Greig's 2010 play *Dunsinane*[10] constructs a provocative account of Gruach, employing many of the same rationalizing and humanizing tropes found in the works described above. A sequel, the play begins when Macbeth has been killed and the victorious English general Siward and his troops encounter Gruach (rumours of her suicide had been spread by a fanatic, malicious Malcolm. Greig's transformation of Lady Macbeth follows several other writers who have turned to Scottish historical sources (unavailable to Shakespeare) to recover, and recuperate, the 'real' Lady Macbeth. Where Shakespeare's Lady Macbeth imploded with guilt after the murder of Duncan, Greig's Gruach is by contrast a strong-willed, charismatic figure, the dynamic centre of the play. Greig 'wanted to see her from another point of view. I was helped by the historical record, which says that she outlived her husband, and may have done so by some distance'. Her character, Greig said, 'emerged very suddenly with a single line ... Siward finds this woman hiding. He says to her, "Woman, what is your place here?"; and she says, "My place? My place here is queen."'[11] Greig's revisionist history results in a powerful, mysterious character who, more or less, represents 'Scotland' against Siward's 'England' (Siward actually introduces himself to Gruach, 'I am Siward. / I am England' [27].)

For Greig,

Too many depictions of Lady Macbeth portray her as a depraved woman, and her sexuality is tied up with a lust for power. I was much more interested in the idea that this is a woman who has a number of very powerful aims, which are rational. She believes that her clan, her faction, should be in charge, and it is her right to be queen. To achieve this she will use all means at her disposal, including her sexuality.

(Brown 2011)

Greig's Gruach becomes the focal point of Scottish opposition to the occupying troops. At one point, she seduces Siward and later, for cynical reasons, agrees to marry Malcolm (only to escape his imprisonment before the ceremony and flee to the countryside). Her resistance is rendered patriotic to the highest degree, inextricably linked to her royal identity. For much of the play, she asserts Lulach's right to the throne even as she hides him in the countryside. In one passage of incantatory rhetoric, she responds to Siward's request that she 'renounce' her son's 'claim' to the throne:

> My son doesn't *claim*.
> My son *is* the King.
> It's not a matter about which he has a choice.
> My son is my son.
> My son is the son of his father.
> My son's father is dead.
> My son is the King. (34)

Siward can only respond by asking 'What would you do—if you were me?' The simple answer is devastating: 'If I were you I would not be here' (34).

After many episodes of increasing savagery, through which the English occupiers hoped to win the hearts and minds of the people, Siward kills a 'Scottish Boy' who may or may not have been Lulach, only to have Malcolm tell him that the Moray do not accept that the dead boy is Lulach, and worse, that 'it's more likely that by killing this boy you have given him eternal life' (125). In the final scene of the play, Siward then takes the boy's body to Gruach, thinking she will give up her resistance, only to be shown a baby said to have been fathered by Lulach: 'This child is now the King' (134), Gruach informs Siward, and she describes to him a lineage of birth and resistance that, in effect, will stretch to the crack of doom. The play ends with Siward not harming the baby, and walking out, without destination, to disappear into the snow: 'And then there is only white' (138). Macbeth is never seen in the play: we learn only that he did not die bravely fighting but 'was running when we caught him. A spear in his back' (25). But Gruach not only survives, she endures: a heroic, mystical figure of beauty, resistance, and agency.

In 'liberating' Lady Macbeth, these adapters employ various strategies: demonizing Duncan, Malcolm, and even Banquo, making the Macbeths patriots, preserving the old Celtic ways, and so on. These adaptations for the most part also deny Lady Macbeth the option of suicide – certainly nothing could be further from the mind of Greig's Gruach or King's Gruadh (nor from the historical records, which show her surviving Macbeth's death).[12] These appropriations openly declare what might be called a 'realist' vision of what the play *should* have been but failed to be, whether through Shakespeare's dereliction or the vagaries of the early modern publication process. Noah Lukeman concluded, in *The Tragedy of Macbeth, Part II: The Seed of Banquo* (2008), that '*Macbeth* is unfinished' (2008: v) in part because Lady Macbeth's 'child' is 'omitted from the play' (vi), so Lukeman produced said child. But Lukeman, to be fair, is in good company, as many recent adaptations of Shakespeare's play have made similar moves.

Recuperating Lady Macbeth

While many adaptations attempt to recuperate, rationalize, and understand Lady Macbeth by turning to the 'historical' record to recover her royal lineage, it is worth repeating that there is not a whisper of this lineage in Shakespeare's play or Holinshed's, Buchanan's, or Leslie's accounts of Macbeth. Nor is there any hint of royal lineage in Holinshed's account of Donwald's ambitious wife (generally considered to be Shakespeare's inspiration for Lady Macbeth), as they join in murdering King Duff. Holinshed's account of Lady Macbeth consists of just a single sentence: the prophecy of the three weird sisters encouraged Macbeth and 'specially his wife lay sore upon him to attempt the thing, as she that was very ambitious, burning in unquenchable desire to bear the name of a queen' ([1587] 1808: 5.269).

Olga Valbuena has made a scholarly case for retrieving Lady Macbeth's historical lineage, noting that historicist critics (such as Norbrook) have thoroughly investigated the conflict of succession

issues in the play but 'have not addressed the historical Lady
Macbeth's dynastic claims and revenge motive lurking at the
margins of historical and dramatic master texts or the public
transcript' (Valbuena 2003: 81). Sid Ray, quoting this passage,
says with satisfaction that this lineage provides a 'motive' for Lady
Macbeth's actions, giving them 'a political rather than personal
resonance' (Ray 2009: 119), as if this is an improvement on the
play. Ray's essay first describes Gruoch's lineage, missing in the play,
as a way to analyse several films which either do not do justice
to Lady Macbeth or exploit the actress playing her (Orson Welles,
Polanski), or 'deepen the character by suggesting that Lady Macbeth
has a history worth revealing' (as in the 2006 Wright film). The
history that is revealed in these films, however, has nothing to do
with her lineage, but primarily her maternity.

When Lady Macbeth's lost lineage is described as one of
the lacunae in the *play*, the implication is that Shakespeare has
suppressed this information. Yet he apparently had no access to
it in the first place, whereas the succession questions (mystified in
the play) were openly treated in Holinshed, Buchanan, and other
probable sources. The retrieval of this information (often in very
partial form, and often incorrect) amounts to a sentimental rescue
mission based on a conflation of a literary character with (some)
elements of a historical figure. Even if Shakespeare had had access
to this historical material, the question that Anna Jameson asked in
1832 still remains valid: 'what is all this [chronicle history] to the
purpose? ... she is Lady Macbeth; as such she lives, she reigns, and
is immortal in the world to imagination. What earthly title could
add to her grandeur? What human record or attestation strengthen
our impression of her reality?' (Jameson 1901: 354)

Ironically, this historical turn even more firmly inscribes Lady
Macbeth in patriarchal discourse than Shakespeare's play does,
as her 'royal' lineage stems entirely (if necessarily) from her male
predecessors. Greig's phrasing of Gruach's defiance – 'My son is the
son of his father. / My son's father is dead. / My son is the King' –
reproduces the early modern parthenogenetic fantasy in which the
female has no role in reproduction and lineage. The resurrection
of Lady Macbeth's royal lineage, moreover, deflects her motivation
to, in part, restoring a past (masculine-derived) right rather than
the play's looking-forward desire ('Thy letters have transported me
beyond / This ignorant present, and I feel now / The future in the

instant' [1.5.54-6]). The 'royal lineage' narrative, finally, ultimately deprives Lady Macbeth of the agency – for good or bad – that the play actually grants her. Bottomley's and Greig's versions are the exception. Based on conversations with a historian of the period, Greig developed his Gruach from a 'speculation' that she 'was the real power in the land ... Macbeth was just the muscle employed by her to hold on to the throne' (Brown 2011).

Finally, in addition to her royal lineage, virtually every recent adaptation has invoked, often on an elaborate scale, Lady Macbeth's maternity (or lack of it) as to a greater or lesser extent determining her actions and identity: she has miscarriages, or her son Lulach must be saved, or she must be reunited with her invented daughter. Reisert's young adult novel *The Third Witch* adopts all three of these mitigating strategies: Lady Macbeth is heard telling Macbeth '*Your* blood is as royal as his [Duncan's]. *My* blood is more royal. My poor, dead babe whose little body moulders in the ground – even the blood of my babe – gnawed by worms and other crawling things of the darkness is more royal than our greedy king's' (Reisert 2001: 115); yet the novel does not really attempt to mitigate Lady Macbeth's behaviour. The narrative of Caroline Cooney's young adult novel, *Enter Three Witches: A Story of Macbeth* follows the action of the play from the point of view (primarily) of Lady Mary, daughter of the Thane of Cawdor. Cooney also resists the maternal theme, for while this Lady Macbeth was 'always in a state of wanting' (Cooney 2007: 37), yet 'Lady Macbeth was not motherly and would not offer comfort [to Mary]' (74), and no hitherto unknown child appears in the novel (though Fleance once again returns in triumph, and marries Lady Mary).[13]

Many recent adaptations have taken the issues of maternity and children to extraordinary lengths. In Woolcock's film *Macbeth on the Estate* (1996), not only has Lady Macbeth given birth to a child now dead, but she remains trapped in grief, preserving the young boy's bedroom – an oasis of innocence in the midst of the grit and grunge of the estate – and is frequently shown holding someone else's child (especially Macduff's). After the murder of Duncan, Macbeth lies next to her in bed, but she suddenly has to get up because of menstrual cramp; when she opens the bathroom cabinet, she begins to reach for a Tampax but then reaches for a home pregnancy test kit, opens and tears it pieces, and throws it away. Her suicide is strongly motivated through her horror at seeing the slaughter of Macduff's family. Realizing what her husband is about to do, she runs to the Macduff's to warn them (with some of the Messenger's lines at 4.2.66-74), but then runs out, looks through the kitchen window to see the slaughter, including the murder by Macbeth himself of the infant she is so often seen holding.

Brozel's 2005 film completely modernizes the play temporally, and preserves comparatively few lines of the play. Its plot moves generally along the same track as Shakespeare's play, taking the trope of food not just as a theme but as its very centre (see **Chapter Four**) in the Michelin-starred restaurant. Lady Macbeth is the *maître d'*, jealous on her husband's behalf as Duncan is merely a celebrity who no longer cooks in the restaurant: she smears his smock with sauce before he appears to the patrons in order to lend credibility to his position as head chef. The culinary elements and blood come together in such moments as Lady Macbeth's long soliloquy in which she refers to her pregnancy:

> Three days and two nights, then they cut me open, and out he popped, clean as a whistle. But tiny, like a bird, with tiny lungs, and a tiny little heart. Then three more days and nights, Joe and I sat looking at him in his little box, all hooked up with tubes. We didn't go to sleep. I held him once. They knew it was over so they gave him to us to hold. He put his little mouth to me, and then he died. The size of the coffin was so small, it made me laugh.

This heart-rending account of her lost child trumps every other emotional moment in the film, gaining its power in part through its links to other things being cut open in the kitchen, as well as to such details as Macbeth's remembrance of eating sparrows as a young boy: 'Ever since I've loved the crunch of tiny little bird bones in my mouth.'

Reilly's 1990 film *Men of Respect* literalizes the issue even further, making an abortion part of the sacrifice that Ruthie/Lady Macbeth has made for the benefit of Battaglia/Macbeth's career. In her effort to convince him to kill D'Amico/Duncan, she says: 'I know what it is to have a life inside me, and squashing it out because it's not the right time, it's too difficult. I know what it is to kill for you, Michael, so don't tell me I don't understand.' And in Bhardwaj's 2003 film *Maqbool*, Lady Macbeth/Nimmi is pregnant, though Maqbool is uncertain of his paternity ('When was the last time you slept with

Jahangir?' he asks Nimmi; 'It's yours, Miyan. I know it's yours. I'll have an abortion if you want'). Nimmi cannot sleep because she relives the murder, but later blames the foetus ('He won't sleep. Keeps wailing all the time [...] I can hear it wail all the time'). After the assault on Maqbool's house, she gives birth and her own life is miraculously saved, but she comes home from the hospital prematurely, and eventually dies. Maqbool returns to the hospital, where he sees the child held by Guddu, and shortly after, Maqbool is shot and dies. By abortion or miscarriage, then, these versions produce the child that Macbeth no longer has. Wright's 2006 film depicted a tragically unmaternal Lady Macbeth, so traumatized by her reproductive failures (and her husband's murderous nature) that she has become a cocaine addict; she gazes at an empty children's swing just as she begins her 'Unsex me here' speech.

Kurzel's 2015 film *begins* with Macbeth and Lady Macbeth setting their dead child on a funeral pyre; the fire that follows will be echoed in the film's final scene of an apocalyptic-scale fire. Throughout the film, the tropes of children and fire recur – Macbeth is haunted by one boy who dies, and several of the witches are children. Before Lady Macbeth – who pressured her husband into murdering Duncan while in the act of sex – descends into madness, Kurzel makes it clear that her murderous ambition derives from her grief; she is embittered and anguished by her maternal emptiness. At one point (**Figure 9**), Macbeth touches his dagger to her womb, visually suggesting that his violence and her maternity are connected.

This focus on Lady Macbeth's maternity or lack of it has of course been prominent in critical studies since Bradley, memorably parodied in L. C. Knights's famous essay, 'How Many Children Had Lady Macbeth?'[14] and many scholars have since responded to the various issues raised by the question itself. Carol Chillington Rutter has recently shown how some recent versions (Adrian Noble's 1986 RSC production and Woolcock's *Macbeth on the Estate*) have made it

the Shakespeare play our theatre has been using for the past twenty years to think through a cultural crisis in 'childness', to make us search our deep anxieties about relatedness and separation, about authority and autonomy, about locating the child in contemporary culture, about valuing the child's life – or not. (2004: 40)

FIGURE 9 *Macbeth and Lady Macbeth.* Macbeth *directed by Justin Kurzel © The Weinstein Company 2015. All rights reserved. Screen grab.*

But the focus on Lady Macbeth's maternity, I would argue, also emphatically reinscribes her in patriarchal discourse, since the activities of her womb constitute her primary identity, and that womb is dysfunctional, capable only of miscarriages and deformity when not simply barren. This move, too, devalues or deflates the agency that Shakespeare grants her in the play: it is a horrific power, and it crumbles into nothingness, but it belongs to *her*. The recently recovered 1958 screenplay for Laurence Olivier's proposed film of *Macbeth* was set to open with this shot:

> Macbeth is turned away but with his eyes slanted back towards Lady Macbeth. She slowly and deliberately leans across the space between them and places her hand upon his arm. He turns round. Holding his gaze steadily and in the tremulous hope that it will cure all ills, she tells him now that she believes she is going to have a child. (Barnes 2012: 268)[15]

Later, 'staring down at her husband' from the ramparts, she watches the burial of her miscarried child. This site also, fittingly, becomes the place of her suicide – from her point of view, as 'the camera ... hurtles down towards the ground' and a 'dark red flash' ends her life (275).

The move to establishing Lady Macbeth's pregnancy and/or her miscarriage(s), before or during the play, has now become standard theatrical and filmic practice. Sian Thomas's essay on playing Lady Macbeth in 2004 reveals that little has changed since Clarke's 'Cormac' died in infancy. Thomas writes that she was influenced (as many have been) by accounts of Sarah Siddons's legendary performance. Thomas felt Lady Macbeth 'saw the murder of Duncan as her one clear chance to escape from being the timid, domestic creature she was afraid she might be' and so played her as 'vulnerable' (Thomas 2006: 97). She and Greg Hicks, the Macbeth, created a coherent if now conventional back-story: 'We decided that we had been married at least ten years, and – in response to the famous "How many children had Lady Macbeth?" question ... – that there had been a child, who had died' (99). Trying not to over-specify the invented narrative, still, 'we did not think they really believed there were any further children to come, for whatever reason – she is utterly thwarted, she depends on him to express herself. She loves him, and is proud of him, in almost a motherly way' (100). Of his role as Macbeth in 2005, Simon Russell Beale writes that he and Emma Fielding (Lady Macbeth),

> like so many people who have played the Macbeths before us, felt the need to invent a precise back-story. I suppose ours was the simplest of all the options. A child was born to the Macbeths who lived only long enough to have been suckled by Lady Macbeth and whose death was as traumatic as any such death would be for a married couple. There were no subsequent children and perhaps even their sex-life has withered under the presence of an incurable grief. Consequently, attacks on Macbeth's virility always hit home. (Beale 2006: 114)

The psychoanalytic assumptions in both Thomas's and Beale's meditations may be persuasive for most contemporary readers and audiences, and certainly for actors and actresses trained in certain styles of performance, but they are still assumptions.

The result of these womb failures, as Adeline Chevrier-Bosseau (2013) points out, is that Lady Macbeth 'becomes some kind of socially acceptable hysteric – not a degenerate woman, perverted by her unnatural lust for power, but a natural descendant of Eve, born to suffer, a "normal" member of the weaker sex, an enduring mother, suffering because of the cruelty of men and heroically taking revenge in the name of her lost children'. Mary McCarthy (1962: 234) offered a similar view: 'the very prospect of murder quickens an hysterical excitement in her, like the discovery of some object in a shop ... the unimpeded exercise of her will is the voluptuous end she seeks'. McCarthy's use of the term 'hysterical' is, in unfortunate ways, typical of the reduction of Lady Macbeth to a set of symptoms. The 1912 analysis of Isador H. Coriat, in *The Hysteria of Lady Macbeth* (28-9), took the now-typical approach: 'Lady Macbeth is a typical case of hysteria; her ambition is merely a sublimation of a repressed sexual impulse, the desire for a child based upon the memory of a child long since dead'. A confirmed disciple of Freud, Coriat focuses especially on Lady Macbeth's 'somnambulism' as indicative of hysterical symptomology, concluding that her hysteria is 'a substitution for her childlessness or rather for the children which she has lost and it may be termed a sublimated sexual complex' (57). The result is that Lady Macbeth does not have free will: 'Determinism is triumphant, because Lady Macbeth cannot emancipate herself from the suppressed complexes which inevitably led to her mental disorder. She thinks she chooses her actions whereas in reality they are chosen for her by the unconscious complexes' (89).[16]

At about the same time as Coriat's psychoanalytic essay, Margaret Lucy, in a talk *Read at a Meeting of Members of a Ladies Literary Circle at Stratford-upon-Avon* in 1911, defended the Lady from such forms of weakness:

> Here then is a woman of great executive ability, abnormal, almost of inhuman strength of will, spurred on by boundless impersonal ambition. Add to this a narrow intensity of vision, which saw nothing except what was necessary to the realising of her desires, and then say whether such a woman could yield to hysteria at this the turning point of her career and his. I think not. (7)

Lucy had also excavated the historical Lady Macbeth's lineage – 'she had a better right to the throne than either Duncan or her husband' (4), but concluded that Lady Macbeth had no motives of her own. Rather, 'she sinned for the sake of the man she loved, and that according to her lights she made him a perfect wife' (4). Lucy never mentions or speculates, however, on whether she had had a child, or a miscarriage.[17]

In Shakespeare's theatre, the role of Lady Macbeth was, as is well known, performed not by a woman but by a male (probably a boy) actor.[18] Some productions, however, have featured female actresses who were themselves pregnant at the time. The Polish production in the 2012 'Globe to Globe' festival featured a heavily pregnant Lady Macbeth. In a striking historical irony, Mrs. Siddons was quite visibly pregnant while acting the part in 1794, but criticized only in personal terms, with no connection to the character *per se*: Mrs. Piozzi wrote that 'She is big with Child, & I fear will for that reason scarce be well received: for people have a notion She is covetous, and this unnecessary Exertion to gain Money will confirm it' (McDonald 2005: 15). By contrast, Anna Jameson's vivid and passionate defence of Lady Macbeth as a woman – 'the woman herself remains a woman to the last – still linked with her sex and with humanity' (Jameson 1901: 361) – proceeded without ever mentioning or imagining the character as (ever) pregnant.

Such moves routinely iron out the wrinkles of eccentricity and the irregularities of the Folio. Many of the efforts described here not only inadvertently deny agency to Lady Macbeth and imagine her in feminine stereotypes, but also more generally attempt to normalize and domesticate the play's wildness, its strangeness, its ellipses, refusals, and erasures. But what's done cannot be undone, as Lady Macbeth herself comes to realize (5.1.57-8).

6

Novelizing *Macbeth*

The process of turning any play into a novel is fraught with technical difficulties but also advantages. Several novelizations of *Macbeth* make use of prose's ability to explore inner consciousness through free indirect discourse, omniscient narrators or first-person voices, and to provide often elaborate descriptions of characters' physical features, battle scenes, and more. We have seen in earlier chapters some of the issues involving point of view and structure as well as genre, from Hartley and Hewson's historical approach to Nesbø's crime novel. Adapters must necessarily decide what sub-genre within the category of 'novel' to appropriate as a structure or reference point. As the cases of Hartley/Hewson and Nesbø illustrate, the choice leads to the difference between faux-gothicism and the 'mean streets' of Dunsinane.

Hartley and Hewson 'wanted to make real use of the novelist's ability to represent more than dialogue, and to do so in a language readers would find more approachable than Shakespeare's, but we also did not want to simply render a pale imitation of the play …. we wanted to make the story – not the play, but the story – our own' (2012: 318), and their effort largely succeeded. Their intention to make the 'story' but 'not the play' their own, however, raises many questions. Unlike Ionesco or some other adapters, they did not seek to 'talk back' to Shakespeare, or offer a strong critique of the Folio; rather, they require a reader's basic knowledge of the play as a skeletal frame on which they construct many new moments, descriptions, and characters. Their target audience seems to be a well-informed reader, who will appreciate the differences they have created. And their marketing strategy includes a full audiobook version on Amazon/Audible, narrated by no less than Alan Cumming (see **Epilogue**). The Amazon blurb promises 'This is *Macbeth* as you have not heard it before: fresh, edgy, and vital. It is a story of valor in battle, whispering in shadows, witchcraft in the hollows of an ancient landscape, and the desperate struggle of flawed people to do what they think is right.'

Similarly, in Ewan Fernie and Simon Palfrey's 2016 *Macbeth, Macbeth*, the authors argue that 'In the same way that [Shakespeare's] scenes invite us to infer and imagine *more*, so too' do his 'dense metaphors … we wanted to enter these words, bringing them to new life, just as we entered other gaps in the play' (2016: 280). The novelty in their approach lies in their choice of a narrative model: 'It occurred to us that *Macbeth* shares the same basic structure as *The Brothers Karamazov*, pivoting on a primal act of parricide.' They proposed that 'the four sons of Karamazov – the errant sensualist, the atheist intellectual, the apprentice saint, and the bastard in the shadows – uncannily evoked different aspects of Shakespeare's anti-hero. What if we had a story in which each one of these sons, in their own awful way, proceeded to repeat the tragedy of Macbeth?' (viii). The result is a 'multi-pronged repetition' – as a sequel, after Macbeth's death – but with one key difference from the Folio that the temptation is a woman, not a crown: Dostoevsky's Grushenka 'became our heroine, Gruoch' (viii), called 'Gru'. This dark novel is formally experimental, mixing modes of narration, typeface font, and dotted with illustrations that can fairly be described as Dostoyeskian in tone. Lisa Klein's 2009 *Lady Macbeth's Daughter*, on the other hand, is written for a young adult reading audience: on her website, Klein describes herself as 'Author of Historical Novels for Teens of All Ages'. Each of her books includes a downloadable pdf 'Discussion Guide' with plot and thematic questions, and project topics for teachers to consider assigning. Hartley, Klein, Fernie, and Palfrey all hold Ph.D.'s in English Literature and/or professorships at major universities. These authors clearly know their subject matter and know how they wanted to diverge from it.

While many contemporary novelizations simply appropriate the title, location, or characters of the play to create a quite different story (as in Freeling's crime novel, **Chapter Five**), or construct a new narrative based on the supposed 'curse', others track the play's plot rather closely. Then there is R. A. Wilson's 2012 version, *The Tragedy of Macbeth: A Novel* which, on its copyright page, documents that it is 'Based on a work at http://nfs.sparknotes.com/macbeth' (Wilson 2012: Loc. 17).[1] As the citation suggests, this work is a kind of third-person prosification of the plot, as it is summarized in the *No Fear* 'translation' on the sparknotes website. The novelization follows scene by scene as 'chapters' in the novel, with the usual euphemisms and literalizations of the text common in such translations: thus Lady Macbeth's 'unsex me here' becomes 'Come to me spirits that tend to murderous thoughts and make me less of a woman and more of a man' (Loc. 423-7) or Duncan's 'silver skin' as 'milky skin' (Loc. 809), the Porter's 'equivocator' as 'con man' (Loc. 702), and so on. Even in a work clearly designed as a scene-by-scene trot for students, however, Wilson could not resist adding scenes not present in the Folio that echo the recurring moves of other adapters. Thus, Wilson shows, in detail, the graphic violence of Duncan's murder: Macbeth enters his room, studies the King and pauses, but then a bead of sweat falls from Macbeth onto Duncan's nose, at which point the king's 'eyes snap open. His pupils contract quickly, and fright shows etc.' (Loc. 611), and Macbeth kills him.[2] Wilson also provides another graphic scene of Lady Macbeth's suicide: 'She pulls a dagger out that was hidden in her cleavage' (Loc. 1684) and stabs herself, which suggests quite a cleavage and/or a pretty small dagger. While many adaptations provide such scenes – Welles's film shows Lady Macbeth throwing herself off a high cliff – Wilson also shows Malcolm in an opening battle scene, fighting bravely but then wounded (1.2) and Donaldbain is described as a weak fop (wearing 'extravagant pieces of armor that are more for looks than actual use with gold leafing and lettering', Loc. 195). Wilson's novelization asks no questions of the Authorized Version, while providing some of the traditional 'missing' scenes.

Charles Lear's 2012 *Post-Apocalyptic Macbeth and the Girls*, by contrast, is a first-person narration by 'Charles', a middle-ageing former punk musician/theatre guy in New York, set in the summer of 2005, when Hurricane Katrina strikes. He and his friends decide to put on a play, 'Shakespeare in the Industrial Park presents Macbeth on the Roof' (Lear 2012: Loc. 1147), to be performed on a Manhattan rooftop. The plot follows Charles as he plans and directs the play, and deals with his friends; at the same time, the rehearsal of the play proceeds in parallel. Although the production is set far in the future, Charles presents the Authorized Version: Malcolm is 'the rightful king' (loc. 1642), the Doctor in

4.3 is deleted, and Lady Macbeth's familiar backstory is invoked ('It had never occurred to me that Lady Macbeth might have been married before and had possibly lost both husband and child ... this would add more depth to their relationship' (Loc. 1588). What stands out in Lear's work at the present moment, however, is the production's scenario as set out in the 'Prologue' in the program. After the United States has been defeated in an energy war with the European Union, Lear produces a quite prescient look at the future – as I quote this, the planet is suffering from the worst days of the coronavirus pandemic: 'All was well until a mutation of the Chinese Monkey Virus became an airborne threat to humans. In 2063, an epidemic wiped out three quarters of the world population .... The time is now 2067, a time of great unrest and war. ... it was meant to be taken in the spirit of the cheesy post-apocalyptic movies we were using as our inspiration' (Loc. 3860-3871).

Ajay Close's 2017 *The Daughter of Lady Macbeth* sounds as if it might belong in a bookstore's young adult section right next to Lisa Klein's identically titled work. Close's novel, however, is an ambitious and certainly adult novel whose chapters toggle back and forth between the narrative present and the early 1970s. The daughter is Freya Cavalle, daughter of Lilias, an actress who had played Lady Macbeth, and had gone into labour with her 'in act four ... during a Saturday matinee at the King's Theatre in Edinburgh .... There was talk of naming me Hecate', but 'instead I got Freya, the Norse goddess of love' (Close 2017: 54). But that story, Freya discovers much later, was fictional. Soon after learning that truth, she also learns that her mother has taken her own life through an 'overdose' (257) rather than face her cancer. The connections to *Macbeth*, slight but powerful, are issues of maternity ('What if you turned out like your mother?' runs a blurb on the cover), inheritance, and identity.

Few authors have more self-consciously proceeded to turn the play into a novel than John Passfield, in his 2019 *Lord and Lady Macbeth: Full of Scorpions Is My Mind*. Passfield's website offers free downloads of two accompanying texts, *The Making of Full of Scorpions Is My Mind* (172 pages) and *Planning Full of Scorpions Is My Mind: A Notebook of the Development of a Novel* (98 pages). Passfield's inspiration for the project seems to have been 'Watching *Macbeth* on video (Ian McKellen & Judi Dench). Both Macbeth & Lady Macbeth are talking about themselves when they talk of each other' (2019b: 1), the first entry in his often stream-of-consciousness Notebook of observations.

The novel itself alternates chapters between Macbeth and Lady Macbeth, in the first-person, following the events of the play's plot closely, but each monologue is also interspersed with 'cycles': e.g. 'The Life-experience Minor Cycle ... in my novels has become the minor cycle of imagery in which the main character reviews his entire life .... [it] would be either an actual exchange or an imaginary exchange of intimate conversation between the two Macbeths' (2019a: 13). Passfield takes on some of the perennial questions about the play – e.g. whether the Macbeths had a child, and here Passfield departs from the frequent resort to the 'real' history behind the play:

> I would say that a recourse to Shakespeare's sources strikes me as a diminishment of the imagery ... the Macbeths both think:
> – of having a child in the present, and
> – of not-having a child in the present,
> so, whatever the play-sources say as to earlier marriages and earlier children of those marriages, ... the novel presents a very rich interplay between [these contradictions] ... a completely literal explanation is not, I believe, possible. The interplay between the two image-patterns is the point. (2019a: 35)

Passfield is certainly not above inventing details – his weak Duncan is given a wife who is 'feeble and helpless' (2019: 45), and Macbeth is given an enormous self-regard that, when denied the kingship in favour of Duncan, led him to bitter self-deluding justification: 'I knew, from the day I was born, that I would be king. Old King Malcolme was reaching his terminus. Duncan's colours were trailing in the race' (19). The decision to seek the kingship doesn't derive from the witches' prophecies, for there are many comments throughout like this by Lady Macbeth: 'We have talked about the kingship from the day we met' (27). Passfield also, like Davenant, has Lady Macbeth meet Lady Macduff, so that her murder is a real turning-point: 'The closest I came to what I take to be friendship was with Lady Macduff. I had invited her and her brood for a visit to this castle, the very day that I heard of your [Macbeth's] assault on their hearth' (91). The novel ends with Macbeth – now the first-person point of view reveals its real limitation – doing battle with

Macduff: 'I grunt and give my sword a mighty heave' (135). The first-person narrator who is dead may seem a rhetorical bridge too far for some readers.

Historical narratives

We have touched on several novels expressly written for either young adult readers, usually females, or with a female audience in mind. Hately describes some crime novels written for young adult readers, such as one which features a first-person narrator young woman who works on her high school's newspaper (2018: 137). As with the many adaptations that produce a counter-history for Ophelia, Lady Macbeth and/or her 'daughter' or other relations often provide a convenient springboard to explore some contemporary feminist issues. Peg Herring's 2016 *Double Toil and Trouble: A Story of Macbeth's Nieces* begins a decade after Macbeth's death, and follows the adventures of the two nieces, Jenna and Jessie, one of whom travels to France and meets William of Normandy 'just before he leaves to conquer England', and both girls 'struggle to put her emotions aside, but their hearts don't know how' (Herring 2016) in a typical young adult plot of self-discovery.

Susan Fraser King's *Lady Macbeth* (2008), however, dives deep into the historical past that Passfield had rejected and Herring had invented. King's novel includes, before the narrative proper begins, the historical origin of Gruoch's name from the Cartularium of the Priory of Saint Andrews, a map of eleventh-century 'Celtic Scotland', and a full-page genealogy of both Macbeths, dating back to the fifth century, and ending with James I, and a 'Historical Note' observing that the novel is 'based not on Shakespeare's brilliant drama ... but rather on the most accurate historical evidence available to date regarding the lives of these eleventh-century Scottish monarchs .... [that history has] been interpreted through the filters of imagination and fiction'. At the end of the novel, King provides a seven-page 'Author's Note' in which she describes what is generally agreed upon in terms of the historical facts regarding the couple, and then a three-page 'Glossary' of names and Celtic terms used in the novel. Unlike Passfield's novel, this first-person narration ends with Lady Macbeth quite alive.

In her concern for historical accuracy, King follows the path of Dorothy Dunnett, whose 700+ page novel, *King Hereafter* (1982),[3] is also framed by maps and genealogies. Dunnett's omniscient narrator novel has relatively little to do with the story as Shakespeare told it. Here, instead, 'Macbeth' is only the rarely used baptismal name of Thorfinn, Earl of Orkney, grandson of King Malcolm of Alba. Groa, the young widow of the slain Gillcomghain, has little in common with Shakespeare's Lady Macbeth or indeed with many of the contemporary versions of Gruach seen in **Chapter Five**. The last two-thirds of the novel treat Thorfinn's career as a basically good king (recalling but transforming Holinshed's remarks about the first ten years of Macbeth's rule), in which he pursues a long and violent feud with his half-nephew Rognvald, builds up Alba's alliances and naval power, then faces increasing troubles as the Norman invasion of 1066 approaches. The novel provides *many* battle scenes, betrayals, blood feuds, and ultimately, Thorfinn's surrender via suicidal duel. Shakespeare's play is visible mainly through section headings ('Now Witchcraft Celebrates', 'Pure as Snow', as well as the title) and occasional echoes. The novel's plot necessarily coincides with the play's plot at some points (Thorfinn becomes king after the very different death of Duncan) and at other times follows the medieval Scottish chronicles (the historical Macbeth's journey to Rome). Dunnett's novel explores the turn to Christianity at the time, and the dense and confusing politics of alliances and betrayals among the Norse, Scots, and Danes, but she chiefly focuses on the relationship between Thorfinn and Groa. Dunnett's novel cannot quite be termed an adaptation of *Macbeth*, but, like King's and many other such works, is unthinkable without Shakespeare's play as inspiration and background.

Fifty shades of Dunsinane

Recent novelizations of the play have produced less and more heated love lives among the major or invented characters. One can discern an erotic scale that, depending on the genre, leads towards increasing frankness. One young adult novel, Klein's 2009 *Lady Macbeth's Daughter*, follows the first-person narrator Albia as she grows into young womanhood, when Fleance (though raised as her 'brother') becomes her object of desire. The relationship between Fleance and Albia develops along the usual contours of young love awakening, as seen from a teenage girl's perspective: the place where he touched her arm remains in her memory, she dreams of him more than once ('His hands on mine, teaching me to hold a sword. His thick brown hair blowing across his face, my hands reaching up to push it back, touching his cheek', 187; 'I see and even feel his arms touching mine … my fate is bound to Fleance's', 196). Despite the overheated prose ('Then I feel his hands at my waist, untying my girdle. I trust his fingers and do not try to stop them', 229), Albia retains her innocence, though she and Fleance share kisses and pronounce their mutual love (228-9).

Klein's audience receives about as much openness as that genre allows. Bonnie Copeland's 1979 *Lady of Moray*, though, turns up the heat to simmering. Copeland's Gruoch weaponizes her sensual allure, even as a young girl, as an instrument of her will. Invoking familiar tropes of the romance novel, aimed at a more mature audience than Klein's, Copeland has Gruoch watch Gillecomgain undress on their wedding night: 'Her blood began to tingle and she felt a surge of desire that hardened her breasts and tightened her loins', but he, alas, is an untutored lover who suddenly 'crushed her down upon the floor and took her in violence, his lust a wild, unthinking eagerness' (1979: 90). Having allowed her rough husband this moment, though, she begins to tutor him through suggestive rhetorical enticement: 'One should play love's tune as on a fine rich instrument, delicately, gently. The body must not be goaded and driven with violence and pain. The love tool is something to be pleasured with sweetness, with tenderness. And at the end will come an ecstasy as fierce as a summer storm' (91). Using the instruments and tools at her disposal, Copeland's Gruoch makes her way through many storms, using her sexuality with full agency.

While the formulae of young adult novels and romance novels allow for some suggestive scenes, few novels have combined erotic *frisson* and female empowerment to the extent that Maggie Power does in her 2008 *Lady Macbeth's Tale*. Power's approach is confusing, however, because while in the latter part of the novel the central character is indeed 'Gruoch', wife of Moray then Macbeth, in the first two-thirds of the novel Powers has imagined that she was originally Gwaina, daughter of the King of Cornwall, who describes – on the first page – how she was raped by Tregennen (who is having an affair with the King's younger and traitorous wife), who eventually, through many trials, becomes Gwaina's husband and king. The novel is in effect a 350+ page prequel to the play.

There is little doubt that Power's Gruoch will do just about anything to survive; beginning with the rape – and yes, she falls in love with her rapist and desires him – and then imprisonment, escape, recapture, voyages from Cornwall to Ireland to England to Scotland, humiliations: she survives everything, maintains her own identity (insisting on her royal blood – her father Boede is a Scotsman, somehow transplanted to and ruling Cornwall), and pursues her own destiny. In this, she is a modern woman. While the young adult novels depict the sexual awakening of the teenage Gruoch or her daughter or, as in Bottomley's play, the mature Lady Macbeth herself, the scenes in these other works remain relatively discreet: heart-throbbing, suggestive, but still somewhat modest: 'At once we lean together, and our arms find their natural fit around each other's bodies. Our lips meet like an arrow and its target, holding fast until I almost faint for lack of breath' (Klein 2009: 228). The heroine, though blushing in heat, reasserts herself and pulls back.[4] Such scenes reflect cultural tropes of thwarted/fulfilled young love dating from Romeo and Juliet to – the more relevant comparison in Klein's case – the *Twilight* films. But Powers goes far beyond these models, providing many soft-core porn scenes of rape, thrusting, probing, tonguing, etc., sometimes with relative nuance, but often as blunt as a hammer: 'before he [Macbeth] can soberly consider the matter, she's thrown back the sheets, straddled his naked body and began fucking him senseless' (Powers 2008: 265). For every vaguely feminist rumination – 'And I reduced to the brood mare of state … no longer Gwaina … yet not a queen in my own right … little more than a womb … providing entry and passage … for men' (163-4) – Power provides a dozen frank sexual scenes, including one that Gwaina imagines (in parallel with an orator's recounting of the story of Othello) that would *really* have troubled Brabantio ('*Even now, very now, that old black ram's being sucked off by our own lost white ewe!*', 213). Power's novel ends as Gruoch and Macbeth have returned from the journey to Rome (though, historically, it occurred after Macbeth had become king), and as the weak and foolish Duncan is beset by military threats from Norway and the Northmen generally. The plotting couple anticipates Macbeth's entrance into battle and victory, and a steady undermining of Duncan's rule.

The eroticism of Power's novel had been anticipated by earlier adapters such as Bottomley, but is not really a contemporary invention, for Shakespeare's play fully (if not grossly) represents the alliance between power and sexuality, providing a great deal of suggestive imagery surrounding the tragic couple's sexual friction, and feminizing Duncan's body so that his murder was conflated with a rape, as we saw in **Chapter Two**. Rebecca Bushnell documented early modern culture's 'association between femininity and tyranny ... in two related images: the lustful and shrewish woman as the mirror image of tyrannical rule, and the "effeminated" prince subjected to his lust while he rules others tyrannically'. In most of these cases, the 'only vulnerability' of 'Renaissance stage tyrants' is 'their lust for women or their uxoriousness'. To the extent that the family was seen as analogous to the stage, Bushnell concludes, 'the shrew's "mannish" authority and her husband's submission to her served as a model of tyranny, the opposite of legitimate sovereignty. The image of "the woman on top" is not just a figure of a rebellion in the lower orders of society: it symbolizes a problem at the heart of sovereignty, located in reason's imperfect mastery of desire' (Bushnell 1990: 68–9). Many adapters have focused on Macbeth's 'uxoriousness', in the first part of the play especially, and the supposed 'unnaturalness' of Lady Macbeth; by the end, when they have chiastically switched positions, both have collapsed in different ways. In plays such as Beaumont and Fletcher's *The Maid's Tragedy* or Middleton's *The Revenger's Tragedy* and *The Lady's Tragedy*, the authors do not hold back, serving up copious amounts of degenerate sexuality – incest, rape, necrophilia, scopophilia – linked to the tyranny of the sovereigns in each play. The very first novelization of *Macbeth*, as we will now see, followed in this tradition while rewriting the play in quite radical ways.

The Secret History

Shakespeare's *Macbeth* has become the sole origin of Macbeth-discourse, the only version of the story known to most modern readers and audiences; but for centuries before Shakespeare's play, and for a century and a half after his play, another version of Macbeth – its afterlife significant in political as well as literary terms – continued in parallel to and at times intersecting with the Shakespearean version. This other version of the Macbeth narrative derives primarily though not entirely from the Scottish historian George Buchanan's account of Macbeth in his 1582 *Rerum Scoticarum historia*. Buchanan's history was condemned by the Scottish Parliament in 1584 and denounced as 'infamous invective' by James in *Basilikon Doron* (McIlwain 1918: 40) for justifying the deposition of James's mother, Mary Queen of Scots. Buchanan's history, along with his *De jure regni apud Scotos* ('The Powers of the Crown in Scotland', 1579), provided historical evidence for European writers seeking to advance a theory of royal succession based on election rather than inheritance, and to counter monarchical claims of absolute powers and prerogatives.[5] Buchanan was used to justify the deposition of Charles I in 1649 by Milton and others. It might seem, after the Restoration, that the Royalist position was victorious, and that the indefeasible right of inheritance would once again become the settled theory of succession for the British monarchy, but the constitutional crises of 1688–9 and at the end of Queen Anne's reign brought the same issues to the boil again with Buchanan's arguments and examples invoked anew.

As Buchanan summarized in his *History*, the real problems in the Scottish monarchy began with King Kenneth III and his son Malcolm II, who 'did strive, to settle the Succession to the Crown in their Families, That the Eldest Son might succeed the Father' (1690: 7.205) – that is, in altering the traditional system of succession through alternation between parallel lines of descent (and sometimes to someone not related at all) to one of inherited lineal descent. These issues resonated throughout the seventeenth century, particularly in times of constitutional crisis, and the narrative of Macbeth would be continually appropriated and re-told by both royalists and their opponents, for the Macbeth narrative foregrounds the same problems of sovereign authority that were then at stake.

As popular as Shakespeare's *Macbeth* was, Buchanan's account also continued to be both available and widely quoted; at times, some writers merged aspects of both narratives, but the differences between the two accounts are crucial. In Buchanan's version, the traitor Macdonwald commits suicide, and Macbeth then cuts off his head 'and hung up the rest of his Body, for all to behold, in a conspicuous place' (7.208). Sweno and the Norwegians are overcome not in open battle, but through the cunning administration of drugged wine ('made of Barly-Malt, mixed with the juice of a Poysonous Herb, whereof abundance grows in *Scotland*, called, *Somniferous Night-shade*', 7.209), sent by the Scots as part of a peace offering. There are no witches or supernatural in Buchanan (see the **Introduction**), as the prophecies appear to Macbeth in a dream. Buchanan mentions Lady Macbeth only briefly, as spurring Macbeth on by 'daily Importunities' (7.210). Once king, Macbeth 'Enacted many good and useful' laws, and governed well for ten years. But eventually 'he converted his Government, got by Treachery, into a Cruel Tyranny' (7.211). After the murder of Banquo, Macbeth 'broke forth into open Tyranny' (7.212) – hence justifying his overthrow, in Buchanan's thinking – and was overthrown by King Edward's invading army. Buchanan's version, by contrast with Shakespeare's, presents a simpler, more admonitory narrative, stripped of the supernatural and other bizarre trappings that the Boece–Holinshed account had produced.

Throughout the seventeenth century, Buchanan's account of Macbeth's reign served both sides of the debates on Stuart legitimacy and sovereignty. As the reign of Queen Anne neared its end, uneasy, ironic parallels between her reign and the end of Queen Elizabeth's became evident, and the same constitutional issues 'were referred to and played out again in the early eighteenth century' (Nenner 1995: 236). The origins of the house of Stuart, and therefore the reign of Macbeth, were rhetorical touchstones. With an ageing queen on the throne and the end of a royal dynasty near, the story of Macbeth – not necessarily Shakespeare's version – still presented relevant issues of succession and sovereign power.

In 1708, as these succession questions were becoming ever more urgent, the London printer James Woodward published an anonymous work, *The Secret History of Mack-Beth, King of Scotland. Taken from a Very Ancient Original Manuscript.*[6] While there were other prose accounts of Macbeth's story in various histories and chronicles – e.g. Peter Heylyn's often-reprinted work[7] – the *Secret History* was the first adaptation of the play as a novel. The work evidently proved popular, because Woodward printed it again in the same year as part of a book entitled *Hypolitus Earl of*

Douglas. Containing Some Memoirs of the Court of Scotland; with the Secret History of Mack-Beth King of Scotland.[8] The *Hypolitus* collection was reset and reprinted again in 1741 with a text virtually identical to that of the 1708 edition. The *Secret History* was then anonymously reprinted again in 1768, in *A Key to the Drama ... Containing the Life, Character, and Secret History of Macbeth.* Here the author/editor made substantial textual changes, to be discussed below, primarily to modernize the text and 'to purge ... [it] of a number of indelicacies' (1768: iii). The *Secret History* made further appearances in 1828 as *The Secret History of Macbeth, King of Scotland* and again in 1841 in *Memoirs of the Court of Scotland.*

The long textual history of the *Secret History*, stretching nearly a century and a half, suggests the continuing fascination of Macbeth's story, and the continuing relevance of Buchanan's version, which the *Secret History* primarily follows. Its evident popularity coincides with, in Ian Watt's well-known phrase, the rise of the novel as a literary form, and the creation of new reading audiences. Such narratives mediated and transformed the tragic drama of *Macbeth* into a more approachable genre, in which dramatic characters could be placed into the current conventions of 'realism', and even characters like Hamlet and Macbeth, though given extensive revelatory soliloquies in their plays, could be put on the couch for deeper analysis. The novel's demand for a form of 'realism', moreover, required even more backstories, filled gaps, explanations, and, as we see here, the exposure of 'secret histories'.[9]

The *Secret History* provides an exemplary account of the dangers, on the one hand, of a weak king in a political culture of unbridled factionalism, and on the other, of an unchecked, tyrannical, monarchy. These situations reflect earlier Scottish narratives, Jacobean politics, and early eighteenth-century English history. At the end of the 1708 version, the Thane of Argyll makes a long speech to Malcolm upon his coronation, distilling his political wisdom.[10] The terms of Argyll's speech suggest how far the story's theory of sovereign power is from Shakespeare's play: 'The Prince therefore of any People shou'd reflect, that he is chose[n], and exalted to that high Post, not to indulge his Appetite, give a Loose to his Passions, and make ev'ry thing subservient to his Will, as if he were the Lord, not Ruler, of his People, and they his Slaves, not Subjects ... a Prince has less Right to indulge, or give way to his Passions, than his Subjects' (1708: f8v); the speech continues in this vein at length. The idea that the king is 'chose[n]' by the people, and that they have the right to a 'Remedy' – i.e. deposition – if the king becomes tyrannical, rests on a contractual theory of kingship derived from Buchanan (among others) that is far more openly articulated here than anywhere in Shakespeare's play.

The 1768 version of Argyll's speech makes the point about limited kingship even more explicitly: 'The affiance between a king and his subjects ought to be held as the most sacred compact ... Like a contract between husband and wife ... an inviolable contract between you and your people; then, my Liege, they will find it their supreme happiness to love and obey their Sovereign, as you, I hope, will find it yours, to cherish, support, and improve the rights of the Public' (1768: u6r, x1r). The contractural language here is now even applicable to the sacrament of marriage.

The *Secret History* relates the story of two powerful factions, one led by the Thane of Caithness and one by Ross, Thane of Gawry. Ross's followers support Mack-Beth, while Caithness's followers stir the court against him. Mack-Beth here is clearly the worthiest, most powerful and respected thane at the court, presided over by an ineffectual Duncan, who was 'A Prince of too sweet, and easie a disposition to be at the Head of a Government so difficult to manage' (1708: a7r). The 1768 version is even more direct on the subject of the weak king: '*Duncan* was of too soft and easy a disposition to be at the head of a government divided into a diversity of factions, every one of which making advantage of their monarch's inactivity, laboured to aggrandize their several families, without any sort of regard to the public-weal' and goes on to assert that Mack-Beth 'was himself of the blood royal' (1768: b1v). Mack-Beth eventually leads a third faction, who call themselves the 'Patriots': 'they wanted a Man of Spirit, Bravery and Resolution to over-awe and quash all the Parties, that had got too great Head for the safety of *Scotland*' (1708: c5r); Duncan, in the meantime, names Malcolm Prince of Cumberland to head off the Patriots. Mack-Beth then kills Duncan, but not personally, as in Shakespeare; rather, as in Buchanan, 'he sent a party of Men, who joining *Bancho*'s, and meeting the King on the Road in *Innerness*, fell on him from their Ambush, and having left him and some of his Train dead, separated without any Pursuit, so odious was the King grown to the People' (1708: c6r). The *Secret History* also follows Buchanan (and Holinshed) rather than Shakespeare's play in the beheading of Macdonwald, with additional sadistic touches: Macdonwald 'fell on his own Sword, expiring the very moment, the Fortress surrender'd. *Mack-Beth* was not satisfy'd with the Execution he had done on himself, but order'd his Head to be struck off on a Scaffold by the Provost Marshal in the sight of his army. Nor was he content with this Punishment of the Leader, but, contrary to the true Policy of sparing the Multitude, he hung up all the Prisoners he took, which drew the hatred of all the People on the King, as done by his Order' (1708: c3r).

The main outlines of the remainder of Mack-Beth's story play out as we know it from Buchanan, though also with some elements – primarily the aggressiveness of Lady Mack-Beth – that may have come from Shakespeare's play. Mack-Beth tries to escape from Dunsinane by donning a disguise, but after he had defended himself for some time against his pursuers, '*Mac-duff* ... encounter'd him with equal Force, and soon brought him to the Ground, with many Wounds, and frequent Exprobrations for the Murder of his Wife and Children' (1708: f7v). Lady Mack-Beth, we are told with none of the ambiguity of Shakespeare's play, hanged herself (1708: f8r). 'Thus fell the Tyrant', the narrator sums up, 'who had rais'd himself by Virtues he had not, and fell by the Vices he cou'd not Master; after he had establish'd his doubtful Throne in Righteousness and Love, he forsook both, to destroy in Seven Years by his Folly, what he had built up in Ten by his Wisdom' (1708: f8r).

If the *Secret History* were no more than a transformation of Buchanan's *History* and Shakespeare's play into the terms of the eighteenth-century politics of faction, it would still be a remarkable testament to the centrality of the Macbeth narrative as an ideological instrument in political self-definition, from the beginning to the end of the Stuart dynasty, and significant as the first full novelization of the play. Like Buchanan, the *Secret History* banishes all traces of the supernatural. The 1768 revision is particularly emphatic on this point, making even a dream of the witches doubtful; rather, 'his ambitious wife ... quickly raised upon it [the dream] the diabolic structure, which from that moment she pressed him to execute with so much vehemence. It has been, I imagine, upon the foundation of that vision, that the ridiculous story was invented of his having been ... saluted by three witches, whom he visibly met in a forest in the middle of a day; and howsoever much the fiction of the witches may be better imagined, as better corresponding with the tyrannical conduct which followed it; yet ... this dream ... was related by [Mack-Beth] himself, long before the story of the witches was ever heard of; and I now consider it to have been nothing else than the effects of his perpetual thoughts, which incited him to form such a dream' (1768: i6r–k1r).

Lady Mack-Beth – a terrifying enough figure in Shakespeare – is even more monstrous and unnatural in the *Secret Life*, motivated solely by desperate ambition, and taking the lead in various schemes. More surprisingly – and we have now arrived at the most elaborate, even bizarre, revisionism in the entire Macbeth narrative – Lady Mack-Beth does not merely wish to 'unsex' herself, as Shakespeare's character does; rather, she is from the beginning blatantly a-sexual, yet willing to play the bawd for her husband: 'The Queen was a Woman, that took so little Delight in the Conjugal Embraces, that she had an utter Aversion to Man in that particular; and the better to engross her principal Delight, the governing of the Nation, she took care to amuse her Husband with the Chace of some Ladies of the Court, while she drew the Dispatch of all Affairs of State into her own Hands' (1708: c8v–d1r).[11] She thus exemplifies a pathological suppression of the 'natural' in the name of power, with more than a hint of being lesbian.

Lady Mack-Beth's demonization in the *Secret History* drains off, as it were, the actual demonic powers present in the other Macbeth narratives. In Lady Mack-Beth's asexuality we find instead an equivalent unnaturalness, antithetical and complementary to Mack-Beth's 'secret' story: his insatiable sexual appetite. Angus's description of Mack-Beth initiates the narrative's move to the erotic: 'his Manners were every way engaging ... This won him the Hearts of all the Men of the Court, whilst his Person and Address, made an easy way for him to the Hearts of the Ladies' (1708: a7r–v). At ages twenty-one and twenty-six respectively, Mack-Beth and Angus were more interested in sex than politics: 'Love chiefly employ'd our Industry; Intrigues with the Ladies took up more of our time, than Intrigues of State' (1708: a7v). The key event in the novel is Mack-Beth's seduction of Annabella, the beautiful young wife of the old Thane of Kyle. The account of his encounter with her, while Kyle is away, features a pornographic voyeurism that amply fulfils the title's promise of revealing what has been 'secret' until this moment. Admitted into her bed-chamber,

I found her in a perfect Undress ... a thin loose Robe, but ill conceal'd the Charming Proportion of her Limbs, and her snowy Bosom was all bare, and discover'd two such beautiful Breasts, as wou'd have tempted an Hermit to have press'd them with his consecrated Hands. They were White, Firm and Round, and heav'd with an agreeable Motion, that betray'd the soft Desires of her Heart; ... her curious Hair hung loosely down her Shoulders, in such Quantity as made her a Natural Veil for her Body.

Mack-Beth cannot resist this vision, needless to say: 'You may imagine this Sight was like Wild-fire in my Blood, and made me immediately throw my self down by her, throw aside the thin Garments that deny'd my Eyes the Beauties of her Naked Body ... I was now scarce got into Possession of this inestimable Treasure, when in the next Room we heard the *Thane's* Voice, which made us start from all our Pleasures into the utmost Confusion' (1708: b1v–b2r). A bedroom farce worthy of Fielding now follows, as Mack-Beth, hiding under her bed, must listen to her and her husband: 'the old *Thane* by the Authority of a Husband made her submit to his Pleasure while I lay in a double Rack' (1708: b2r–v). Still, after Annabella steps into a bath in order to cleanse herself of her husband's pollution, Mack-Beth becomes aroused again and joins her, with predictable consequences. The redactor of the 1768 version, who had promised 'to purge ... a number of indelicacies' (1768: iii), in fact found himself unable to resist adding new details to this next scene from his own fevered imagination: 'She threw aside her loose attire, and plunged into a well prepared bath. The floating beauties which now inflamed my agitated soul, enhanced, if possible, the extacy I had felt before!' (1768: e1v).

Once Mack-Beth becomes king, his satyriasis briefly abates. The people enjoy tranquility, and present no resistance to his rule: 'All Obstacles being remov'd ... he began to give way to that Amorous Inclination, which Hurry, and Ambition, and Business had along [sic] while lull'd asleep' (1708: c8v). While his attention is diverted, through Lady Mack-Beth's procuring genius, she takes on more and more power to herself. The *Secret History*, following Buchanan here, ends without a second set of prophecies, and Mack-Beth falls because of his tyranny, his failure to suppress faction, and because of 'the [personal] Vices he cou'd not Master' (1708: f8r).

This account of Mack-Beth reflects Malcolm's testing of Macduff in Shakespeare's version by claiming to be 'luxurious':

> But there's no bottom, none,
> In my voluptuousness. Your wives, your daughters,
> Your matrons and your maids could not fill up
> The cistern of my lust; and my desire
> All continent impediments would o'erbear
> That did oppose my will. (4.3.60–5)

The *Secret History* makes Mack-Beth not the least bit uxorious, at least in the sense of being under his wife's sexual powers. Rather, Mack-Beth's lechery and Lady Mack-Beth's wifely status are completely distinct. Neither seems jealous or concerned over the other's activities. Mack-Beth's pursuit of Annabella receives the greatest attention, but it is hardly his only such transgression: he even pursues Banquo's beautiful nineteen-year-old half-sister, Inetta. When Mack-Beth asks Banquo to intervene with Inetta on his behalf, Banquo is shocked, and the split between them, engineered by Lady Mack-Beth, leads to Banquo's death. As part of the plot, Mack-Beth has asked Banquo to sleep with Lady Mack-Beth in order to produce an heir; when Banquo crawls in bed with her, she stabs him to death, claiming he had attempted to rape her. Mack-Beth then has his way with Inetta, who has been drugged, but when she awakens she continues to resist him. Eventually she and a number of other virtuous characters escape from the court. Mack-Beth himself goes to Lady Macduff, rapes, then kills her and the children (1708: e1r–v).

Thus Mack-Beth as Caligula.[12] The conclusion to the *Secret History*, with speeches on the responsibilities of sovereign power, offers a tone of high-philosophical seriousness, but it hardly mitigates the salacious vision of Mack-Beth, now an early eighteenth-century rake, for a new reading audience. The *Secret History* reflects the continuing influence of Buchanan's history of Macbeth into the early eighteenth century, and, at least in this case, the relative unimportance of Shakespeare's version. This relation between the two Macbeths was soon, and permanently, reversed: novelists from the nineteenth century on took on Shakespeare's text, not Buchanan's history, as their starting point for adaptation. *The Secret History* has remained largely unknown, but its novelization of the Macbeth story, at least one version of it, anticipates many others to come. The new audience of readers and the traditional audience of theatre-goers no doubt often overlapped but are in many ways distinct, certainly in terms of generic expectations: what could not be shown on the stage could be described at length in prose; blank verse soliloquies could become stream-of-consciousness explorations; invented back stories could fill problematic lacunae in depth. Moreover, the limitations and difficulties incurred in attending a live theatrical performance could now be replaced by an inexpensive book on the home shelf, even in the furthest reaches of the kingdom. From the pre-1606 prose chronicle histories to Heylyn's oft-reprinted *Microcosmus* through the multiple editions of *The Secret History* to the Lambs' *Tales from Shakespeare*, and on to the contemporary explosion of self-published novels and fan fiction, the story of Macbeth found more and more life in the medium of prose, and in doing so, that story was continually reshaped through this new genre.

7

Global and racial *Macbeth*

Previous chapters have alluded to adaptations from many countries beyond the United States and the UK: most of Europe, Russia, Brazil, India, Japan, and others. Discussing adaptation without reference to these other cultures is impossible. Equally impossible: any individual's ability to master such a range of languages, cultures, and adaptations. The MIT Global Shakespeare project alone has posted thirty-five full or partial versions of the play from countries ranging from China and the Philippines to Yemen.[1] The MIT site only begins to reflect the multitude of global adaptations, and by its very nature it omits all non-visual adaptations. If one considers translation as a form of adaptation – and it clearly is, particularly in cases such as Ducis – then the range of adaptations of Shakespeare's *Macbeth* has been global for over three centuries. Non-Anglo adaptations, moreover, are necessarily 'political': they are appropriations by another culture and language; they invoke Shakespeare's immense cultural capital to enhance prestige; or they write back against Shakespeare's cultural capital as a tool of imperialism.

Given this globalizing process, I was not surprised to learn, for example, that 'the first translation into Finnish of a Shakespeare play' was – *Macbeth*, in 1834, by Jaakko Lagervall (Aaltonen 1997: 61). Like many global adaptations, the translation was not from the English, and somewhat surprisingly, not from Ducis, but from a Swedish version of Schiller's translation, with other influences floating around, demonstrating once again the rhizomatic nature of adaptation. The play's title, *Ruunulinna*, was 'the name of both the protagonist and his castle' (Aaltonen 1997: 60). The clothing of the titular figure on the front page (see **Figure 10**) 'suggests

FIGURE 10 Ruunulinna, *the Finnish* Macbeth, *1834. Public Domain.*
http://creativecommons.org/publicdomain/mark/1.0/deed.fi

some connection with the singing or collection of folk poetry ... playing the *kantele*, a traditional Finnish stringed instrument' (60). Lagervall justified his changes by noting that Sir Walter Scott 'didn't think it [Shakespeare's play] happened in Scotland either' (Töyrä 2020). But even when the Scottish play was translated into Scots, the adaptation reflected its own cultural moment. As McClure (1999: 40) notes, Lorimer's 1992 translation included a decidedly revisionist moment: 'Shakespeare's "show of eight Kings" [in 4.1] became *a paidgean o seiven Kings & a Queen*: restoring Mary Queen of Scots, whom Shakespeare may have thought it tactful not to mention, to her rightful place in the Stewart royal line'. In one way or another, every culture remakes the play to meet its own needs.

To return to that Finnish adaptation: it makes familiar choices we have seen in previous chapters. With the setting in Finland, Macbeth became a general fighting in the Finnish army on behalf of the king. The Finnish Macbeth, according to Aaltonen (1999: 146) 'was a famous guerrilla leader of the eighteenth century', while Lady Macbeth became an 'evil Finnish woman whose persistent yearning for power was not innate but suggested by the witches'. Against the witches – who 'embodied, both in name and behavior, afflictions such as pain, hardship and worldliness' – were the 'positive powers of Nature and Love' which, nevertheless, failed to prevent tragedy. Moreover, 'The witch scene was made prominent and it had links with Finnish mythology'. While Lady Macbeth's sleep-walking scene was omitted, and 'her madness was edited out', Aaltonen notes that the sleep-walking scene 'became important as a dramatic fragment in the Finnish theatre some forty years later'. Thus, there are both one-to-one equivalencies (Scottish thane=Finnish general), radical rewritings (the sleep-walking scene), and an overlay of a radically different culture (Finnish mythology). In some ways, this is the pattern of most global adaptations.

I will proceed here with a closer look at some non-English adaptations: two less canonic (Griselda Gambaro's *La Señora Macbeth*, Argentina; Pavel Kohout's *Play Macbeth*, Czechoslovakia), and then one quite well-known (Kurosawa's *Throne of Blood*, Japan). The chapter ends with a survey of additional non-Western adaptations, especially those emphasizing racial and ethnic issues. I cannot pretend to know the cultures or languages of all these countries well, or at all. The world is a very large place, I've (re)discovered.

Griselda Gambaro:
La Señora Macbeth (2002)

Gambaro is a prolific Argentine playwright, novelist, and essayist. Forced into exile during the 1980s 'Dirty War' under the military junta dictatorship, she created a body of work analysing forms of resistance and subjugation, and the often disturbing relation between victims and victimizers.[2] Her 2002 play, *La Señora Macbeth* (apparently not yet translated into English), reflects post-dictatorship conditions in Argentina, overlaying Shakespeare's play with the guilt of survivors and witnesses of the horrors, particularly the role of women, ranging from the resistance of the Mothers of the Plaza de Mayo to the complicity of those who remained silent.

Gambaro's play includes just five characters: Lady Macbeth, three witches, and Banquo's Ghost; the witches act out other scenes like the slaughter of Macduff's family. Unlike many adaptations centring on Lady Macbeth, Gambaro's is not interested in her pre-history (e.g. Clarke, Bottomley, Klein) or her post-Macbeth life (e.g. Greig). Rather, the play focuses closely on her reactions to what she learns about Macbeth's actions, and what she learns about her own guilt. Shakespeare's play occurs offstage, more or less contemporaneously, with reports of the Folio's plot regularly reported by the witches. Many Folio speeches are quoted verbatim, though not always by their original speakers; Gambaro in effect releases the play's discourse into the void of Lady Macbeth's consciousness. Finally, like many other adaptations, Gambaro expands the witches' roles far beyond that of uttering prophecies: they become a kind of expressionist chorus,[3] a malevolent stream of conscience for Lady Macbeth. They are present throughout, and preside over Lady Macbeth's death at the end. With the exception of a brief appearance by Banquo's ghost, all the male characters in the Folio are absent. The focus is purely on Lady Macbeth, the witches, and their relation. As the First Witch says, 'Being a woman is an important issue' (36); in many ways, it is *the* issue of the play. Gambaro's Lady Macbeth is very far from the tradition of the 'fiendlike' queen who, in Copeland's novel, signs a pact with Satan. Instead, she is herself a victim, a product of the masculinist social order in which she is trapped, and deluded by her love for her husband even as he (literally and symbolically absent throughout the play) marginalizes and manipulates her.

Gambaro's play opens onto a 'kind of baroque sculpture' that includes a throne, swing set, and a slide. Lady Macbeth is planning the banquet for Duncan, and she wants to invite as guests 'the poorest children', whose feet she will wash, and prisoners released from their dungeons; her naïve, unaware 'goodness' extends even to saving a little bird with a broken leg, placing it 'on my breasts' (15). When she says that she will not accuse the murderers – 'always the victim offers herself as a prostitute, she only knows how to tempt the murderer' (19) – the play begins to contextualize Lady Macbeth within a patriarchal culture. The witches point out that certain thoughts 'should not be thought', to which she replies 'I don't think anything, I leave it to Macbeth who does it for both of us' (20). The Second Witch says that Lady 'is a transvestite but a creature that does not hide her soul' (25) – through dress, gesture, and voice, she is a woman in performative terms; but within, she is masculine. As the play proceeds, the conflict between inner and outer leads to frequent eruptions of frustration: 'I will beget myself. I will be queen with king power!' (29). The deepening contradictions result in her being able to call Macbeth's name only by 'squawking like an animal' (32). Preserving her sense of innocence proves impossible. She reports that when Macbeth said 'We're not going through with this', she looked 'at myself as if I'm his accomplice. But I hadn't said a word'; the First Witch responds: 'It doesn't matter being mute, señora. It is convenient. He will tell you in due time the words that he wants to hear. And he will increase his love for you because your tongue will be a mirror of his tongue' (35). And 'just as he puts words in my mouth, he moves my body in actions that my body does not want' (40). Of all the Lady Macbeths we have seen who lack voice and agency, Gambaro's might be the most tortured case.

After Duncan's murder, Lady Macbeth deludes herself with the thought that 'It wasn't Macbeth, it wasn't Macbeth's idea, it was Duncan who put his head on the block. It was Duncan who moved the dagger in Macbeth's hand and directed it at his chest so that the dagger passed through' (39). Victim and victimizer are locked in a horrible relation. When Banquo's ghost appears to report on his actions in the banquet scene, he tells her that 'my son [Fleance], who was able to flee from the ambush, will take revenge' (48). After the ghost disappears, Lady Macbeth wonders 'But if only the murderer suffers the punishment of seeing the specter of his victim, why did I see him?' (53), and her downward spiral accelerates. Upon learning of the slaughter of Macduff's family, she insists even more strongly that 'Macbeth will never touch a child's hair. He knows that if he touches a child he will be rejected even by hell' (60-1). 'He is not a butcher, my Macbeth!' she insists, 'Just a man with ambitions. If someone is to blame, it is me, who did not know how to stop him' (61). Her sense of responsibility grows, exacerbated by a scene in which the witches 'act out the scene at Macduff Castle' (63), which includes the Folio's dialogue between Lady Macduff and her son about traitors. Echoes of the recriminations against the Argentines who were silent now seem inescapable: 'What use, then, this feminine defense of saying: I have not hurt anyone?' (68). Finding it difficult to believe that 'such an awkward representation' as the witches have given can 'be true' (70), Lady Macbeth looks to her hands, now covered in blood. The play now implies that a second spectre inhabits Lady Macbeth on the inside, the transvestite dual identity that can no longer be denied:

Am I a man and I only wear women's dresses so that my acquiescence is pretended to be tender, natural, and with this disguise of my dresses I accompany, without the blush of a man, without the pride of a man, the power of Macbeth? Or am I a woman and even though I am a woman I want the power of Macbeth, if it were mine I don't know if it would have been different from his? I know it myself. Oh, what a terror! ... I myself forgot my love for Macbeth! (73)

As Magnarelli points out, 'she temporarily achieves something of a partial "awakening" ... although her position as his pseudo accomplice causes her to suffer the guilt he apparently does not feel' (2008: 370–1), as in the Folio. Witnessing her handwashing and delirium, when she mistakes the ground for a bed, the witches discuss Macbeth's offstage death, eventually offering her a 'sweet antidote to oblivion' (82), which Lady Macbeth greedily drinks. But the drink is a poison, bringing her the oblivion of death. Her final words: 'My Macbeth ... will he live?' But she receives no answer, and 'She is already dead' (85), the Second Witch announces.

Gambaro's focus on gender within a regime of state violence amplifies, in her own context, issues that the Folio also surveys.

The place of women in Argentine history had been suppressed until some forms of resistance had been developed. Gambaro knows that even a woman subjugated to her husband's will, her voice not her own, cannot simply invoke the 'feminine defence': complicity produces blood on the hands. The tragic fate of Señora Macbeth, and women in Gambaro's culture, is that they have become what the play calls 'transvestites': ostentatiously 'female' on the outside, male on the inside. Señora Macbeth dies of poison, even as she is already poisoned.

Pavel Kohout: *Play Macbeth* (1978)

Kohout's play, which premiered in 1978 in the Living Room Theater, has become well-known, in name and concept if not in detail, through Tom Stoppard's *Cahoot's Macbeth*, which Stoppard wrote after meeting Kohout in Prague (Worthen 2007; see **Chapter One** on Stoppard). But Stoppard's sun seems to have eclipsed Kohout's actual play, even as it elevated it to world-wide status. Kohout's adaptation merits attention on its own. It seems not to have been translated into English or German, according to Kohout's own website.[4] Remarkably, though, a full-length colour film of the production was made by cinematographer Stanislav Milota, the husband of the actress Vlasta Chramostová (who played Lady Macbeth). The recording was secretly exported abroad, presented on Austrian television ORF and, most importantly, saved for future generations. The play was performed 'about eighteen times' in 1978–9 (Worthen 2007: 120), until a production in the home of Vaclav Havel's brother was interrupted by state police – thus leading to Stoppard's meta-adaptation. Kohout wrote Stoppard that the

two great and forbidden Czech actors, Pavel Landovsky and Vlasta Chramostová ... are starring Macbeth and Lady, a well known and forbidden young singer Vlastimil Tresnak is singing Malcolm and making music, one young girl, who couldn't study the theatre-school, Tereza Kohoutova, by chance my daughter, is playing little parts and reading remarks; and the last man, that's me ... ! is reading and a little bit playing the rest of the roles. (Stoppard 1993: 142–3)

Shakespeare, Kohout felt, 'wouldn't be worried about' the adaptation: 'it is nevertheless Macbeth!' (**Figure 11**).

The most remarkable feature of Kohout's adaptation is that it took place at all. As many scholars have documented, the Living Room Theater became a form of resistance irrespective of what play was being performed; as Prochazka (1996: 61) notes, its repertory 'was fairly traditional. No absurd dramas or avant-garde experiments were staged'. The choice of *Macbeth*, then, was only partly the consequence of the play's use in previous 'political' moments in Czech history.[5] Stoppard's policeman reflects the authorities' ambivalent relation to Shakespeare as both a cultural value to be appropriated and at the same time feared, but Kohout's relation to Shakespeare as a tradition to be resisted, Prochazka notes, is not important, 'nor is the idea of resistance expressed by the encoding of language' (62), as we saw in various post-war adaptations in Chapter One. Rather, the 'resistance' here was the forging, in the act of performance itself, of a communal space of relationships and wonder, as a ritual process. The boundaries between artist, director, actors, and audience were no longer hierarchical or static, but now elements in a 'representational fluidity' (Worthen 2007: 124). One Czech critic saw Kohout's play, 'staged on the policed border of Socialist society ... as an absolute exigency, "our last possibility" to discover and preserve freedom'.[6]

Even without knowing Czech, the structural contours of Kohout's adaptation are apparent in the ORF film. Many of his revisions reflect choices made by many other adapters, while some reflect the fact that there were only five actors, three of whom had to play multiple parts. First, there are the necessary and the considered cuts: the Porter's speech (2.3); much of 4.1 (the Show of Kings); Hecate; Siward and his son; the Doctor in 4.3; and others. The result is a running time of about seventy-five minutes. Secondly, stage directions were read aloud, facing the camera (a Brechtian effect). Thirdly, many passages – monologues by minor characters, in particular – were put to music, sung as more or less protest songs. These songs, accompanied on guitar, worked against the spoken blank verse, as Prochazka notes, 'by stressing authenticity over artificiality', in contrast to 'the inauthentic relation to speech and acting of the central pairs of heroes. Their inauthenticity was conspicuously thematized by Macbeth's "asides"' (Prochazka

FIGURE 11 *Macbeth 'Is This a Dagger' in* Play Macbeth *directed by Pavel Kohout, 1979.* Österreichischer Rundfunk; *https://youtu.be/ TMbsAn2DGHM. All rights reserved. Screen grab.*

1996: 63). In their very nature, the songs reflected the totalitarian world and resistance to it outside of Chramostová's apartment.

Perhaps the most significant staging choice concerned Malcolm. We have seen before how the representation of Malcolm varies according to political perspectives. For seventeenth-century royalists and adherents of the Authorized Version, Malcolm is the rightful, triumphant king at the end, while by the time of Ionesco and Müller, he had become a monstrous killer. In some post-war European countries, however, he was still a righteous figure ushering in a new order. In *Play Macbeth*, Malcolm's lines are sung, thus marking him off from the tonal register of Macbeth's and Lady Macbeth's lines. Here, Malcolm was 'the innocent victim of the tyrant's cruelty, a "dissident" forced to emigrate and seek foreign help to overthrow the regime' (Prochazka 1996: 63). The final lines of the play were sung by all, as the new community formed by and during the performance itself: 'The new ruler is joined by his subjects in introducing justice into the country where the time is free' (Stříbrný

1994: 277–8). After the four actors each speak the line 'We will perform in measure, time and place' (5.9.39), Malcolm's final line – 'So thanks to all at once, and to each one' (5.9.40) – is sung, with all facing the camera.[7] The play's final line, about Macbeth being 'crowned at Scone', is omitted: in Kohout's version, Malcolm's assumption is not a restitution of a former social order, but a wholly new one. Thus Malcolm, as we saw in Chapter Two, can be either a new tyrant or as here, a dissident triumphing over tyranny.

Akira Kurosawa: *Throne of Blood* (1957)

Kurosawa's renowned film has frequently been called the greatest adaptation of *any* of Shakespeare's plays, and it is difficult to disagree.[8] Kurosawa's genius extends beyond the astonishing camera work, stunning imagery, and adroit use of black-and-white film, to his entire re-conception of Shakespeare's play. The film's world is essentially that of the forest, as the play's title in Japanese suggests.[9] Kurosawa sets his film in the 'Age of the Country at War' (1392–1568). This warrior culture, embodied in the samurai code, produces a dark and threatening world. Like Kott, Kurosawa evoked a world of repetitive cycles, represented in part by the Witch's spinning wheel, but mainly by the film's overall frame shots. After the swirling fog begins to clear, the film begins with shots of graves, and a wooden marker that reads 'Here stood Spider's Web castle', followed by a dissolve showing the castle. The film ends where it began, with fog, the same bleak landscape, and the refrain 'Look upon the ruins / Of the castle of delusion / Haunted only now / By the spirits / Of those who perished / A scene of carnage / Born of consuming desire / Never changing. / Now and throughout eternity. / Here stood Spider's Web Castle'. The circularity of language, image, and sound (wind, flute) reminds one of the many contemporary adaptations that have seen Malcolm's dispensation of rewards, and the presence of a traitor's severed head, as a repetition of the beginning. But Kurosawa's film offers no Malcolm, no hope for the future. Nor, more unusually, does it contain a Macduff. Without these 'moral' counterparts, the destruction of Washizu (=Macbeth) is communal, as he killed by hundreds of arrows – made from wood from the Spider's Web forest – shot by his formerly loyal soldiers.

Among his other revisions, Kurosawa famously adopted techniques from the Noh theatre tradition, reflected in acting styles, costumes, music, and especially, the absence of soliloquies. He also introduced an off-screen chorus. Certainly the illusion of a deep interiority in Macbeth and Lady Macbeth is one of the hallmarks of the Folio, and of most adaptations. Shakespeare gave them soliloquies, adapters revised and expanded them, contemporary novelists delved further into their minds through narrative techniques such as first-person narration or free indirect discourse. But Kurosawa shows only surfaces, sounds, and movements to represent that interiority. Asaji (=Lady Macbeth), for example, remains preternaturally still during most of the film, but her occasional explosive movements betray her inner anxieties and guilt. While Washizu is murdering Lord Tsuzuki, Asaji's to-and-fro shuffling produces uncanny sounds – her slippers on the wooden floor, the swishing of her robe[10] – that represent her interiority, just as the often-present fog reflects Washizu's and Miki's (=Banquo's) mental confusion.

Like other adapters, Kurosawa also depicts a pregnant Asaji/ Lady Macbeth who suffers a miscarriage: the child is born dead, 'dead within her'. She had told Macbeth of her pregnancy ('I am with child') just as he is about to name Miki's son as heir to the throne and pronounce that 'we are barren'. The timing is fortuitous, to say the least, but there is no doubt that she later suffers a miscarriage (the maid says 'My lady has given birth. The child was stillborn'). When the maid later cries out 'My lady', Washizu goes to her, sees her empty kimono hanging on a screen, and behind it, in her madness, she attempts to wash the blood off her hands. However, Kurosawa does not, as many adapters do, link Asaji's maternal condition to her ruthlessness. She convinces him to do the deed by reminding him that the Great Lord had murdered his own predecessor, and in a Kottian insight, she describes the violent principle of succession in this world: 'In this degenerate age, one must kill so as not to be killed'.

Surely the most noted aspect of Kurosawa's adaptation is his conception of the witches – not three or fifty, but one: a mysterious figure (**Figure 12**) turning a spinning wheel within a wooden cage. The wheel reminds the viewer of the Parcae or the Fates, but also as a metadramatic metaphor for the film projector (Donaldson 1990: 76). When Washizu and Miki enter the witch's cage, they

FIGURE 12 Throne of Blood *directed by Akira Kurosawa © Toho International Company 1957. All rights reserved. Screen grab.*

have crossed a liminal threshold into a different world, marked in part by the cage's sudden disappearance, and then by the equally sudden disappearance of the witch, or Forest Spirit. He or she is androgynous both in appearance (as in the Folio text) and in voice: the figure is played by a female actor, whose distorted voice has been re-recorded by a male actor (according to the DVD Commentary); moreover, Kurosawa turned off the treble range of the male voices to estrange the voices even further. The result is an utterly brilliant adaptation of one of the compelling elements of the Folio.

Washizu's shock at the later prophecies' fulfilment – the coming of Birnam Wood, especially – is exceeded only by his shock at the warriors turning against him. The famous scene of the hail of arrows reinterprets the Folio's death scene: there is no beheading, no triumph of a restored sacramental kingship, no Malcolm to pronounce the final victory – just the chorus's return, Washizu disappearing into the ground fog as he dies, and the swirling fog where 'here stood Spider's Web castle'. Kurosawa's film has profoundly influenced many later versions, as Burnett (2013: 163–94) has demonstrated.

Racialized *Macbeths*

Welcome Msomi's well-known 'Zulu' *Macbeth*, *uMabatha*, is far from the first transformation of the play in terms of race. Long before Msomi's adaptation, Orson Welles's production, the so-called 'Voodoo Macbeth', placed the play in Haiti and linked Macbeth to the Haitian Emperor Henri Christophe; employing an all-Black cast, Welles's production is probably the most famous 'racial' adaptation of the play. Yet it too is far from the first. The Black American actor Ira Aldridge had performed as Macbeth as early as 1830 (Lindfors 2010: 48), and before him, James Hewlett had assayed the role in the 1820s, first at New York's African Grove Theatre, then on tour. His 'agonies of death' and his delivery of the line 'enough!' were said to be 'equal to any improvement in reading made by Kean' in an 1822 review.[11]

Even before 1606, however, the Scots in the Scottish play had been marked as a different race, certainly as an inferior people: uncivilized, often wild and savage, because descended from the Picts rather than the English descent through Anglo-Saxon-Norman lines. In his 'Description of Britain', William Harrison described the Scots as 'a people mixed of the Scithian and Spanish blood' who came from Ireland, and eventually called Picts 'because they painted their bodies' (Holinshed 1587: B2r). Harrison then repeats, as many anti-Scottish writers did, an anecdote first related by Saint Jerome, who when he was a youth in Gaul, saw Scots feeding on human flesh, 'and therefore called Anthropophagi' (as Othello claims to have seen); they 'used to feed on the buttocks of boys and women's paps, as delicate dishes' (B2v). There were further racial/ethnic distinctions made as well between Highlanders and Lowlanders (Floyd-Wilson 2006). The racialization of the play, in short, extends over five hundred years.

Returning to more recent times, Welles's famous production was a huge success, seen by upwards of 150,000 people in New York alone (Rippy 2010: 84). It adapted the Folio to fit the new setting in Haiti: voo-doo was invoked as an equivalent to witchcraft magic, and primitive drums were heard. Hecate, played by a male actor, became a central figure with lines both added and taken from other characters, even participating in the murder of Banquo; almost as a chorus, Hecate often ended scenes, and has the final line in the production, 'Peace, the charm's wound up' (1.3.35), towering above the three witches and the severed head of Macbeth. (Welles would end his 1948 film with one of the three witches speaking the same line.) Welles's production, like many others, also produces a closed frame, undermining Malcolm's claim that 'The time is free'. The racial politics of this production are complicated, as many writers have noted. Its positive force rested, above all, in the fact that it provided work – it was sponsored by Roosevelt's WPA as part of the Federal Theater Project – and entertainment for communities of colour, and then later on a national tour. Some of the reviews were typically racist, however, and the entire venture has seemed to some to be a white colonialist fantasy of primitive darkness – the mashup of Caribbean and African elements was, so to speak, whitewashed through Shakespeare's cultural capital. The production was certainly a landmark for Welles, having been hired at just the age of twenty for his first major directing opportunity. His reputation suffered when he later claimed to have performed the part of Macbeth in blackface, after the lead actor fell ill during a tour; his acting was so convincing, he claimed, that no one realized that he was a white actor (Rippy 2010: 83).

Msomi's *uMabatha* (**Figure 13**) has, like Welles's production, been wildly successful in terms of audience reception, world-wide tours (1973–82; 1997; in 2001 it was part of the 'Globe-to-Globe' project, where the play's language was Zulu, not English), and the approval of no less than Nelson Mandela after his release from prison: the play, he wrote, 'illustrates vividly the universality of ambition, greed and fear. Moreover, the similarities between Shakespeare's *Macbeth* and our own Shaka become a glaring reminder that the world is, philosophically, a very small space' (Msomi 2000: 165). But, also like Welles's, Msomi's adaptation has also been critiqued as a Western tourist's fantasy of 'Africa', no matter that Msomi is himself South African. He wrote *uMabatha* at the urging of Elizabeth Sneddon, a white drama professor at the University of Natal, after her suggestion that his play be 'about the great African nations, based on universal epics' (McLuskie 1999: 159), but Msomi went his own way, finding that in '*Macbeth* ... the intrigue, plots and counter plots of the Scottish clans were almost a carbon copy of the drama that took place with the early nations of Africa ... As in *Macbeth*, Shaka the great warrior king was also murdered by those closest to him' (Ryan 2002: 5). Shaka was a

Zulu chief ruling in the early nineteenth century, noted for his cruel and often violent rule; he was murdered by his bodyguard and half-brothers in 1828 (*South African History* 2020).

Msomi's adaptation follows the play's plot closely, and at times seems a direct translation from one culture to another: instead of reading aloud Macbeth's letter in 1.5, for example, Kamadonsela (=Lady Macbeth) listens to a *'Distant drumbeat'* (Msomi 2000: 172) and interprets its message aloud; her 'unsex me' monologue becomes 'Let my heart be like the devil's thorn / My blood of mamba's poison … Dry up my woman's tears / And let my breasts shrivel with serpent's milk' (173). As with many Lady Macbeths, *'She faints* and *is carried out'* (177). Similarly, Macbeth's 'tomorrow' speech becomes 'Our wishes are but empty calabashes, / Our lives have withered slowly / Since Mdangazeli's (=Duncan) branch was hacked away. / It is no matter, let all things / Turn against me, I will fight / Until the last drop of blood is shed' (186). Msomi quite

FIGURE 13 uMabatha *directed by Welcome Msomi 4 January 2011. Trailer: https://youtu.be/XqUsqerEV8g. All rights reserved. Screen grab.*

consistently translates the Folio's imagined Scotland (heaths, forests, fog) into the natural world of South Africa (stones, rivers, thorns): birds and horses become a 'hissing mamba' (173), a 'scorpion' (174), or 'poisonous beetles' (181), while the English court becomes 'Swaziland' (183). The three witches are the three Sangoma, traditional healers linked to ancestral spirits; their prophetic powers follow the Folio's closely: 'Mabatha! Chief of Dlamasi! ... Chief of Mkhawundeni! ... The bones rattle for a mighty chief' (170).

Msomi does make some significant revisions. As Kamadonsela enters the sleep-walking scene, she *picks up the makhweyana* [a musical bow] *and caresses it*, then *moves off, singing* (185), an allusion to Ophelia, it would seem. In the final scene, closing one of the Folio's missing frames, Msomi's Mbatha *fights DONEBANE* (=Donaldbain) *and slays him* (186), though Folose (=Fleance) escapes when his father is killed (180), and never reappears. Mafudu (=Macduff) slays Mbatha, but does not behead him or present it or any other token to Makhiwane (=Malcolm). Msomi's play ends, as Kohout's and many others have done, with the unclouded triumph of Makhiwane who is hailed, three times, by all at the end. Makhiwane does not, however, distribute new honours to the warriors, but instead urges the return of those who fled the 'tyrant': 'All those loyal warriors who fled / From the tyrant's cruel hand / Can return and live in peace. / The spear has broken', and *'He throws the spear into the ground'* (187), which seems roughly parallel to Davenant's Macduff presenting Macbeth's sword to Malcolm. Msomi created, in effect, a Zulu equivalent to the Authorized Version. The controversies surrounding Msomi's adaptation, particularly in its vibrant, exciting productions, have primarily concerned whether it enacts white Western conceptions of 'Africa' and Zulu culture – that 'Africa' is tribal, superstitious and warlike (like 'Scotland'). The production also was criticized because of its use of bare female breasts on stage; such display was said to be traditional, but in a Western context seemed voyeuristic.[12] But the supposed parallels are imprecise and unstable at best. Mandela had praised the 'similarities between Shakespeare's *Macbeth* and our own Shaka' – between Shaka and the play, not Duncan. Shaka's historical cruelty and tyranny find no place in Msomi's play: Dangane is a purely good Duncan ('His praises are sung as the wisest councillor / His words are greeted with the Royal salute', 174) whose only mistake is to 'pronounce ... my eldest son, / Chief of Mkhambathini' (172).

If Msomi's project now seems slightly opaque, another production set in South Africa but conceived and directed by a white Englishman, Max Stafford-Clark, staged an openly political adaptation worth noting. The cast was all-Black – except for the white actress playing Lady Macbeth, whose outsider status in a violent masculinist society was thus racially marked. The setting was a modern-day African dictatorship, modelled, according to the program notes, on the reign of Idi Amin (Uganda) and the story of Emma McCune, 'a British aid worker in southern Sudan who married the warlord Riek Machar and earned the nickname "Lady Macbeth" for her ruthless behavior' (Scheil 2006: 116). If Msomi's production was occasionally critiqued as a nostalgic fantasy, Stafford-Clark's seems to have aimed for the opposite, producing a nightmare Africa of violence and danger – sadly, not imaginary, but hardly the whole truth about Africa. Like Msomi's, this production used 'Frenzied dancing to pulsating drums [that] transported us far from the mists of Scotland to the African setting' (116), so, from one imaginary to another.

Stafford-Clark has said that after reading Daniel Bergner's *Soldiers of Light* he wanted to commission 'a play [about Africa] concerning child warriors, genocide and the appalling brutality of "a collapsed state" .... Child actors play[ed] child soldiers – Fleance, Donalbain and the young Macduff' (Jones 2010: 1); the play's imagery was intended to remind viewers of 'child soldiers in Sierra Leone, Rwanda and the Sudan ... [with] Pictures of children brandishing guns, of African voodoo dolls strapped to a foliage covered jeep *"Birnam Wood comes to Dunsinane"*' (7). Malcolm's exile in England was represented as 'a kind of colonial country club' (9). As with many other adaptations, Lady Macbeth had given birth by a former husband, but there were no children with Macbeth. The witches were distinguished as Other by having them 'originate in French speaking African Zaire or Cote d'Ivoire or perhaps Cameroon, their dialect add[ed] to the unease of the audience by removing the well-known spells and charms that make the play familiar' (2). This was an immersive production, intended to make the audience uncomfortable: Macbeth's asides were delivered directly to individual audience members, '[r]andom audience members were seated at the banquet table' (Scheil 2006: 117), and 'spectators were invited to "come and take a look" at the carnage' of the Macduff's family slaughter (118). The production ended with the familiar closed frame, 'as Malcolm became just another African warlord to take over the land, differentiated only by a different tribal dance and drumbeat' (118).

Stafford-Clark's production originated in the UK, toured throughout the world, and then came – to Nigeria. His own account of the performances in Nigeria, organized by the British Council, is sardonic and more than a trace condescending (local corruption, ten-year-old prostitutes, security men with AK-47s): 'The dancing is sensational. The booty action is plentiful – backsides shake like blancmange. I find myself very awake all of a sudden. As for Macbeth – people still flick through their mobiles but the performance is more resolute' (Stafford-Clark 2005). The reference to 'blancmange' offers almost too much to comment on; it's not quite clear if the booties in question are black, but certainly even the 'blanc' or white members of his 'Restoration audience: ageing beauties, the aristocracy, wits, bankers and armed members of the public', sitting in Africa and watching an 'African' production, seem bored. The production's greater successes came before largely white audiences in Europe and the United States.

Other South African adaptations include two episodes of a 2008 mini-series on television. First, *Entabeni* takes place in a very different world from Msomi's:

> the world of black business ... we follow the rapid rise and downfall of Kumkani, a talented, fearless, young prodigy in the world of investment banking. Loved, admired as well as feared by all, Kumkani is what everyone wishes to be. Young, rich, gifted, powerful, with an incredibly bright future, and married to the most beautiful woman in all Southern Africa. (*Entabeni* 2008)

Kumkani has 'just landed the biggest contract for Entabeni Security Holdings, a major company owned by his distant and beloved cousin Matthews. And most importantly he has done so almost single-handedly. The story begins at the peak of this young man's amazing life which has captured the attention of the world'. He meets a 'strange homeless woman' who utters the usual prophecies ('Kumkani, CEO of Entabeni') including a mysterious old, homeless woman whom he meets on his return from overseas.

The second film, *Death of a Queen*, features Prince Malôrô (=Macbeth) who 'with Mugudo, his right-hand man and friend, [returns victorious] from negotiations to ensure the preservation of the Kingdom'. He 'encounters three male witchdoctors who address him as "Guardian of the Sacred Forest" and future King of Mapungubwe'. The twist here is that 'For the prophecy to come to pass, history would have to be turned on its head and his own younger sister, the Rain Queen, would have to die'. His wife, ironically named Grace, urges him on to kill his sister, which he does, but he is then unable to produce the rain the country needs. This Lady Macbeth eventually takes her own life, and when King Malôrô dies, the rains return (*Death of a Queen* 2008).

Adele Seeff's detailed analysis shows how both versions internationalize Shakespeare's play in terms of three topics of keen interest to contemporary post-Apartheid South Africa: 'changing gender roles and the place of women in a patriarchal society'; 'the role of the supernatural' in both traditional ancestral terms and modernized versions; and third, 'the concern with sovereign power, succession, and lineage' (Seeff 2013: 175; see also Seeff 2018). The entire series of six plays works, she notes, to re-globalize the 'hybrid product [of Shakespeare and local settings] through export to the international entertainment community' (174). Both *Entabeni* and *Death of a Queen* appropriate not only Shakespeare's play, but some essential conventions and tropes: film *noir* for the first, ancestral myths for the second. Both films employ some of the familiar adaptive moves we have seen before: in *Queen*, Grace is pregnant, but miscarries and dies onscreen, smearing poison on her lips (Seeff 2013: 193, 194), while the Malcolm equivalent is the young Puno, who is female, representing a hope for the future. *Entabeni*, on the other hand, works in part like Almereyda's *Hamlet*, as a critique of modern capitalism, and its ending follows the trajectory of *noir* when the Macduff character, 'gun in hand, enters the Macbeths' apartment and records their mutual admissions of guilt. He promptly send the evidence to the Police Chief' (185). In a number of ways, then, these two adaptations map out a quite different 'Africa' than those of Msomi and Stafford-Clark.

There are many – too many to take up here – other race-conscious adaptations from Africa, Asia, Oceania, and South America. Among the most notable is *Makibefo*, a 1999 (release date: 2001) black-

and-white film shot in Madagascar that has gained considerable attention from Anglo-US critics.[13] Its cast is the indigenous Antandroy peoples; the majority of the actors, according to the director, have never seen a television or a film, and had never acted before in their lives (Burnett 2008: 240). The prophecies are spoken by a witch doctor; when he goes mad, Makibefo sees visions of his victims in ghostly white-painted faces. Abela has said he wanted to unite two cultures and 'engender a communal and intercultural reading of Shakespeare' (240). The English-speaking narrator reads some of the play's text from a leather book, while the cast speaks in Malagasy (the national language of Madagascar). This film is a perfect instance of a 'glocal' adaptation of *Macbeth*.

In the western hemisphere, the Shakespeare Theatre Company's 2017 production (Washington, DC) set the play in an unnamed contemporary African country suffering from civil war. There are, again, child soldiers, and witches (mixed-gender) that are not only not supernatural, but 'actually Western intelligence operatives manipulating Macbeth into destabilizing the political structure of this country in order to gain easy access to its natural resources'. They are also the only Caucasian members of a mixed-race cast (Hurley 2017). With Hecate as their supervisor, 'they spied on and actively aided Macbeth in his coup and military campaigns' (Joubin 2018: 243). The transposition to Africa 'reflected the life experience of Liesl Tommy, an African American director who was raised in Cape Town, South Africa, during the apartheid era' (Joubin 2018: 241).[14]

The film *Macbett (The Caribbean Macbeth)*, according to a pre-release blurb, takes place in a world where Black West Indians rule: 'General Macbett encounters the weird sisters, who are the spirit daughters of Mother Africa and reign over water, fire, earth and sky' (*Macbett* 2012?) and so on. Directed by a Black woman, Aleta Chappelle, the cast features many well-known Black actors: Terrence Howard, Harry Lennix, Blair Underwood, and Danny Glover.[15]

One of the more symbolic castings of a Black American actor occurred in a 2009 production by the Chicago Shakespeare Theater, which featured 'a Malcolm who bore a stunning resemblance to … Barack Obama', who had just been elected president (Gaines 2019: 43); hence a positive Malcolm, bringing in a new and just order. The impulse to reflect US contemporary racial politics travelled across the border to the Stratford Canada Shakespeare Festival's 2009 production, set in 'colonial Africa in the 1960s' with explosions and machete combat; the cast was mixed race, in which the Black Lady Macbeth was said by one reviewer to be at times 'just a bit too Michelle Obama', which would seem a complete antithesis between character and historical figure (Ouzounian 2009). The director of this production saw the play's subjects as 'startlingly familiar': 'unsolved assassination leading to civil war, military invasion, regime change, moral cowardice, inbred corruption, unchecked dictatorial powers and the diseased politics of terror' (Jones 2009). It would seem difficult to fit Michelle Obama into such a concept. Thus 'Africa' is too often projected either as a drum-beating world of (at times bare-breasted) savages, rituals, and colourful dancing, or a tyrannical dictatorship of assassinations and terror. While the seventeenth-century English construction of 'Scotland' reflects many of these tropes, it seems clear that these representations of 'Africa' construct an imaginary from popular western fantasies and some realities.

Beyond these culture- and ethnic-specific adaptations, colour-blind casting has long become standard practice in Western film, opera and theatres, and *Macbeth* has been part of this trend. A film like *Shakespeare on the Estate* employs the practice extensively, though making little or no connection to problems of race. So too does the 1999 film, *Macbeth in Manhattan* – a 'meta' film of a production of the play within the film, with the characters toggling back and forth into their characters; the entire plot turns on the legend of the supposed 'curse'. The white director Greg Lombardo uses a Black actor as a Chorus-figure/stage hand, relaying the plot through the fourth wall. The cast is multi-racial, but the film makes nothing of the potential racial issues (in Manhattan, no less).

Macbeth in Asia

The increase in the number of Asian adaptations of *Macbeth* is staggering: I cannot do any kind of justice to it here. The new scholarship on the subject is equally prodigious.[16] Many adaptations stemmed initially from residual British imperialist practices in theatrical and educational institutions, but vigorous new directions have also emerged. The national Shakespeare associations in China,

Japan, Korea, and India are large and energetic. One sign of Asian prominence in Shakespeare studies was the location of the 4th World Shakespeare Congress in Tokyo (1991), with the 11th World Shakespeare Congress slated for Singapore (now on-line) in 2021. For some US/Anglo audiences, Kurosawa's great film (see above) has overshadowed many other distinguished adaptations. For example, Yukio Ninagawa's *Ninagawa Macbeth* was staged in 1980, and toured extensively in the following decade. Incorporating elements of Kabuki and Bunraku (or puppet theatre), the *Ninagawa Macbeth* was set, like Kurosawa's film, in the violent Azuchi-Momoyama period (*c.* 1558–1600) (Ninagawa 2015), but with allusions to the violence of contemporary politics, including pre-war imperial Japan and Red Army attacks in 1972 (Kliman 2004: 162–3). Ninagawa said his production

> is set within a Buddhist family altar and everything happens within that frame. There is such an altar in all Japanese houses, but that does not mean that it is a religious frame. The altar is where your ancestors dwell, and the Japanese will talk to their ancestors within this setting quite naturally. It is a link between the living and the world of death.
>
> (Braunmuller 1997: 87)

The most pervasive visual image of the production was, Ninagawa noted, the 'cherry blossom … [they combine] regret at human madness and folly with awareness of earthly beauty' (88); the imagery combined beauty and eros with transience and death (when Macbeth died, the cascade of falling blossoms suddenly ceased [Kliman 2004: 177]). The production design featured huge sliding screens, which became semi-transparent when backlit, turning the stage into a space that the audience's vision could not fully penetrate, and forming a metadramatic frame through which the play's action was mediated. The ending gave us an ambiguous Malcolm: 'his last words were heard from behind the closed, darkened screen' (Kliman 2004: 162).[17]

Other Japanese productions include the *Shogun Macbeth*, staged by the Pan Asian Repertory Theatre in the 1980s, which recently returned to New York. It relocates the play from eleventh-century Scotland to the feudal military dictatorship of thirteenth-century Japan, a time of warring clans. Other important productions include

Tadashi Suzuki's 1992 intercultural *The Chronicle of Macbeth*, a shortened (seventy minutes) adaptation in which '"Macbeth" is a sickness, a disease of the soul, and the protagonist has hallucinated himself as Macbeth. He is visited by members of a religious cult who attempt to release him from his illness by freeing him (and all humankind) of the burden of history and memory' (Pronko 1993: 110). The cult members double as the witches and murderers. The play text itself 'is presented as a play within a play into which the patient steps'. Suzuki kept 'only the scenes which deal with Macbeth and his Lady' (110), thus shrinking the play. Suzuki's notion that the play itself is in the protagonist's mind would find an even more intense echo in Alan Cumming's one-man performance (see **Epilogue**). Many other Japanese productions could be noted: as Kliman notes, there are so many that it is 'impossible to point to one particular style or interpretation as *the* Japanese *Macbeth*' (159),[18] just as there is no definitive Chinese, Korean, Philippine etc. much less 'Asian' format. The Japanese productions, above all Kurosawa's film, have become better known to Anglo/US audiences, but the advent of YouTube and repositories like the Global Shakespeare website have made many other productions available, from China, Taiwan, India, South Korea, and many more.

Finally, under the category of non-English but difficult to categorize, there is *Pidgin Macbeth*, by English writer/actor Ken Campbell, written in Pidgin, a language spoken by numerous inhabitants of the South Pacific Islands. Campbell pushed for Pidgin to be adopted as a world language, as simpler than Esperanto and much easier to learn. Campbell's production was performed throughout Melanesia as well as in London. Relocated to the islands of the New Hebrides, with many cuts, the play ran about ninety minutes. The anthropological implications of the production were of great interest (Kingston 1999: 1), but beyond the play's relocation, the linguistic issues were most striking. Campbell said (one hopes with tongue in cheek) that Pidgin is 'a huge improvement, there's none of that iambic pentameter rubbish which is Shakespeare's main drawback' (Smurthwaite 1999). Thus Macduff's discovery of Duncan's corpse ('O horror, horror, horror!') became 'Maktup' saying 'Bagarap, bagarap, bagarap!'[19] This adaptation's identity politics are complex: 'Despite the liberating sense of Melanesians being used as a model for utopian future rather than primeval past, the inversion and the humour really only works because of their identical banishment from our present ... Pidgin is used to present an image of a unity that has roots in notions of the distant past as much as the future' (Kingston 1991: 2).

If Campbell wanted to overcome Babel by looking to a future lingua franca, a mixed-race multi-lingual production on another Pacific island, Hawai'i, by Paul Mitri in 2008 offered the Babel of the present as something positive. The racial composition of Hawai'i's population – 'the largest multiracial population [of any state in the United States] with 24.1% ... identifying with two or more races'[20] – was reflected in Mitri's production. The set consisted of multilevel ramps, platforms, and sewer grates, from which the witches slithered in and out, and into which the play's many corpses conveniently fell. Banquo's ghost rose and fell eerily without the distraction of awkward stage business. Fumes and harsh sounds belched forth occasionally. The above-ground view was post-apocalyptic: eleventh-century Scotland by way of Samuel Beckett and *Blade Runner*. The costumes indicated that the inhabitants of this strange world were Scots, samurai, and Russians, among others. The casting included students of Anglo-Saxon, African-American, Japanese, and Chinese descent, among others, while Mitri self-identified as 'of Egyptian descent' (Mitri 2009). This multi-ethnic adaptation was also elaborately multilingual. The witches spoke several different languages; Duncan and his clan spoke a great deal of Japanese, and were of Japanese descent; Macduff and his family spoke Russian. There was a smattering of Gaelic (the Gentlewoman in 5.1) and Arabic (the Doctor). The Macbeths spoke Spanish as well as English. The choices, Mitri said in his Director's Notes, 'create a cohesive world populated by remnants of our present world' (Mitri 2008a). Macbeth and Banquo's entrance in 1.2 give a flavour of the result (in Mitri's Working Script the different languages were parti-colored):

BANQUO.   How far is't call'd to Forres? *Nanda are wa,*
                  So wither'd and so wild in their attire,
                  Kono yo no montomo omowarenga,
                  Tashika ni soko ni oru? – Live you or are you
                  aught
                  That man may question?
MACBETH.   *Habla,* if you can: *¿qué eres?*
FIRST WITCH: *¡Gloria a Macbeth! Gloria a ti, noble de Glamis!* (Mitri 2008b)

The results, for an English speaker familiar with the play, were fascinating: an alienation effect that both forced greater attention to the dynamics of power on display, and the otherness of the experience. While some English-only speakers were disappointed with Mitri's babel, the majority of the audience might have found the English to be the distraction.

In staging this and an earlier 2007 production in Japan in 1997, Mitri said he had a three-fold purpose, which might be invoked for almost any non-English adaptation: (1) 'to make a play that could be understood by any audience member' (i.e. in a multicultural, multilingual audience; (2) to provide an experiment for actors; and (3) for actors and audience to 'use Shakespeare's works as a way of exploring their changing global commitments' (Mitri 2007) – to question their own beliefs.

* * *

Macbeth has an extraordinary international history: from the Globe to the global. This story of ambition, husband/wife struggle and regicidal violence, seems irresistible wherever it is known, in whatever language and culture it survives.

8

Macbeth, the musical

'Macbeth' was the name of a Milan-based gothic metal band with its own YouTube channel and Facebook page, relevant-sounding albums like *Superangelic Hate Bringers*, and an online store with Macbeth key holders, tote bags, and T-shirts. 'MacBeth' was also the name of a Taiwanese 'post-punk indie rock' band from about ten years ago.[1] There is a 'Macbeth Song Compilation Project' that includes music by Green Day and Red Hot Chili Peppers that *may* be linked to the play.[2] The band 'The Brothers Grimm' composed an electronic soundtrack for a performance piece called *This Is Not Shakespeare's Macbeth* (2013), a 'site-specific work, built atop the original Shakespeare, [that] examines the intrinsic connection between conscious [*sic*] and conscience: the idea that retribution comes from within and it is the demons of our own minds that bring us the greatest grief in the wake of our actions'. Using 'imagery and practices of sanatoriums and asylums of old … devices of hospital lore become the stuff of nightmares … the mania of two particular patients who seem to be violently reliving the events in their lives that continue to torture their souls'.[3] Lana Lane's 2005 rock album, *Lady Macbeth*, takes the point of view of Lady Macbeth, beginning with 'The Dream That Never Ends', and ending with 'Dunsinane Walls'.[4]

Many albums or bands are simply titled 'Macbeth', including the album *Macbeth* by 'The Frail Ophelias'[5] and a competitor album by the appropriately named band 'Skeleton Worm'.[6] The German heavy metal band *Rebellion*'s debut album was 'Shakespeare's Macbeth – A Tragedy in Steel', with ten songs and spoken dialogue, from 'Disdaining Fortune' to 'Die With Harness on Your Back'.[7] And how could a metal band named 'Megadeth' *not* have some link to its punning namesake?[8] Their song 'Kill the King' is right out of Kott. The attraction between Shakespeare's dark play and heavy metal/industrial/punk music seems inevitable: machismo, violence, darkness. Moreover, an uncountable number of lines from the play are quoted in popular music. Elvis Costello's song 'Miss Macbeth' includes somewhat sympathetic lyrics – she has been done wrong – but ultimately suggests she will have no redemption.[9] The late rapper Tupac Shakur included a song 'Something Wicked' with hypnotic repetitions of the play's 'Something wicked this way comes'. There must be hundreds more songs borrowing lines or ideas from the play.

On a lighter note, Paul Boyd's 1992 *Macbeth the Musical* was loosely based 'on Shakespeare's infamous Scottish play, populated with comically re-imagined versions of ... Lord and Lady Macbeth, a plethora of Macduffs, the doomed King Duncan, the beautiful Banquette, as well as an entire Scottish army in disguise, the Glasgow Operatic Chorus in full voice, and three beehived witches in training. The musical features a soundtrack of original rock, pop, and West End/Broadway-style songs'.[10] A darker adaptation, the *XXI Century Macbeth*, a 2003 chamber ballet version, includes scenes such as (in English translation) 'Prophecy', 'Death of the Lady', and 'Revenge'.[11]

Shakespeare's *Macbeth* was, to be sure, musical from its inception: there are numerous calls in the play for sennets, flourishes, hautboys, and dancing. Most famously, the songs in 3.5 and 4.1 probably added by Middleton were expanded and added to in Davenant's adaptation (see **Introduction**), to the extent that his version has sometimes been called the 'first opera'. While Simon Forman's account of a 1611 performance did not mention any music, the playgoer/diarist Samuel Pepys, who saw Davenant's version several times, explicitly praised its 'dancing and musick' in 1667 (Pepys 1908: 2.219), and a few years later, after likely further revisions following Davenant's death, the former actor John Downes wrote that this version, 'with all the singing and dancing in it: the first composed by Mr. Lock, the other by Mr. Channell and Mr. Joseph Preist; it being all excellently performed, being in the nature of an opera, it recompensed double the expense'. It still proved, he concluded, 'a lasting play' (Brooke 1990: 38), but by then it was no longer Shakespeare's nor quite Davenant's either. In 1809, J. C. Cross repurposed the music 'of the late Matthew Locke' (B2v) in his

Ballet of Music and Action. As we saw in the **Introduction**, singing and dancing witches multiplied in numbers and routines for the next century or more. Parodies and burlesques in the nineteenth century produced music hall versions of the music, as it became ever less 'serious'.

This chapter will consider some more-or-less 'serious' musical treatments of *Macbeth*, looking at the ways in which composers have understood and adapted the play's narrative: which parts or elements of the play recur in musical treatments, which are suppressed, and in some cases, how the play is staged. After a survey of some musical adaptations, I will turn to three operas – by Verdi, Bloch, and Sciarrino – that have transformed Shakespeare's play.

Film and theatre scores

Every production of *Macbeth* – stage, theatre, television – has produced some kind of musical soundtrack, often original. The English composer William Walton's best-known Shakespeare compositions were for Olivier's films (*Hamlet, Henry V, Richard III*), but he also wrote a pastiche for a 1941 *Macbeth* directed by and starring John Gielgud. Another distinguished composer, Jacques Ibert, who had at one time worked as a silent-film pianist, wrote the score for Orson Welles's 1948 film; the 'Suite symphonique' published separately includes, after the Overture, five key scenes: 'Murder of King Duncan', 'Macbeth after the Murder', 'The Ghost of Banquo', 'Death of Lady Macbeth', and, in a reprise of the Authorized Version, 'Triumph of Macduff's Armies'. As we saw in **Chapter Three**, however, Welles's film ends with the return of Fleance, picking up the fallen crown. Williams (2006) notes how Ibert quoted from other films and music: the drums during Cawdor's execution evoke Welles's earlier 'voo-doo' production, while the music around the drunken, crowned Macbeth 'parodies themes associated with ... Prokofiev'.

More recently, the contemporary British composer David C. Hëwitt[12] composed an intense score for Nicholas Paton's (still unreleased) 2008 film set in 'London ganglands ... Part of a noble gang, feared by the villainous, respected by the community, the vigilante Macbeth protects his friends and neighbors from the violent crime committed by malevolent street gangs', but turns into a brutal, immoral gang leader.[13] The National Theatre of Northern Greece commissioned a complete score by *Daemonia Nymphe* in 2018; the first track, 'Macbeth's triumph', is suitably martial, then blending into bagpipes, while the last, 'Malcolm's victory', features a Celtic-sounding alto singing 'When the battle's lost and won etc …. fair is foul and foul is fair' with bagpipes doing 'Scotland the Brave' to end the track (and presumably the play, with pretty clearly a Good Malcolm).[14] Yuri Kochurov's 1940 incidental music was for a production which he then developed over several years into his *Macbeth Symphony for Grand Orchestra*. Richard Strauss's influence is evident throughout. As Barnard (2010) observes, in Kochurov's program notes for the premiere 'there is not a single reference in it to the witches or the supernatural only "evil growing in Macbeth's heart" and "dark forces"' – omitting the witches seems unique among composers, whether instrumental or operatic. Kochurov was fortunate, Barnard believes, to evade censorship for this piece, which ends in a 'positive' cymbals-clashing triumphant march. The Scottish composer Geraldine Mucha composed a score for a 1965 ballet version, parts of which were condensed into a twelve-minute Suite of key scenes: after an overture, 'Witches', 'Banquet', 'Lady Macbeth Sleepwalking', and an exciting finale, 'Death of Macbeth and Conclusion'. A Slovenian music group called Laibach composed a score for a 1987 production in Hamburg, Germany. The avant-garde industrial music – often dissonant, bombastic and exciting – has an eerie final section titled 'Agnus Dei (Exil und Tod)'.

Songs without words

'Classical' composers who work without words have a real challenge in taking on the play, but many have made the attempt. There were many Shakespearean musical compositions in the long Victorian era, following the exaltation of Shakespeare's 'word music' in Romantic aesthetics. Berlioz, Dvořák, Tchaikovsky, Liszt, Wagner and others took on various Shakespeare plays. Among those drawn to *Macbeth* was Bedrich Smetana, who composed a short piano piece, 'Macbeth and the Witches' (1859; printed posthumously in 1912). After an intense minor-key excursion, with Lizstian influences, the piece improbably ends on a major chord. Arthur Sullivan (of Gilbert and Sullivan) composed incidental music in 1888 for the production by Sir Henry Irving (as Macbeth and Ellen Terry as Lady Macbeth). Of the thirteen individual numbers (some music was lost in a fire at the Lyceum Theatre in 1898), most are for the first part of the play, and very little for Lady Macbeth. The musical highpoints are the sections for the witches, and the Overture (see DeLong 2008). Richard Strauss's first symphonic poem was his *Macbeth* (1887–8; revised later), influenced by 'Wagner's use of the *leitmotif* to associate 'abstract ideas [such] as power and ambition, with particular musical themes, also using them to represent specific dramatic events – Duncan's murder, the crowning of Macbeth, and, toward the end, distant fanfares representing the triumph of Macduff' (Kirzinger 2015: 36). Hans von Bülow criticized the original score's ending: 'It is all very well for an Egmont Overture to conclude with a triumphal march of Egmont, but a symphonic poem *Macbeth* can never finish with the triumph of Macduff', so Strauss dampened it down, 'leaving only suggestions of a distant triumphal march for Macduff' (Mandel 2015: 40). A thematic unit 'marked *appassionato* and starting sinuously in the winds, is clearly meant to represent Lady Macbeth, some of whose words are printed at this point in the score: "Hie thee thither [etc.]"' (41). Basically a character study of the two principals, there is little attempt to follow the plot of the play closely.

The Moravian composer Ignaz Brüll's 'Macbeth Overture' (1884) is filled with thrilling and dramatic gestures. Finally, the nineteenth-century German-Swiss composer Joseph Joachim Raff wrote an orchestral prelude to *Macbeth* in 1882. 'The work begins', as Thomas (2017) describes, 'with swirling woodwind depicting the three witches in Raff's best spectral fashion, followed by short statements of the themes which seem to represent Macbeth and his companion Banquo – the one full of nervous strength, the other rather calmer and nobler, showing the Thane's alter ego. All three are then mixed in a stormy passage depicting the play's opening scene'. Lady Macbeth, the writer suggests, is represented by 'a new and slippery melody', while the piece as a whole focuses around 'Macbeth's persistent struggle with his conscience'. The finale once again provides a Good Malcolm, as shown 'by the triumphant peroration of his theme to have succeeded his father to the Scottish throne'. Leichtling's detailed analysis (2004) shows the 'motivic layout', step by step and second by second, of this complex eleven-minute piece. Leichtling's invitation – 'Imagine, if you will, Shakespeare's great five act drama being condensed into an eleven minute long newsreel, or flashback sequence in which there is barely time to expose the characters, the situations, or the overall dramatic scope of the play. Instead of complete scenes, you have the briefest of excerpts' – reflects the enormous difficulty of adapting a play like *Macbeth*, or indeed any play, into music. As with much programmatic music, it would be difficult to guess the play without such notes. Perhaps the most effective way of representing *Macbeth* musically is through opera.

Operatic *Macbeth*[15]

As seen in the **Introduction**, Beethoven discussed the idea of an opera based on *Macbeth* with Heinrich Joseph von Collin, the playwright responsible for *Coriolan,* for which Beethoven had written an overture. Traces of this never-completed project survive in Beethoven's notebooks: the overture 'fällt gleich in den Chor der Hexen ein' (begins with a chorus of witches; Johnson 1985: 213). Collin's first act was printed in 1809, but he died before completing the libretto, and nothing more seems to have come of the project. The libretto includes Hecate and the Chorus of Witches singing 'Where the wild storms rage ... All around, / Around and around, / Lightning flashes, thunder cracks; / The open jaw yawns. / All around, / Around and around' (Nottebohm 1887: 226). A not entirely successful attempt was made in 2001 to reconstruct the few traces of the overture by melding it with other, known works of the time and proximity in the notebooks.[16] Beethoven's only completed opera, *Fidelio*, ends with a triumphant chorus celebrating the overthrow of tyranny; possibly his *Macbeth* would have ended in a similar way, as Verdi's does.

Perhaps the earliest completed opera of the play, by Hippolyte Chèlard, premiered at the Paris Opera in 1827 – a failure cancelled after five performances, though later, after revision, quite successful in Germany and at Drury Lane (Primmer 2001). Chèlard's libretto might have been part of the initial problem: it covers only the first two acts of the play; it eliminated Banquo, Macduff, and Malcolm altogether; Duncan's only child is a girl, which, to say the least, complicates the succession issues; the murder of Duncan is concealed until the end of the play, when Lady Macbeth reveals it in the sleep-walking scene. Dean (1964: 157) summarizes the opening: it 'begins with a chorus of depressed soldiers who propose to discard their arms and bury their flags because they cannot find Macbeth'. The libretto also invents the Ghost of Duncan (see **Chapter Two**). Dean also describes a lost opera by Lauro Rossi, *Biorn* (1877), for which none of the music survived in print, so disastrous was its premier (Budden 2001). The action of the play was transferred to Norway: the witches became Norns; Lady Macbeth was named 'Editha' (Dean 1964: 161).

Speaking of Norway, Oslo Norway television showed the premier of the compelling 1989 opera *Macbeth* by the Italian-Norwegian composer Antonio Bibalo.[17] The English libretto follows the Folio closely. The staging was surrealist/expressionist with off-kilter sets and giant paper crowns (**Figure 14**). The highly dramatic music perfectly reflects the production's extremity of emotions. Unlike

FIGURE 14 Macbeth *opera by Antonio Bibalo, directed by Antonio Pappano. NOR Oslo Norway Television production 1989. https://youtu. be/ziZII4ede90. All rights reserved. Screen grab.*

many adapters, Bibalo retains an abbreviated version of the Porter, who wears a clown's makeup/face with red bulb on his nose. As Duncan's dead body is carried out, Lady Macbeth takes the crown off his head and holds it: she certainly is not one to faint. The second act begins with Macbeth crowned, his back to the audience on his throne, hiring the murderers to go after Banquo; his death and Fleance's escape are shown in a scene with violent atonalities. The Cauldron scene opens on a stage littered with bodies, the three witches (as before) clad in black with mysterious white runes all over their bodies. At the end, after Macduff crowns Malcolm, who walks slowly towards the back of the stage followed by his thanes, Macduff looks towards the audience, and the witches slither out to give him another giant crown, under whose weight he falls. The witches mark runic symbols on his body: thus Bibalo provides a circular ending, as the process will begin all over again. This work deserves a wider audience.

Giuseppe Verdi

Verdi's opera of *Macbeth* is, in the judgement of most critics, his first great opera and also considered the greatest of all musical versions of the play; as one critic has said, Verdi was 'the most Shakespearean of all opera composers' (Schmidgall 1990: 61). The scholarship on the opera is immense and enlightening.[18] Verdi worked from an Italian translation by Rusconi, though he may have consulted as many as six translations (Weaver 1984). His librettist, Francesco Piave, played a secondary role to Verdi (who had written out the entire plot – from Rusconi – in prose) and to others whom Verdi consulted. The translations Rusconi and others provided in turn derived from yet other translations (Letourneur's in French; perhaps Schiller's in German). Verdi's wife knew English, but he did not, and he had never seen the play performed (nor had it yet been, in Italy). To complete the rhizomatic diagram, Verdi's work was itself almost immediately adapted and transformed in performance in ways that parallel the Folio's transformations.

Verdi's opera could easily have been a case study in **Chapter One**, as it is 'political' in many ways. Its first performance, coming just a year before the European-wide revolutions of 1848, was in Florence, a city that permitted Verdi to write the plot he wanted. The 1847 version – I discuss the 1865 revision below – required a chorus of at least eighteen witches, in three covens, and the focus was primarily on Macbeth and his Lady, with almost all the Folio's dialogue from other characters removed, along with the Porter, the on-stage murder of Macduff's family, and so on. Indeed, Verdi wrote in an 1865 letter that 'there are three roles in this opera and three is all there can be: *Lady Macbeth*, *Macbeth*, and the *chorus of witches*'; moreover, 'The witches dominate the drama; everything derives from them ... They are truly a character, and a character of the utmost importance' (Rosen and Porter 1984: 99). Verdi's narrowing of focus might at first seem less 'political' than psychological, but when the Fourth Act begins and the Chorus sings '*Patria oppressa*', the immediate relevance to Italy was clear: Verdi's support for the *Risorgimento* and the revolutions of 1848 was strong. In any event, his 1847 *Macbeth* did not travel well outside of Florence. In Austrian-occupied Milan, the offending lines were not sung: so '*Patria oppressa*' became '*Noi perduti!*' and '*La patria tradita*' became '*La fede tradita*' (356). In Rome, references to the supernatural had to be erased, so there were gypsies telling cards rather than witches, while in Sicily regicide itself, always a dangerous topic, was erased – Duncan became Count Walfred, 'a very rich Scottish nobleman, King Duncan's first military general' (356). Some had objected to Verdi's Duncan, who not only has no lines in the opera but has none of the sacred aspects that made his murder so heinous.

The ending of the two versions, as we will now see, differs considerably. In 1847, Verdi's final scene provides Macbeth with a long dying speech; though it does not seem to have been taken from Garrick's, it too provides a moralistic resolution:

I have sinned, for I have trusted in
The prophecies of hell.
All the blood that I have shed
Cries to the face of the Eternal!
On the brow of the accursed
Its revenge will strike!
I die! Abandoned by earth and Heaven,
Accursed crown! And only for you. [*dies*]

Macduff then announces that distressed Scotland can 'breathe again' and all hail Malcolm, 'now our king' (*il nostro Re*).[19]

Shortly after his work's premier, Verdi travelled to England, where he saw his first performance of *Macbeth*, acted by William Macready. As Bradshaw (2004: 48–9) points out, had Verdi stayed in London a little longer, he could have seen Samuel Phelps's 'unprecedented but short-lived attempt at an authentic staging, which reduced the army of witches, eliminated the dying speech, and even reinstated the Porter and the Macduff family'. But Verdi, having discovered that there was no dying speech, did drastically reduce Macbeth's final words in the 1865 revisions for the Paris production. Now, Macbeth simply says '*Cielo*' ('Heaven'), and Verdi provided a new, massive chorus of praise for 'Victory!' and thanks to Macduff, '*A chi ne liberò*' ('to him who has set us free'), who has 'saved our homeland and our king'. Malcolm ends the 1865 version with an even more positive message than the Folio's: 'Scotland, trust in me. / The tyrant is dead. / I shall make everlasting / The joy of such a victory' (Fisher 2017: 64–5). This great chorus of victory is wholly positive: the terms 'victory' and liberation carried enormous political weight. The contrast between the two endings has provided adapters fertile ground for staging.

In both 1847 and 1865 versions, Lady Macbeth is at the centre of events: she has far more agency and is far more dominant than in most adaptations. She prompts the murders, actively prodding Macbeth to murder Banquo, whereas in the Folio she is to 'Be innocent of the knowledge' (3.2.46). In neither version does Lady Macbeth faint or get carried out. In the 1865 revision, Verdi gave her a new aria, in which she speaks Macbeth's words from the Folio ('Light thickens' etc., 3.2.51) as '*La luce langue*'. In both versions, the sleepwalking scene is 'the musical high point of the opera', as Barish (2004: 149) notes. Verdi had termed the scene one of the 'two principal numbers in the opera' (Rosen and Porter 1984: 67), along with the duet between her and Lady Macbeth. Verdi's letters reveal his exceedingly close attention to the vocal qualities he required of the singer: 'I would like the Lady to have a harsh, stifled, and hollow voice', the vocal equivalent of her appearance: 'I would like Lady Macbeth to be ugly and evil' (67).

Verdi's adaptations thus intensely focused the story onto the two main characters and the witches, while at the same time, especially in the 1865 version, emphasizing liberation and delivery from tyranny. Most productions now present the 1865 text and music more or less as written – a musical equivalent to the Authorized Version. But as with Folio adaptations, more cynical readings of the rhetoric and politics of 'liberation' have become prominent. Many modern productions have rewritten the triumphant 1865 ending, as we saw in the return of Fleance (**Chapter Three; see Figure 6**) in particular. And Verdi's opera, no less than the Folio, has been translated into far different periods of history and locations. A 2018 Berlin production, for example, opens on a battlefield, with smoke rising against a ruined post-apocalyptic landscape; Lady Macbeth enters carrying a sword in one hand and a doll in the other. The set switches back and forth between this wasteland and a castle with white leather sofas. The projection of burning oilfields, ruined castles, and industrial wastelands underscores its temporal moment, the twentieth century, complete with refugees and Fascist military garb; a whole platoon of caped soldiers waylays Banquo and Fleance. This version ended without any chorus of victory, but with Macbeth's death speech taken from the 1847 version; even then, the production offered neither the 1847 entry of Malcolm and Macduff and the final chorus '*il nostro Re*', nor the chorus and promise of the 1865 ending, but with Macduff and Malcolm each holding a side of the crown (actually, in this production, a royal sash), looking at one another, as the curtain falls. As the program note said, 'The battle for succession begins immediately' (Giese 2018: 48): it is about as Kottian a vision of future division as could be offered.[20]

Shakespeare's play is performed and adapted probably thousands of times more frequently than Verdi's opera, but any number of productions of the opera as an Authorized Version could be described, even in updated settings and time periods; yet others, like the Berlin production described above, adapt the play in ways similar to many post-war stage and film productions of the Folio. One of the most radical reimaginings of Verdi's opera was by the (white) South African director, Brett Bailey, in 2014. A series of title cards at the beginning set the location as 'North Kivu Province, Democratic Republic of Congo, 2013'. Here,

A troupe of refugee performers flees a war that has killed several million in the past 20 years / They discover an old trunk containing the paraphernalia of a colonial-era amateur production of Verdi's MACBETH / They use the material they find to tell the story of conflict in their region.[21]

Bailey worked with the composer Fabrizio Cassol, who composed a second score in parallel and often in conflict with Verdi's. The company, Third World Bunfight, was joined by 10 South African opera singers and the 'renowned trans-Balkan "No Borders Orchestra"'. The Chorus of witches[22] is reduced to three village women, being threatened by a guard; the opera is shrunk to ninety minutes; the Italian lyrics are translated into completely different meanings (*Che faceste? Dite su!* – What have you been doing? Tell us! – becomes 'How much do you reckon we'll make?', Wong 2017: 272). Wong sums up Bailey's project succinctly: this 'adaptation-within-an-adaptation foregrounds the socio-economical landscape of a postcolonial Africa by addressing the on-going, and yet little-known, ethnic and military conflicts in the DRC fueled by greed and corruption of multinational corporations and regional governments and generals' (269). Bailey thus, for want of a better term, deconstructs both Verdi and Shakespeare through inventive techniques of Brechtian-style alienation: screen projections of scenes, projections of text, puppet-like movements of some characters, modernizations such as smartphone texts, all while pursuing the political narrative: 'Driven by their greed for minerals, a cabal of multinationals – the witches – manipulates the rise and fall of the Macbeth regime'. The globalization of *Macbeth* and of Verdi's opera is thus set into a context of globalized entertainment capitalism in post-colonial Africa.

Ernest Bloch

Bloch's opera of *Macbeth* was first performed at the Opéra-Comique, Paris, in 1910; at the time, Verdi's version was unknown to Bloch, as the 1865 Verdi production in Paris ended after only fourteen performances and essentially disappeared from the French repertoire for decades. Eventually, Verdi's version far outpaced Bloch's in terms of popularity and performance; indeed, Henig shows the intermittent history of Bloch's through 2014: 'Slightly short of one hundred performances [anywhere in the world] over slightly more than a century', though enough to establish it as 'surely permanent on the outer fringes of the wider operatic repertoire' (Henig 2016: 167) – as further indicated by the lack (as far as can be determined) of any video version of the full opera, just brief excerpts from a few productions.

Musicologists who have heard or studied the score offer praise, noting similarities or influences from Debussy and Moussorgsky. In a 1908 letter, Bloch commented on his intentions:

> I conceive the prologue in my music and orchestration in a manner very vague and nebulous, drowned in the fog of twilight. There is an atmosphere of emotion and mystery proper to the suggestions of the witches. In writing my music, I have been constantly haunted by lighting. It must play also a role and one of the most important. As much as the settings must be static, crude and barbaric, so the lighting is mobile, alive and expressive. I have also taken notes on the concordance and the music, mainly in the dark cavern of the witches barely lighted, but where some certain harmonies a bit cabalistic come out like a mysterious glow. (Hening 2016: 152)

Commenting on Bloch's 'emerging originality' in this opera, Kushner (2002) singles out the sleepwalking scene: 'Instead of a full-blown aria, Bloch provides the dishevelled Queen with pitches more closely associated with the speaking voice, allowing Shakespeare's words to be the focus of attention. This approach, far removed from the high drama accorded this scene in Verdi's version, makes all the more powerful the tremendous climax that follows.'

Bloch followed the Folio closely, though in some later productions the scene in which Macduff's family is murdered was often cut, partly to shorten the opera, partly because it seemed too brutal to reviewers. It seems clear, from Bloch's own comments, that he saw the play as the Authorized Version. He saw Lady Macbeth as 'the veritable pivot of the drama, the soul even of the crime: one must constantly feel her presence, which is always decisive' (Henig 2016: 152), though Bloch's Lady is not as dominant a figure as Verdi's. The three main roles – Macbeth, Lady, and Macduff – Bloch said, 'are essentially in motion. They evolve constantly' (152). Several years before Freud's famous comments on the Macbeths in *Some Character-types Met with in Psycho-analytical Work* (1916) – that

'Together they exhaust the possibilities of reaction to the crime, like two disunited parts of a single psychical individuality' (Freud 1970: 137) – Bloch had intuited their chiastic relationship in musical terms: 'Honest and weak, [Macbeth] becomes at the end terrible. His line is a gigantic crescendo. Contrarily, Lady Macbeth … falls before Macbeth. Her line is a diminuendo'. The ending of Bloch's opera rests on an optimistic, royalist reading: while Macduff becomes 'bloodthirsty' for a time, after he kills Macbeth he 'finds himself again, containing the mob and designating Malcolm as King. A new life begins … Forget the past'. Duncan is of course Good Duncan, with 'the sole scene of light in the drama' and Malcolm is the 'worthy son of the father' (Henig 2016: 152). The positive nature of Bloch's ending was noted in a 2009 performance in London – the first time it was staged in full in 'Shakespeare's own country' since its premier (165). The production (in English) was set in the First World War, even though, one reviewer commented, 'precise parallels were not entirely clear' (Miller 2009: 62), with a 'potent' 'final victory chorus, with Birnam Wood marching on Dunsinane'. The crowning of Malcolm was 'celebrated with a melodic lilt and choral vigour pre-echoing Kurt Weill' (63) – a somewhat odd comparison, given Weill's often ironic and sardonic take on politics.

Sciarrino

Salvatore Sciarrino worked on his 2002 opera *Macbeth: tre atti senza nome (da Shakespeare)* for twenty-five years; in it, he is trying to 'awaken our social consciences' and shake 'us out of indifference'. The premier in Frankfurt deployed 'optically contorted imagery' to 'give visual reality to the eerie and nightmarish soundscape',[23] with overlapping distorted perspectival lines, as if Fritz Lang had been involved in the geometric chaos. This set seems to have reflected the stage direction to Act Two, Scene Two of Sciarrino's libretto (his own), which calls for a perspective which is 'dizzyingly foreshortened from below, and yet it develops horizontally towards the bottom, where the ceiling stands out, so that the presence of the protagonists in the foreground – or looking out of real people from the arcades, give a strong sense of dimensional imbalance' (Sciarrino 2002: 5).[24] The set designer, Achim Freyer, was said to have been inspired by perspectives by the sixteenth-century architect Jan Vredeman de Vries. Hodges (2003) describes the staging's effect at the US premier in New York: 'some of the stagecraft was absolutely startling. At one point Macbeth appeared to walk down the left wall, his body parallel to the floor. (And make no mistake, he was singing in this position, also.) Lady Macbeth made a similar entrance, rising up horizontally from the floor on the left side. But later the back wall became the floor, as if we were now gazing down from high above, with silhouettes of cast members visible in the tiny windows far below.' There was a completely different set and staging at the 2014 Opera Lab Berlin production, disturbing and disorienting in a completely different way, judging by the brief videos available.[25]

Sciarrino's libretto condenses and compresses the plot considerably, with several of the Folio's secondary figures given few if any lines. The witches are '*Voci*', voices, uttering lines from their own Folio speeches but also from other figures in the play, as if the agency of Shakespeare's witches 'has become dispersed and generalized throughout the musical texture of the piece' (Bishop 2013: 145).[26] The plot's action produces even more gaps than the Folio text, moving from the murder scene (2.2), omitting the Porter scene and Macduff's entrance, to the very abbreviated and only suggested murder of Banquo (3.3) directly into the Banquet scene (3.4). Perhaps Sciarrino's most distinctive innovation comes in the long (relative to the rest of the libretto) banquet scene, in which – for one of the few times in *any* adaptation – the Ghost (*lo spettro*) of Banquo *speaks*, his disturbing lines punctuated by the *Voci*, as in this sequence:

> MACBETH It stands in front of me. It would scare even the devil
> THE SPECTRE you mock all human strength:
> VOICES The eye breaks on a new gorgon (6)

When the Ghost returns later in the scene, it not only speaks some of the prophecies from 4.1, accompanied by the *Voci*, but Sciarrino ratchets up the tension by adding another Ghost (*Lo spettro si moltiplica*), with a mirror in its hand (7), as in the Line of Kings in 4.1. Sciarrino further marks the uncanny appearance of the ghosts through musical quotations from Mozart's *Don Giovanni* and from Verdi's *Macbeth*.

The third act introduces a formally named Chorus in the sleep-walking scene. The stage direction here is as detailed as earlier ones: 'The same space as the previous scene, but with an inverted perspective foreshortening; at the bottom stands the floor seen from above. The loggia now appear almost deserted. Backing away, Lady seems to fall very slowly into the void, and the fall will continue almost to the end of the scene. It is night' (9). Lady Macbeth here begins her monologue exactly as Verdi began – '*Una macchia*' – with many further verbal quotations. At the end of the scene, her 'fall accelerates suddenly ... as if she is sucked into the space in the background. Her bundled-up body remains at the bottom' (9). She implodes into a void.

Bishop notes how Sciarrino 'cuts from his libretto all elaboration of a specific political environment for the action, beyond the few mere place-names retained from Shakespeare' (Bishop 2013: 138), but the libretto's ending reflects some familiar politically adaptive moves. Since Malcolm is not in the opera at all, the ending suggests that Macduff takes over. The stage directions at the end indicate a transferal not only of power but of identity: Macduff, moving toward Macbeth, extends his hand toward Macbeth's face, repeating Macbeth's gesture in the first act. Macduff then 'tears off the mask' and puts it on his own face. Macbeth is revealed to be 'disfigured by a monstrous disease' ('*un morbo mostruoso*'), as 'darkness engulfs' him (Sciarrino 2002: 11). The work ends with a *Congedo*, a leave-taking, which begins 'Not a trace. / The unspeakable is too sacred / to disperse [or "lose"] it in signs' (11). While many productions of the play and the opera evoke the terror that Ducis struggled with or the horror of the Goold film, Sciarrino has, as few others have done, combined them into a profound spectral eeriness.

Metal Macbeth

To move from the sublime and terrible to something very different, this chapter concludes with a Japanese rock-musical adaptation, *Metal Macbeth* (2006). Hidenori Inoue, the director, places this long post-apocalyptic metal/rock version of the play on two parallel temporal planes. The first is Tokyo in the 1980s, when a heavy metal rock band named Metal Macbeth, starring Macbeth Uchino (members include Banquo Hashimoto and Macduff Kitamura), rises to prominence. The second time frame is the year 2206, when a warrior named Randomstar (who is the reincarnation of Macbeth Uchino, played by the same actor) meets three witches who greet him as 'Macbeth' and hand him a CD of the 1980s band. Seeing that he looks like the 1980s rocker, Randomstar uploads the CD's contents into his own brain; the songs on the CD ('None of Woman Born', etc.) prophesy his future.[27]

Metal Macbeth does so many different things at the same time that it is difficult to unpack. There are invocations and parodies of the academic Shakespeare industry, for example: in one scene, a character outlines some of the stage history of *Macbeth*. There are allusions to Kurosawa's *Throne of Blood*, among others specific to Japanese culture that Yoshihara explicates. The visual aesthetic of the film reflects both traditional stagings (e.g. the sleep-walking scene) and contemporary dystopian films such as the *Mad Max* franchise.[28] Inoue stages a frenetic ending: first, Lady Macbeth is shown (on a projection screen) jumping to her death. Then, the ghost of Duncan appears to Randomstar as Macduff enters the scene. As Randomstar and Macduff battle, the ghost of Lady Macbeth appears, and Macduff takes advantage of the distraction to slash Randomstar with his sword. The final moments of Randomstar's life come during a phantasmagoric strobe light/ electrical storm blowout, his arm in the air with his fifth and second fingers raised (in the 'rock on' sign). In the smoking ruins of the castle, and civilization itself, Macduff enters with both Randomstar's guitar and his severed arm. The final image is of Macduff raising the arm in grisly triumph, as the head-banging music reaches a crescendo, while the spectral images of Macbeth Uchino and 'Rose' (Lady Macbeth) rise in the background. Yoshihara has explained the significance of the film's dating of Macbeth Uchino's death in 1989: that year 'was, globally, the year of the Tiananmen "Incident", the dismantling of the Berlin Wall and the beginning of the end of the Cold War. Locally, it was the year of the death of Emperor Hirohito, and the beginning of Japan's long economical [*sic*] recession after the bursting of the economic bubble' (140). Inoue's musical adaptation of *Macbeth* is boldly transgressive and disorienting, reflecting popular culture and the global commodity known as 'Shakespeare' to an extraordinary degree.

FIGURE 15 Metal Macbeth *directed by Hidenori Inoue* © *Village/ Gekidan Shinkansen 2006. All rights reserved. Screen grab.*

Music may or may not be a 'universal language' (as Longfellow said) or the 'language of the soul' (Hegel), but many composers have sought a musical language to represent the narrative of *Macbeth*, and have remade the play as their own. The operas created from the play parallel the history of stage adaptations in many ways, with familiar cuts, emphases (it is a rare composer who does not find musical inspiration in the witches), and 'political' revisions or enhancements. While Verdi and others usually saw the play in terms of the Authorized Version, more recent composers and stagings have turned the narratives in Kottian and post-modern directions.

Epilogue: *Macbeth* 3.0

Whole worlds of adaptation have not yet been considered, especially many contemporary parodies. There is the Second City's 'Sassy Gay Friend: Macbeth', in which Lady Macbeth's madness and death could have been prevented by the helpful eponymous friend's intervention ('Queen of Scotland? Really? I mean, it's lovely, but it's smaller than Ohio')[1]; the 'Letter from the Condo Association to Mr. and Mrs. Macbeth', notifying them of breaches of the 'association's regulations and rules of conduct' such as 'the unauthorized use of a cauldron, in non-conformity with Article 32.7: "Installation of Appliances"' (Murray 2020); the full-length play *Scots on the Rocks*[2]; the compilation of anecdotes (most about the supposed curse) in *There Is Nothing like a Thane*; and on and on. Then there is fan fiction,[3] comic books, versions for children below the young adult market, karaoke, graphic novels, computer simulation games, and an entirely green screen film that 'magnifies the raw, dark, imaginative power of the text with an extraordinary, dynamic modern aesthetic – making the play both viscerally entertaining and giving it contemporary relevance'.[4] The proliferation of streaming sites and digital innovations has made almost any written commentary obsolete before it even reaches print.

Popular television versions abound, from Black Adder ('Don't Mention Macbeth') to the Simpsons' *MacHomer* ('Is this a dagger I see before me? Or is it sauce?').[5] There are multiple references in the *Star Trek* series, from episode titles ('Dagger of the Mind', 'All Our Yesterdays') to a play-within-the-episode performance of the murder scene in *Macbeth* in Season One's 'The Conscience of the King'. The episode begins with a theatre group on Planet Q performing the scene: the first image is the dagger, which Macbeth then plunges into the sleeping Duncan, thus showing the murder in exceptional openness. The actor Karidian is recognized, however, as actually Kodos the Executioner, former governor and mass murderer. The episode then shifts into a *Hamlet*-like revenge plot, a poisoning, and a production of *Hamlet*. This proliferation of texts and objects demonstrates once again the rhizomatic nature of the adaptive gesture, long since unmoored from the Folio text.

The past few decades have also witnessed many radical reimaginings of the play's plot. The 2017 play *The Macbeths* compresses the entire action into seventy minutes: 'Set entirely on and around the couple's bed, it explores the destructive relationship at the heart of the story.'[6] In one reviewer's words, 'The result is a sweaty, erotic and breathlessly self-destructive re-imagining that casts the Macbeths as serial killers driven to extremes by their own distress' (Cooper 2017). Versions like this concentrate their focus on the domestic couple and their crippling psychological problems; another reviewer described them as 'like victims of post traumatic stress trying to kill their partners in sleep' (McMillan 2017). Similarly, a 2016 Welsh production offered an adaptation which 'stripped back action and character to zoom in on the dynamics of the killer couple, tracking their murderous ambitions, escalating anxieties and disintegrating bonds against a backdrop of sensual pleasure and normalized violence'.[7] Surely no adaptation of the play has taken the idea of mental illness further than Alan Cumming's one-man version of the play, in which 'Macbeth' is a patient in a Victorian-style mental asylum, observed by a doctor and nurse, who come onto the set to sedate him when he is too far gone: the entire play is in his head. The witches are Cumming on three TV monitors; as both Macbeth and Lady Macbeth in 1.7 ('Bring forth men-children only'), he assumes both positions in a charged representation of sex. Cumming's virtuoso performance offers perhaps the most desperate mentally ill Macbeth on record, gaining enormous power through its claustrophobic focus, but at the same time in effect erasing the 'outside' world altogether.

Recent years have also seen an increase in what might be called oblique adaptations – spinning off a character or an issue to create an entirely new version. *Queer Lady M* (2020) is a one-person play in cabaret style which 'brings together drag, devised performance and Shakespeare while exploring the real-life experiences of working-class, gender-fluid artist Shane Gabriel'.[8] As I write this, the Chicago Shakespeare Theater is streaming a one-man (plus Fleance) performance called *I, Banquo*, written by Tim Crouch, in which Banquo, who 'had a rough go of it' in Shakespeare, here 'considers how he might have responded to the prophesies of the Weird Sisters had he been in Macbeth's position – questioning his own motives, desires, and temptations'.[9] Among the most successful such adaptations was Bill Cain's 2009 play, *Equivocation*, playing off the Porter's allusions to the Gunpowder Plot, the trial of Henry Garnet and the doctrine of equivocation in the political context of 1606. Garnet's persecutor, Robert Cecil, is the real equivocator in Cain's play, having invented the plot as a way to justify his persecution of Catholics. He commissions the playwright 'William Shagspeare', or 'Shag', to write a play celebrating the defeat of the Plot and justifying Cecil, but Shag – his political principles at work – instead writes *Macbeth*, part of which is performed before King James as a play-within-the-play, punctuated by commentary from the actors and audience. With the defeat of Macbeth and the severing of his head, the cast cries to King James, 'Hail, King of Scotland!' (Cain 2014: 118). James notes that Shag has written a play about 'a man of no conscience, with ambitions above his station, a killer of royalty, careless of his wife, with a spy in every house who dies utterly unpitied. They did a play – (*Then, to Cecil.*) about YOU!', at which point the stage direction reads: '*James tosses Cecil Macbeth's severed head. Cecil catches it. Looks at it*' (119). In his 'Author's Note' to the printed text, Cain justifies his approach: 'The only thing we know with certainty about the event [the Gunpowder Plot] itself is that it could not possibly have occurred in the way the government claimed. What follows offers a plausible alternative' (4).

Immersive *Macbeth*

At the 2018 annual Verdi Festival in Parma, a 'Macbeth Immersive Experience' was created:

> A large cube, an apparently empty box, in the center of the Piazza del Duomo ... Inside, a world made up of images, lights, shadows, dreamlike visions and music that expand the space, cancel the horizon and project the viewer into Macbeth's

world. Ambition and the supernatural are translated into visual and sound elements ... [At night], the installation enters into dialogue with the surrounding space, projecting its images on the historic buildings of the square ... each passer-by can immerse themselves'.[10]

The brief advertising video gives only a hint of what it must have been like – a totally non-verbal adaptation associated with the most famous musical adaptation.

The Verdi/Parma immersive experience takes one far away from the Folio, but the most renowned immersive experience of recent years – Punchdrunk Theatre Company's *Sleep No More* – places its audience in a complex relation to the 'play' as it is scattered through several stories of a building; the production is site-specific, having premiered in London (2003) and then produced in Brookline, Massachusetts, New York, and Shanghai. Punchdrunk's production was one of those you-had-to-be-there events – an *experience* – which prose accounts struggle to represent.[11] The production omits most of the spoken text of the play, staging scenes between Macbeth and Banquo, the witches' prophecy and so on through dance and movement. Scattered throughout the site – the 'McKittrick Hotel' in New York, with 'over 100,000 square feet of playing area, divided into about a hundred richly imagined rooms' (Worthen 2012: 80) – the 'audience' wanders through the rooms, occasionally encountering 'characters', occasionally being drawn into a given room for a private 'conversation'. The experience was made to be disorienting in the extreme: the entrance (in New York) was through a dark tunnel, all audience members were required to wear a white mask ('a kind of cross between Star Wars storm trooper, Area 51 alien, and Venice carnival', Worthen 2012: 79) and forbidden to speak. Richardson and Shohet (2012: 2) show how even the Program book for the New York production also lured 'its users into a codicological counterpart of theatrical voyeurism, both hiding and revealing what's inside. The booklet doubles many of its pages, conventionally folding them, then cutting the doubled pages at top and bottom but leaving them uncut, unusually, on the side.' The result is, like the performance itself, an 'absence of words and refusal of full access'.

Thomas Cartelli compared the effect of the production to 'an opened up, interactive digital environment or alternate reality game

(ARG), drawing on some of the same logic of role-playing scenarios from established texts/plays/films – as, in this instance, Shakespeare's *Macbeth*, du Maurier's novel *Rebecca*, and Hitchcock's film version of the same' (Cartelli 2012: 1). The Hitchcock allusion – murder at the heart of things, with some erotic *frisson* – was essential to the feel of the production, along with several other allusions (Stanley Kubrick's *Eyes Wide Shut*, Hitchcock's *Vertigo*). The production, in each city, was widely heralded for its ingenuity and overall effect, though some were unconvinced.[12] Fan-based websites and blogs dissected the productions in each city, generating another world of related discourse: interpretations, complaints, descriptions of encounters, comparisons of sites, and marketing in different cities.

Despite its radical, deconstructive nature and dispersal of the Shakespearean text, *Sleep No More*, Worthen points out, 'is predicated on a surprisingly conventional view of dramatic performance: that the stage reveals fully formed, organic, psychologically knowable and responsive "characters" to whom the audience (or, often, readers) respond much as they do to human beings in the social world off the stage' (Worthen 2012: 83). In blurring, if not reversing, the traditional actor/audience, play/reality boundaries, *Sleep No More* succeeded in generating substantial, often contradictory responses in those who experienced it. In seeking to materialize and 'spatialize' (86) elements of the play, *Sleep No More* foregrounded basic concepts of how a 'literary' work can be adapted and performed. One problem with the production: it requires so much space – and in each city it played, the space was different – and so many logistics, that it is essentially irreproducible.

Pandemic Macbeth

A 2020 German production, *Macbeth Macbeth Macbeth*, stemming from the global pandemic, was performed 'in isolation' by thirty actors from Germany, Switzerland, and Austria, with homemade props, costumes and makeup, and interpolated images (such as Lego figures). At the end, 'Malcolm' holds up a printed paper, stained with ketchup and grease from a Macdonald's (!) fast food meal, with Malcolm's final speech typed out (in German) retrieved from inside a packet of French fries and held up to the screen; after offstage sounds of gunfire and battle, a cheerful version of the Minuet/Trio from the Brandenburg Concerto No. 1 closes out the performance.[13]

Joji is the first film of *Macbeth*, as opposed to a video or Zoom production, to come out during and refer to the pandemic; it might be the first such film of any Shakespeare play. Appearing in the US in April 2021 on *Amazon Prime*, the film is set in Kerala, India; its language is Malayalam with English subtitles. The director Dileesh Pothan begins with a screen card: 'Inspired from Shakespeare's Macbeth', but, knowingly or not, a fair amount of *King Lear* also suffuses the film. There is a tyrannical father, Kuttapan, who terrorizes his three sons, the youngest of whom, Joji, is the Macbeth figure (and by no means a Cordelia equivalent). Even after the father suffers a stroke, Joji cannot wait for him to die and inherit his wealth, so Joji poisons him (as witnessed by his sister-in-law, Bincy, who is more than complicit in the act but not quite a Lady Macbeth). One murder leads to another – one of his brothers – Joji is eventually exposed, and commits suicide. At the end, the camera pans up to a sign on the door to his room: 'Joji's Palace'.

The resemblances to *Macbeth* are rather slight, but as another example of *noir*, the film succeeds in many ways – a perfect example of the glocalization of the play, fusing the local cultural context with the perceived 'universal' aspects of the play. The film's nuanced references to the pandemic are of particular interest – at the beginning of the film, the father 'is in quarantine', and a delivery boy rolls up to the family home wearing a mask. In the hospital waiting room, after Kuttapan's stroke, everyone wears a mask. Eventually, masking becomes figurative as well as literal. Retreating to his room during the wake for his father, Joji is summoned to come out by Bincy – 'Put on a mask and come' – while the faithful outside sing 'Earthly pleasures cause inner sorrow'. Joji looks into a mirror as he conceals himself; earlier, Bincy had seen him in a mirror as he switched his father's pill box for one with poisoned pills. The film thus fuses pandemic mask imagery with *noir* mirrors and shadows, indicating how 'disease' has disseminated throughout this world – perhaps an allusion to Macbeth's complaint to the Doctor, 'Canst thou not minister to a mind diseased, / Pluck from the memory a rooted sorrow, / Raze out the written troubles of the brain, / And with some sweet oblivious antidote / Cleanse the stuffed bosom of that perilous stuff / Which weighs upon the heart?' (5.3.40-5).

Macbeth is referring to Lady Macbeth, but as the Doctor indicates through his shift to a masculine pronoun, Macbeth is really describing himself: 'Therein the patient / Must minister to himself'. In this film, as in the play, Joji cannot heal himself: the pandemic of greed and violence wipes away his identity as surely as masks conceal the face.

* * *

We have seen how the play's formal and thematic elements have mutated over the centuries, particularly in terms of its place in political discourse: from seeing the play as a valorization of hierarchical power and the restoration of 'moral' order to seeing it as a critique of totalitarian rule and social collapse into a repetitive cycle of violent regime change. Lady Macbeth has fluctuated among multiple identities, from a dessicated housewife, or a synonym for a murdering mother, to a valiant woman claiming her own identity and royal heritage. Diverse forms of popular culture, exemplifying Lanier's trope of rhizomic adaptation, have moved further and further from the Folio text; indeed, the play has entered the cultural lexicon – soaps, advertisements, souvenirs, heritage tourist groups – often floating free from the Shakespearean text. Novelists have transmuted the play into a wholly different genre, with immense advantages and some disadvantages: the central characters have been put on the psychiatric couch in ways far beyond what Freud imagined. In Shakes-*noir*, Scottish chieftains have become gangsters, and drugs have taken the place of the supernatural. Backstories of astonishing depth have been produced for Macbeth but more often for Lady Macbeth – and hardly any other character in the play.

As we approach one thousand years since the beginning of the historical Macbeth's reign in 1040, Shakespeare's version, close to the middle of this line, certainly stands above all the other versions, but it could not exist – as a Folio text, or in the contemporary imagination – without all these other versions, both those preceding and those following 1606. If there is anything to be learned from this strange, eventful history of *Macbeth* adaptations, it is this: what is done is never done.

NOTES

Introduction

1 https://bookshop.org/books/awakening-macbeth/9781543209808; accessed 5 August 2020.

2 https://bookshop.org/books/the-island-of-macbeth/9781478742012; accessed 5 August 2020.

3 https://bookshop.org/books/american-macbeth-the-overthrow-of-abraham-lincoln/9781483420325; accessed 5 August 2020.

4 http://news.bbc.co.uk/2/hi/uk_news/scotland/4232221.stm; accessed 5 August 2020.

5 https://www.visitscotland.com/info/tours/the-real-macbeth-tour-406c4336; accessed 5 August 2020.

6 https://theculturetrip.com/europe/united-kingdom/scotland/articles/a-tour-of-macbeths-scotland-in-13-places/; accessed 5 August 2020.

7 https://www.andantetravels.com/tours/uk-tours/the-archaeology-of-macbeth/; accessed 5 August 2020.

8 https://macbeth-international.com/; accessed 26 March 2021.

9 https://www.metoperashop.org/shop/lady-macbeth-soap-16669; accessed 6 August 2020.

10 https://www.metoperashop.org/shop/macbeth-bracelet-1393; accessed 6 August 2020.

11 https://www.etsy.com/listing/813883200/adult-face-mask-macbeth-print?ga_order=most_relevant&ga_search_type=all&ga_view_type=gallery&ga_search_query=macbeth&ref=sr_gallery-1-9&frs=1; accessed 6 August 2020.

12 https://www.cafepress.com/+macbeth+gifts; accessed 6 August 2020.

13 https://shop.shakespearesglobe.com/collections/macbeth/products/macbeth-spot-cufflinks; accessed 6 August 2020.

14 https://masses.com.my/sneakers/history-101-macbeth-footwear/; accessed 26 March 2021.

15 https://esra2021.gr/seminars/; accessed 9 August 2020.

16 Middleton may only have added the two songs in 3.5 and 4.1, though many have argued that he also wrote the Hecate scenes. See

the discussion in Clark and Mason (2015: 321–38). For a counter-argument to the Oxford editors' claims of substantial revision, see Vickers (2010); Taylor responded in 2014: 296–305. For convenience I will refer to the Folio text as by Shakespeare, while acknowledging that Middleton had some kind of role in revising it.

17 Kinney echoes and anticipates many other substantial analyses of the Folio text's inconsistencies; see Brooke (1990); Braunmuller (1997); Taylor and Lavagnino (2007); Clark and Mason (2015).

18 Part of Gamboa's argument fails to convince, as when he claims '*our* sense of justice demands that Malcolm regain his father's crown' because 'his claim on the throne is legitimate' (48; my emphasis).

19 William Empson had anticipated this line of argument as, more simply, the play's details were '*meant* to seem puzzling', to 'keep the audience guessing but fogged' (1986: 146, 143).

20 See Barnes (2012) on the recently recovered 1958 screenplay for Laurence Olivier's proposed film of *Macbeth*; see also **Chapter Five.**

21 See Levin's useful account of the Porter scene (1982: 48–68).

22 The term 'rewriting' limits adaptations to textual events, but I intend the term more broadly to include viewers, inter-actors, listeners and other types of consumers across genres

23 Farrow points out that the Latin verb used – *occiditur* – does not necessarily mean 'murdered' (1994: 8).

24 The third prophecy, that he 'should be / A man of great state and bounty', was made later by the Devil. I have silently modernized these quotations and those following throughout this book.

25 See also Farrow (1994: 14–6).

26 See Adam (1957); Farrow (1994); and Aitchinson (1999).

27 I modernize here John Bellenden's Scots translation of *c*. 1536 [Boece 1821].

28 Norbrook (1987: 116). Norbrook argues that Shakespeare seems to have been aware of Buchanan's account of Macbeth, perhaps through direct knowledge, perhaps through the 1587 edition of Holinshed's chronicles of Scotland, as the editor Francis Thynne had drawn 'on Buchanan to correct some points in earlier sections of the chronicle and to bring the narrative up to date beyond the point at which Boece had broken off' (81).

29 Thomas Duffett parodied Davenant's singing and dancing witches almost immediately in the Epilogue to his burlesque *The Empress of Morocco* in 1673 (the witches were simply prostitutes working the city; see Carroll 1999: 178–84). Garrick commented in 1833 that 'It has been always customary – heaven only knows why – to make low comedians act the witches, and to dress them like old fishwomen ... [with] jocose red faces, peaked hats, and broomsticks' (Braunmuller

1997: 68). Samuel Phelps attempted to break this tradition in an 1847 production: he would show 'Macbeth from the original text, dispensing with the Singing Witches' (Clark and Mason 2015: 99) – but such sobriety soon failed and many later productions continued with comic witches.

30 See Bladen (2013). Some recent films and productions borrow from noir, horror and slasher film genres in attempting to outdo even the Folio in terms of demonism and the grotesque.

31 Thomas argues that the publication of prophecies was prohibited by Tudor and Stuart authorities because political prophecies were usually deployed *after* some act of political radicalism: 'at the heart of the belief in prophecies, there lay an urge to believe that even the most revolutionary doings of contemporaries had been foreseen by the sages of the past ... Their function was to persuade men that some proposed change was not so radical that it had not been foreseen by their ancestors. This had the effect of disguising any essentially revolutionary step by concealing it under the sanction of past approval' (1971: 423).

32 Clark and Mason point out, in spite of some claims, that 'there is nothing to suggest that Shakespeare actually knew it or was even present in Oxford at the time; and the resemblances between it and the words of the Sisters [in *Macbeth*] may well be due to a common source in Holinshed' (2015: 91).

33 The words 'tyrant' and 'tyranny' appear eighteen times in the Folio, two in 3.6 and the rest from 4.3 onward; they are applied to Macbeth as a way of casting his murder as a justifiable tyrannicide, not simply regicide.

34 See Stallybrass (1982); Callaghan (1992); Callaghan et al. (1994); and Purkiss (1996).

Chapter 1

1 For counters to this reading, see Goldberg (1987).
2 Hadfield (2005).
3 Paul (1950), Kernan (1995).
4 For more on Malcolm, see **Chapter Two.**
5 See Tuck (1974).
6 Astington 2011 analyses *Macbeth* allusions in Howard Brenton's *Thirteenth Night* and the TV series *House of Cards* (both written in the 1980s) in relation to the politics of the Thatcher era.
7 On the scene's politics, see Carroll (2014).

8   Calderwood is typical of this reading: 'Macbeth's rule is a tyrannic interlude between the gracious reigns of Duncan and his rightful successor Malcolm' (1986: 72).

9   Such spectacles, Foucault notes, failed to produce the anticipated obedience, as did Malcolm's, historically.

10 'This above all: to thine own self be true / And it must follow as the night the day / Thou canst not then be false to any man' (1.3.77-9).

11 See Stone (1941) on Garrick.

12 On *Macbeth*'s English stage history, see Bartholomeusz (1969); Rosenberg (1978); Kliman (2004); and Wilders (2004). Later actors continued to personalize the role. Perhaps the most self-congratulatory comments came in William Charles Macready's diary entry of 26 April 1841: 'I have improved Macbeth. The general tone of the character was lofty, manly, or indeed as it should be, heroic, that of one living to command. The whole view of the character was constantly in sight: the grief, the care, the doubt was not that of a weak person, but of a strong mind and of a strong man' (Prescott 2004: 90). By contrast, Orson Welles would say that 'Macbeth is always a weakling. The nature of his weakness remains to be found. He's not a strong man who is defeated and collapses. He's sick from the outset' (Miola 2014: 115).

13 I am greatly indebted to Golder's superb study (1992: 163–230). English translations from the French text in Golder, as here, are mine. Gregor notes 'nine distinct manuscript versions ... between mid-1782 (or even as early as 1778) and January, 1784' (2014: 62).

14 Golder suggests that this scene might have been inspired by Louis XVI's promise, in 1791, to uphold the Constitution and act as first citizen under the law (220).

15 For accounts of later adaptations in France, see Fayard (2006) and Pemble (2005). Ducis's pleasure at Napoleon's attendance in 1798 eventually turned into embittered criticism after Napoleon was crowned Emperor in 1804.

16 The first recorded performance of a Shakespeare play in Spain (4 October 1772) was an adaptation by none other than Jean-François Ducis – his Hamlet, in a Spanish translation by (probably) Ramón de la Cruz (Gregor 2010: 7).

17 Carlson (1985: 184–206) lists, by year, the English and American tours, dates, and performances of Ristori, Salvini and Rossi. See also Coduri's history of Shakespeare in Italy (2013).

18 See Moschovakis (2008: 1–72) on 'dualistic' interpretations of *Macbeth*.

19 These modernizing impulses still ran in parallel with more traditional staging, often set in an imagined eleventh-century Scotland, ranging from Orson Welles's 1948 film to Branagh's 2013 production and Kurzel's 2015 film.

20 My translations; German text at Schuhmacher (1938: 254).

21 German text in Brecht (1991). The majority of this text was reprinted, in English translation (translator unknown), in *TLS* in the Shakespeare issue of 23 April 1964. English quotations are from the *TLS* version unless otherwise noted, but other passages – omitted in *TLS* or omitted from the original spoken text – are my translation and will so be noted.

22 Brecht – or his 'friend' – mistakenly takes the prophecy to be that Banquo's *son* Fleance will inherit, whereas the play gives the more ambiguous 'thou shalt get kings, though thou be none'; many adaptations, beginning with Davenant, bring Fleance back in the final scene. See **Chapter Three**.

23 While the *TLS* text gives 'inconsequentiality' for *Zusammenhanglosigkeit*, I think 'incoherence' (a sense of logical disjointedness) is more in keeping with Brecht's critique of trying to make *Macbeth* more logical.

24 This is the *TLS* translation of the German *Dümmeres*; it could also be 'more foolish', or as harsh as 'stupid'.

25 Brecht amplified the problem of the unfulfilled prophecy in a passage deleted from the final radio script: 'Prophecies, where they are aids of the theater, tend to come true in the theater, if not, a theater effect tends to arise from them. Prophecies in life – it is pleasant to be allowed to utter this platitude – do not all come true and not all do not come true' (Brecht 1991: 471n.).

26 As in, for example, John Webster's *The Duchess of Malfi* 5.3.

27 See **Chapter Four** for Brecht's other *Macbeth* adaptations.

28 For a provocative reconsideration of Kott, see Worthen (2010).

29 On developments in Portugal, see also Homem (2008).

30 Kiss analyses films of *Hamlet* and *Macbeth* in these terms, as well as five stage productions from 1994–2011.

31 On Eastern European productions post-Second World War, see also Shurbanov (1998); Matei-Chesnoiu (2006); Makaryk (2006); Makaryk and McHugh (2012); Kiss (2013); Drábek (2014); and Drábek (2016).

32 The play is dedicated to Pavel Kohout, who had been banned from working in the theatre after he had drafted the original document founding 'Charter 77'; Kohout adapted *Macbeth* to be performed in living rooms. Drábek describes *Cahoot's Macbeth* as 'a Westernised imaginative impression' of Kohout's *Play Macbeth* (2017: 8). A *Makbet* – the first Shakespeare play translated into Czech – was performed in Prague (in Czech from a German translation) as early as 1786 (Drábek 2014: 54–9). As Worthen notes, 'As a canonized author, Shakespeare had been performed on the official stage and had been long associated with Czech cultural and political identity' (2007: 121). See **Chapter Seven** for Kohout's play.

33 For Ducis's influence in Romania, see Matei-Chesnoiu (2006: 35–41) on translations across Europe.

34 Billington (2002) reported seeing three on stage; see **Chapter Five** on the production and multiplication of Lady Macbeth's children.

35 See Pfister (1986); Pfister (1994); Zimmerman (1994); and Höfele (2016a).

36 See Höfele's excellent brief overview of Shakespeare's reception in Germany (2016b).

37 *Macbeth* was clustered as 'Nordic' alongside *Hamlet, King Lear* and *Richard II* (23). One writer in 1940 described the play as 'a myth of Nordic winter', but also an expression of the 'yearning for salvation' (Höfele 2016a: 205n46).

38 See Case (1983) and Kalb (2001). Müller said: 'It's treason to use Brecht without criticizing him' (Weber 1984: 18).

39 In his collage adaptation – *A Macbeth* – Charles Marowitz also split Macbeth into three figures, speaking various lines by Malcolm and the witches in the Folio (Marowitz 1978: 82, 95–7).

40 French text at Kamenish (1991: 15).

41 See Kern (1974) on the links to Brecht. For Lamont (1973), Shakespeare's Duncan is the 'gracious sovereign' of the Authorized Version, while Ionesco's is 'Ubu-Stalin-Hitler-Mao-Castro rolled into one'.

42 *Ubu Roi* was performed (only once) on 19 December 1896 in Paris. It features a usurper, tempted by his wife, who kills the king and then is himself deposed by the king's son. Jarry's play signaled a revolutionary and deconstructive (long before the term was known) turn in politico-theatrical aesthetics. See Kern (1974), Cohn (1976), Perry (2000), and Morse (2004).

43 French text at Bonnefoy (1966 & 1977: 161, 162).

44 The printed edition notes its hybrid genesis: 'The National Theatre of Scotland presents the Royal Shakespeare Company's production of *Dunsinane* in association with the Royal Lyceum Theatre, Edinburgh' (Greig 2010). Ironically, this Scottish play, which talks back to The Scottish Play (written by an Englishman who had never been to Scotland), was produced by the most iconic English heritage institution on the planet.

45 He 'received the crown, as lawful inheritor' and ruled briefly until Macduff 'slew him' on behalf of Malcolm Canmore (Holinshed [1587] 1808: 5.278).

46 As in Richard Loncraine's 1995 *Richard III* film, with Richard as a Hitler-figure.

47 Fyodor Komisarjevsky's 1933 Stratford production invoked both 'Soviet Constructivism' via 'a metaphoric structure of burnished aluminum with curved screens, scroll work, and turning staircases' and included as well 'eclectic visual references to the First World War' (Kennedy 2001: 129).

48 The 'TR' is 'wordplay on "terrain", referring to the hotchpotch of spaces in Warsaw where they have performed' (Dickson 2012).

49 Rosenberg (1978: 78–9) cites a 1948 production in Hamburg, and in a 1968 staging, the two murderers of 3.1 were 'hardened SS men, in black clothes, jack-booted, brutal' (398).

50 Cf. the film and novel *The Last King of Scotland*, and Max Stafford-Clark's 2005 production of *Macbeth* (see **Chapter Seven**).

Chapter 2

1 See the **Introduction**.

2 Goldberg (1987: 248) points out that this line is spoken, in Holinshed, by a witch, who prophesies to King Natholocus (Bullough 1975: 7.478).

3 See Adelman (1992).

4 For negative views of James's person, see Wilson (1719); for more varied views, Ashton (1969).

Chapter 3

1 *Fleance*: 'The moon is down; I have not heard the clock.' *Banquo*: 'And she goes down at twelve.' *Fleance*: 'I take't 'tis later, sir.'

2 This is the Arden emendation; New Cambridge reads: '*show of eight kings, and [the] last with a glass in his hand*[; *Banquo's Ghost following*]' (4.1.127). The Folio is '*shew of eight Kings, and Banquo last, with a glasse in his hand.*'

3 It has often been claimed that the unnamed play performed at Hampton Court on 7 August 1606 'was Shakespeare's new play *Macbeth*' (Kernan 1995: 72), but there is no specific evidence, such as a listing of play titles performed; see Braunmuller (1997: 8–9), and Clark and Mason (2015: 19).

4 For the ways in which various *Macbeth* films (mostly those not discussed here) code 'Scotland' (via kilts, accents etc.), see Lehmann (2003) and Burnett (2006).

5 See **Chapter Eight** for a fuller discussion of Verdi.

6 See **Chapter Four** for fuller accounts of Reilly's and other *noir* films.

7 The 'He' of this passage may instead refer to Malcolm, who has not shown sufficient sympathy in trying to comfort Macduff.

8 The novel covers the time period 1032 (Prologue, v) to 1047 (217), when Klein's Macbeth is dead, though this historical specificity does not for some reason correlate with the historical Macbeth's death (in 1057).

Chapter 4

1   See Lanier (2018) on the theoretical issues raised by the Hogarth project; Nesbø's *Macbeth* had not yet appeared.

2   Nesbø however has been quoted that the novel's city is 'one-part Seventies New York, one-part rainy Bergen, but most of all it is the Newcastle of Get Carter, the 1971 Michael Caine film. "I visited Newcastle in my early teens, my parents took me as there was a ferry between Bergen and Newcastle"' (Millen 2018: 2).

3   Max Beerbohm invented the legend in 1898; see Wells (2001), and Maguire and Smith (2013: 150–5).

4   As Rosenberg (1978: 426) notes, the Third Murderer is often meant to be a 'person Banquo knows', hence an even greater kind of 'treachery' (3.3.16).

5   See discussion in **Chapter One** of Brecht's other *Macbeth* adaptations.

6   According to Brecht (1997a: 550), there were three manuscript copies: (1) the first, in Brecht's handwriting, has the title 'Lady Macbeth of the Yards', and lacks the opening scene in a Chinese restaurant; (2) the second typescript's title is 'All our Yesterdays', but with a subtitle '*Macbeth 1946*', and carries all three authors' names. The title 'A Lady Macbeth of the Yards' appears in Reyher's handwriting, with corrections by Brecht and Reyher; (3) the third and latest version bears the title 'Lady Macbeth of the Yards', with all three authors listed, and Reyher's handwritten corrections. This version contains a Foreword bearing the initials of all three authors. Brecht at some point struck through Lorre's name. I will refer to 'Brecht' as the author; the proportions of collaborative work are unclear.

7   The title may allude to Shostakovich's opera 'Lady Macbeth of the Mtsensk District' (1932).

8   Quoted and translated in Cohn (1976: 91), but without citation.

9   John Turturro, Peter Boyle, Rod Steiger, Vincent Pastore, Michael Badalucco and Aleksander Krupa.

10 The exact quotation is 'There is nothing but what has a violent end or a violent beginning' (Hazlitt 1845: 15).

11 See French (1992) and Adelman (1992) on masculine values in the play.

12 Woolcock's Macduff, the Black actor David Harewood, speaks in a Jamaican lilt.

13 For a brilliant reading of the film's spectral nature, see Calbi (2013).

14 Rosenberg notes that 'Twentieth-century stagings avoided the scene [3.5], as unnecessary and unlikely to sustain the continuing illusion for sophisticated audiences' (1978: 494); Welles included Hecate in his 'voodoo' production (see **Chapter Seven**).

15 The witches are 'beautiful skull-faced women with wild hair that peek their heads up from behind a mound of trash' at the 'municipal dump' (17).

16 The gender of this child is unclear: the name in the 'Dramatis Personae' is the feminine 'Donalbina', and when the Ross figure asks where the 'little sister, Donalbino' is, the Lennox figure answers 'He is not with them' (94). If the gender confusion is deliberate, it's not clear why.

17 Wray (2011) provides a comprehensive analysis of the film's context in Northern Ireland's prison and social systems; she notes that it 'is the first Shakespeare film to deploy a behind-the-bars location' (347). See Ko (2014) on a prison performance by Shakespeare Behind Bars in Kentucky.

18 As Wray notes, 'Early modern models of kingship and the social order find a ready analogy in the internal organization of prison paramilitary operations' (2011: 347).

Chapter 5

1 Auerbach observes that Terry's resistance to Mrs. Siddons's portrait of Lady Macbeth as a virago exposed a conceptual crux: 'If Lady Macbeth was not a monster, she exposed a side of woman's nature that most men and many women did not want to know about' (1987: 252). On Victorian conceptions of Lady Macbeth, see (among others) Poole (2004). McDonald (2005) analyses each actress's career (Mrs. Siddons 36–48; Terry 94–100).

2 Things did not improve when Clinton ran for president herself. Smith (2010) surveys how 'Lady Macbeth entered American politics and eventually the White House' (1), matching actresses' landmark performances with their current First Lady; her analysis does not include the more recent texts analysed in this essay.

3 In Rae Shirley's 2010 feminist play, *A Merry Regiment of Women* (alluding to John Knox's 1558 misogynist diatribe, *The First Blast of the Trumpet Against the Monstrous Regiment of Women*), Lady Macbeth laments that 'I have no name. Nameless – anonymous! I live and have my being only through MacBeth – an echo of his name' (2010: 18).

4 Terry had written in her notes that Lady Macbeth 'is full of womanliness ... capable of affection – she loves her husband – Ergo – she is a woman – and she knows it, and is half the time afraid while urging Macbeth not to be afraid as she loves a man. Women love men' (Auerbach 1987: 255).

5 See Lanier (2006) on Gothic associations in some contemporary versions.

6 Clarke's *Girlhood of Shakespeare's Heroines* found a recent echo in James Chalmers' 2015 novel, *Lady Macbeth: Her Early Life*.

7 On succession theory in the period, see Nenner (1995).

8 On tanistry in *Macbeth*, see Stevenson (1927) and Rolls (2002).

9 'We liked the sound of it', rather than Gruoch, the authors said (Hartley and Hewson 2012: 319).

10 See **Chapter One** for other aspects of Greig's play.

11 The actual lines in the printed text are '*Siward*. What is your place here? *Gruach*. My place here is Queen' (27).

12 In Lagervall's nineteenth-century Finnish version (see **Chapter Seven**), Lady Macbeth 'met her fate in trying to close the gate in order to stop the supporters of Macduff from entering: she was crushed under their feet' (Aaltonen 1999: 146).

13 Jennifer Flaherty analyses Klein's and Cooney's novels in terms of the genre conventions of young adult fiction and the romance novel while also showing how they encourage 'young women to embrace their own agency rather than being defined by relationships' (2018: 113).

14 Rackin (2005: 123) examines Shakespeare's 'radical revision of the descriptions of [lactation by] ancient Scotswomen he found in his historical source'.

15 In the screenplay's second draft, the last two sentences were deleted, perhaps prompted by the fact that Vivien Leigh (Olivier's wife, who acted Lady Macbeth) had suffered a miscarriage two years earlier (Barnes 2012: 290n24). On the financial/business aspects of the failure to produce this film, see McKernan (2009).

16 Coriat contrasts her with Clytemnestra, who 'is essentially and fundamentally criminal, deceitful, voluptuous, coldly calculating in her motives and shows none of the symptoms which make Lady Macbeth the irresponsible victim of a definite psychoneurosis. Lady Macbeth reacts only as her unconscious complexes make her react' (34).

17 See Peterson (2010) on the early modern theory of hysteria, especially its differences from the post-Freudian conception often applied to Lady Macbeth.

18 Wills (2011: 25–30) argues that the actor was John Rice.

Chapter 6

1 The advent of the Kindle platform has made it easier for anyone to publish their novels.

2 The scene thus closely resembles Duncan's murder in Polanski's film.

3 King may have known Dunnett's work, as King's following novel, about Margaret, queen to Malcolm III, is entitled *Queen Hereafter* (2010). See Hopkins (2018) for an analysis of the novels by Dunnett, Hartley and Hewson, King, and Klein in terms of their representations of 'Scotland' in the context of the independence movement and Scottish national identity.

4   In Alan Gratz's 2009 *Something Wicked*, however, the Lady Macbeth
    character promises, if the Macbeth character will commit the murder:
    'You do this and you will have The. Best. Sex. *Ever*' (Hately 2018: 136).
5   See Skinner (1978) and Nenner (1995).
6   The characters' names will be 'Macbeth' and 'Lady Macbeth' in
    reference to Shakespeare's play, and 'Mack-Beth' and 'Lady Mack-
    Beth' in reference to the *Secret History*.
7   Heylyn, *Microcosmus, A Little Description of the Great World* saw
    seven editions from 1625 to 1639.
8   The 1708 *Hypolitus* was reprinted yet again in 1711. Authorship of
    the *Secret History* has been attributed to the French author, Marie-
    Catherine D'Aulnoy (*c.* 1650/1–1705), on the grounds that she is the
    author of the *Hypolitus* (published in France in 1690). Seventeenth-
    century editions of the *Histoire d'Hypolite*, however, do not include the
    Secret History, which seems purely an English invention.
9   There was a vogue for similar titles, promising (and sometimes
    delivering) revelations of royal scandal: *The Secret History of K.
    James I and K. Charles I* (1690), *The Secret History of the reigns
    of K. Charles II. And K. James II* (1690), *The Secret History of the
    Most Renowned Q. Elizabeth, and the E. of Essex* (2 parts, 1680 and
    1695).
10 Aitchison (1999: 131) suggests this is an allusion to Archibald, ninth
    Earl of Argyll, 'who was executed in 1685 for his opposition to the Test
    Act [of 1681] and the succession of the Catholic James VII and II'.
11 The 1768 reviser is even more hostile: 'her thoughts were so totally bent
    upon that one object [to rule], that she never suffered herself to dissolve
    into the natural softness of her sex, and was truly incapable of making
    herself desireable in amorous enjoyments ... that his [Macbeth's]
    mind might not be diverted from the Chace which she had in view, by
    employing too much of his time in the other scent, she herself would
    often procure for him!' (1768: k5v).
12 One character in the *Secret History* has studied the Roman tyrants
    Caligula and Nero (1708: e3r); see Bushnell (1990: 30–2) on Caligula
    and Nero as ancient prototypes of the tyrant.

Chapter 7

1   https://globalshakespeares.mit.edu/; accessed 12 December 2020.
2   Her best-known plays (because they are in English translation and
    have been produced in the UK) are much earlier: *Siamese Twins* and
    Antigona Furiosa.

3   They are both '*brujas*' (witches) and '*doncellas*' (maidservants; maidens; virgins).
4   http://www.pavel-kohout.com/stories-on-stage.html; accessed 13 January 2021.
5   Jaroslav Pokorný noted that Macbeth 'became the most translated of Shakespeare's dramas in the literature of a nation which for 300 years had been oppressed by foreign domination' (Worthen 2007: 114).
6   Jindřich Černý (Worthen 2007: 130).
7   My thanks to Prof. Igor Lukes, who translated the final lines of the film for me.
8   Donaldson (1990) is still one of the best analyses.
9   'The Castle of the Spider's Web'; Kurosawa said the forest was named 'the wood of spider's hair' (Donaldson 1990: 72). Translations of the film's dialogue come from the subtitle track on the Criterion DVD.
10 See Tribble (2005) on the film's soundscape.
11 The *Commercial Advertiser* (Thompson 1998: 83). The essays in Newstok and Thompson 2010 discuss other racial adaptations, from the minstrel show tradition and colour-blind casting to appropriations in contemporary African-American plays.
12 See Distiller (2004) for the critical reception of the various tours.
13 Burnett 2008 analyses the film's 'transnational exchange'.
14 The director 'revised the role of Hecate to comment on the Trump administration' after the 2016 election (Joubin 2018: 243).
15 Announced in 2012, the production website, dated 2020, says the film is still 'in development'.
16 Some recent studies: Kennedy and Lan (2010); Lei et al. (2017); Hart (2019); Joubin (2021). The *Asian Theatre Journal* prints many important essays on the subject.
17 See Kliman's entire chapter, co-authored with Paul A. S. Harvey, for a detailed analysis of this production.
18 For a Japanese musical production, *Metal Macbeth* (2006), see **Chapter 8**. Japanese-inspired artists have also produced *manga* versions, an art form whose 'sense of freedom and possibility comes from its border-straddling, transcultural nature and its ambiguous aesthetic identity .... the Shakespeare manga is a salient example of how the global dissemination of Shakespeare intermingles with the global dissemination of new forms' (Myklebost 2013: 110–11).
19 Peter Chrisp reads the play, with commentary, at: https://soundcloud.com/peterchrisp/macbeth-in-pidgin-english.
20 https://www.censusscope.org/us/s15/chart_multi.html; accessed 6 March 2021.

Chapter 8

1 http://www.taipeitimes.com/News/feat/archives/2010/06/18/2003475789; accessed 7 March 2021.

2 https://sites.google.com/site/macbethsongcompilationproject/; accessed 7 March 2021.

3 https://grimmusik.bandcamp.com/album/this-is-not-shakespeares-macbeth-ost; accessed 7 March 2021.

4 http://www.thetank.com/lllmb.htm; accessed 9 March 2021.

5 https://thefrailophelias.bandcamp.com/album/macbeth; accessed 9 March 2021.

6 https://skeletonworm.bandcamp.com/album/macbeth; accessed 9 March 2021.

7 http://shop.rebellion-metal.de/?action=showItem&id=6; accessed 11 March 2021.

8 The band's website says their name refers to 'Unit of measurement equal to the death of one million people by nuclear explosion'. https://megadeth.com/band-faq/; accessed 11 March 2021.

9 https://shakespeareinpopularmusic.wordpress.com/2016/04/20/elvis-costello-miss-macbeth-from-spike-1989/; accessed 7 March 2021.

10 http://www.pbmusicals.com/macbeth-the-musical; accessed 7 March 2021.

11 https://port.hu/adatlap/szindarab/szinhaz/xxi-szazadi-macbeth/directing-7218; accessed 12 March 2021.

12 https://afxindustrial.com/; accessed 14 March 2021.

13 http://bufvc.ac.uk/shakespeare/index.php/title/av68511; accessed 14 Mar 2021.

14 https://daemonianymphe.bandcamp.com/album/macbeth; accessed 15 March 2021.

15 This section regrettably omits Chinese opera. See Peide (1988), Lei (2008) and Xingxing (2020) for useful surveys.

16 The National Symphony Orchestra performed the reconstructed Overture 20 September 2001. A version can be heard at https://www.youtube.com/watch?v=6N8hXT3fsBs; accessed 9 April 2021.

17 https://youtu.be/ziZII4ede90; accessed 30 March 2021.

18 Wills's *Verdi's Shakespeare* (2011) is highly readable. Rosen and Porter's *Verdi's* Macbeth: *A Sourcebook* (1984) is indispensable; virtually all the facts I cite in the ensuing pages derive from this collection.

19 Rosen and Porter print a facsimile of the original libretto (1984: 471–8); my translation.

20 https://youtu.be/_4wOX5Ecg8s; accessed 24 March 2021.

21 https://vimeo.com/153378008; accessed 26 March 2021.

22 Wong (2017) analyses the witches, from the Folio and Davenant
   through to Bailey's adaptation.
23 https://sequenza21.com/062303.html; accessed 31 March 2021.
24 My translations.
25 https://www.opera-lab-berlin.com/en/macbeth; accessed 2 April 2021.
26 See Bishop's entire insightful analysis of the music.
27 Recounting the entire plot would take many pages; see the excellent
   summary and analysis in Yoshihara (2007) and the briefer analysis in
   Lee (2018: 138–41).
28 The greatest homage to *Mad Max* is probably the 2017 Albanian film,
   Mad Macbeth, in which gypsies fight for the crown of King Dushkan
   in a post-apocalyptic future: https://www.thefilmcatalogue.com/films/
   mad-macbeth; accessed 5 April 2021.

Epilogue

1 https://youtu.be/sJLvl9vk-eE; accessed 2 April 2021.
2 http://www.shakespeare-parodies.com/macbeth.html; accessed 2 April
   2021.
3 Yost (2018: 205) quotes one fan who wonders '"what happened to
   Fleance. You never see him after Banquo dies," and so imagines a scene
   between Fleance and the Witches'. Indeed: see **Chapter Three**.
4 http://www.macbeththefilm.co.uk/; accessed 4 April 2021.
5 http://www.machomer.com/; accessed 2 April 2021.
6 https://www.citz.co.uk/whatson/info/the-macbeths-online-streaming;
   accessed 5 April 2021.
7 https://volcanotheatre.wales/macbeth-directors-cut-2018/; accessed 5
   April 2021.
8 http://www.1623theatre.co.uk/; accessed 5 April 2021.
9 https://www.chicagoshakes.com/ibanquo; accessed 5 April 2021.
10 https://www.teatroregioparma.it/spettacolo/macbeth-immersive-
   experience/; accessed 30 March 2021; my translation. Video is at:
   https://vimeo.com/313975834; accessed 30 March 2021.
11 Worthen (2012) remains one of the best accounts.
12 Worthen (2012) makes an excellent case for the production, but see
   the more mixed reactions in Cartelli (2012), Grunfeld (2012), and
   Richardson and Shohet (2012).
13 https://vimeo.com/418617321; accessed 29 March 2021.

WORKS CITED

Modern Editions

Braunmuller A. R. ed. (1997), *Macbeth*, Cambridge: Cambridge University Press.

Brooke, Nicholas, ed. (1990), *The Tragedy of Macbeth*, Oxford: Oxford University Press.

Carroll, William C., ed. (1999), *Macbeth: Texts and Contexts*, New York: Bedford.

Clark, Sandra, and Pamela Mason, eds (2015), *Macbeth*, London: Bloomsbury.

Hunter, G. K., ed. (2005), *Macbeth*, London: Penguin.

Miola, Robert S., ed. (2014), *Macbeth*, New York: W. W. Norton.

Rowe, Nicholas (1709), *The Works of Mr. William Shakspeare*, vol. 5, London.

Taylor, Gary, and John Lavagnino, eds (2007), *Thomas Middleton: The Collected Works*, Oxford: Oxford University Press.

Films, Television and Opera

Death of a Queen (2008), Dir. Pieter Grobbelaar. https://www.tvsa.co.za/shows/viewshowabout.aspx?showid=721 (accessed 20 February 2021).

Entabeni (2008), Dir. Norman Maake. https://www.tvsa.co.za/shows/viewshow.aspx?showid=412 (accessed 20 February 2021).

Joe Macbeth (1955), Dir. Ken Hughes. Columbia Pictures.

Joji (2021), Dir. Dileesh Pothan. Amazon Prime.

Lady Macbeth (2016), Dir. William Oldroyd. Creative England, BBC Films and BFI.

Macbeth (1948), Dir. Orson Welles. Mercury Productions for Republic Pictures

Macbeth (1971), Dir. Roman Polanski. Playboy Productions, Caliban Films.

Macbeth (1979), Dir. Philip Casson. A&E Home Video.

Macbeth (1983), Dir. Paul Almond. BBC.

Macbeth (1989), Opera by Antonio Bibalo, Dir. Antonio Pappano. NOR Oslo Norway Television production. https://youtu.be/ziZII4ede90; accessed 30 March 2021.

Macbeth (1998), Dir. Michael Bogdanov. Channel Four UK and The English Shakespear Company.

Macbeth (2001), Dir. Gregory Doran. Illuminations/Royal Shakespeare Company.

Macbeth (2002), Dir. Franz Welser-Most. Opera by Giuseppe Verdi. Zurich Opera. Image Entertainment.

Macbeth (2005), Dir. Mark Brozel. *Shakespeare ReTold*. BBC ONE, UK and Acorn Media UK.

Macbeth (2006), Dir. Michael T. Starks. Ionogen Studios.

Macbeth (2006), Dir. Geoffrey Wright. Revolver Entertainment, Film Finance Corporation Australia, Film Victoria, Arclight Films, Mushroom Pictures Production.

Macbeth: 2007 (2007), Dir. Grzegorz Jarzyna. Warsaw: Narodowy Instytut Audiowizualny. [DVD]. Live streamed on 13 August 2012 for the 2012 World Shakespeare Festival/Edinburgh Festival.

Macbeth (2010), Dir. Rupert Goold. PBS Home Video/WNET.org.

Macbeth (2012), Dir. Daniel Coll. MGB Media.

Macbeth (2015), Dir. Justin Kurzel. The Weinstein Company.

Macbeth in Manhattan (1999), Dir. Greg Lombardo. Tribe Enterprises.

Macbeth O Rei Do Morro [*Macbeth King of the Favela*] (2019), Dir. Quentin Lewis. Canal Demais.

Macbeth on the Estate (1996), Dir. Penny Woolcock. BBC.

Macbett (The Caribbean Macbeth) (2012?), Dir. Aleta Chappelle. https://cinando.com/en/Film/macbett_93429/Detail; accessed 8 January 2021.

Makibefo (1999), Dir. Alexander Abela. Blue Eye Films, 1999; Scoville Film, 2008.

Maqbool (2003), Dir. Vishal Bhardwaj. Kaleidoscope Entertainment/NH Studioz.

Men of Respect (1990), Dir. William Reilly. Arthur Goldblatt Productions/Central City Films/Grandview Avenue Pictures.

Metal Macbeth (2006), Dir. Hidenori Inoue. Village/Gekidan Shinkansen.

Mickey B. (2007), Dir. Tom Magill. Educational Shakespeare Company Production.

Play Macbeth (1979), Dir. Pavel Kohout. Österreichischer Rundfunk. https://youtu.be/TMbsAn2DGHM; accessed 2 January 2021.

Rave Macbeth (2001), Dir. Klaus Knoesel. 2K Filmproduktion, Falcon Films, and Framewerk Produktion.

Scotland, PA (2001), Dir. Billy Morrissette. US Abandon Pictures, Paddy Wagon Productions and Veto Chip Productions.

Throne of Blood (1957), Dir. Akira Kurosawa. Toho International Company.

Adaptations and Scholarship

Aaltonen, Sirkku (1997), 'Macbeth in Finland', *In Other Words: The Journal for Literary Translators*, 8/9: 60–7.

Aaltonen, Sirkku (1999), '*La Perruque* in a Rented Apartment: Rewriting Shakespeare in Finland', *Ilha ho Desterro*, 36: 141–59.

Adam, R. J. (1957), 'The Real Macbeth: King of Scots, 1040–1054', *History Today*, 7.6: 381–7.

Adelman, Janet (1992), *Suffocating Mothers*, New York: Routledge.

Aitchison, Nick (1999), *Macbeth: Man and Myth*, Thrupp, UK: Sutton.

Alfar, Cristina Leòn (2003), *Fantasies of Female Evil: The Dynamics of Gender and Power in Shakespearean Tragedy*, Newark: University of Delaware Press.

Anderson, Alan O., ed. (1922), *Early Sources of Scottish History A.D. 500 to 1286*, 2 vols, Edinburgh: Oliver and Boyd.

Anonymous (1708), *The Secret History of Mack-Beth, King of Scotland. Taken from a Very Ancient Original Manuscript*, London.

Anonymous (1708), *Hypolitus Earl of Douglas. Containing Some Memoirs of the Court to Scotland; with the Secret History of Mack-Beth King of Scotland*, London.

Anonymous (1768), *A Key to the Drama; ... Vol. I. Containing the Life, Character, and Secret History of Macbeth. By a Gentleman, No Professed Author, but a Lover of History, and of the Theatre*, London.

Anonymous (1828), *The Secret History of Macbeth, King of Scotland; with Interesting Memoirs of the Ancient Thanes. (Originally from a very old MS.)*, Peterhead, Scotland.

Anonymous (1841), *Memoirs of the Court of Scotland ... Containing the Secret History of Macbeth*, Edinburgh.

Anonymous (2016), 'Playwright David Greig on William Shakespeare and the Unmatched Brilliance of Macbeth', *The Herald Scotland*, 3 June. https://www.heraldscotland.com/arts_ents/14535495.playwright-david-greig-on-william-shakespeare-and-the-unmatched-brilliance-of-macbeth/#comments-anchor (accessed 29 December 2020).

Ashton, Robert ed. (1969), *James I by His Contemporaries*, London: Hutchinson.

Astington, John H. (2011), 'Macbeth and Modern Politics', in Randall Martin and Katherine Scheil (eds), *Shakespeare/Adaptation/Modern Drama*, 93–109, Toronto: University of Toronto Press.

Auerbach, Nina (1987), *Ellen Terry, Player in Her Time*, New York: Norton.

Barish, Jonas (1984), 'Madness, Hallucination, and Sleepwalking', in David Rosen and Andrew Porter (eds), *Verdi's Macbeth: A Sourcebook*, 149–55, New York: Norton.

Barnard, Nick (2010), 'Review: Yuri Vladimirovich KOCHUROV', *MusicWeb International*, http://www.musicwebinternational.com/classrev/2010/June10/Kochurov_Macbeth_NFPMA9981.htm (accessed 15 March 2021).

Barnes, Jennifer (2012), '"Posterity Is dispossessed": Laurence Olivier's *Macbeth* Manuscripts in 1958 and 2012', *Shakespeare Bulletin*, 30.3: 263–97.

Bartholomeusz, Dennis (1969), *Macbeth and the Players*, Cambridge: Cambridge University Press.

Bassi, Shaul (2016), 'The Tragedies in Italy', in Michael Neill and David Schalkwyk (eds), *The Oxford Handbook of Shakespearean Tragedy*, 691–705, Oxford: Oxford University Press.

Beale, Simon Russell (2006), 'Macbeth', in Michael Dobson (ed.), *Performing Shakespeare' Tragedies Today*, 107–18, Cambridge: Cambridge University Press.

Berger, Harry (1980), 'The Early Scenes of *Macbeth*: Preface to a New Interpretation', *Genre* 15: 1–31.

Bickley, Pamela, and Jenny Stevens (2020), *Studying Shakespeare Adaptation from Restoration Theatre to YouTube*, London: Bloomsbury.

Billingham, Peter (2007), *At the Sharp End: Uncovering the Work of Five Contemporary Dramatists*, London: Methuen.

Billington, Michael (2002), 'Blood and Guts', *The Guardian*, 30 March 2002. https://www.theguardian.com/culture/2002/mar/30/culturaltrips.art (accessed 13 Mar 2017).

Bishop, Tom (2013), '*Macbeth: Three Nameless Acts (after Shakespeare)* by Salvatore Sciarrino', in Stuart Sillars et al. (eds), *The Shakespearean International Yearbook: Volume 13: Special Section, Macbeth*, 135–58, New York: Routledge.

Bladen, Victoria (2013), 'Weird Space in *Macbeth on Screen*', in Sarah Hatchuel, Nathalie Vienne-Guerrin and Victoria Bladen (eds), *Shakespeare on Screen: Macbeth*, 81–106, Rouen and Le Havre: Presses Universitaires de Rouen et du Havre.

Boece, Hector (1821), *The History and Chronicles of Scotland*, trans. John Bellenden, 2 vols, Edinburgh: W. and C. Tait.

Bonnefoy, Claude (1966&1977), *Eugène Ionesco: Entre La Vie et Le Rêve: Entretiens*, Paris: Pierre Belfond.

Boswell, James, ed. (1821), *The Plays and Poems of William Shakspeare*, vol. 11, London: F. C. and J. Rivington, et al.

Bottomley, Gordon (1921), *Gruach and Britain's Daughter*, Boston: Small, Maynard, & Company.

Bradley, A. C. ([1904] 1968), *Shakespeare Tragedy*, New York: Fawcett.

Bradshaw, Graham (2004), 'Operatic Macbeths: What We Could Still Learn from Verdi', in Bernice W. Kliman (ed.), *Shakespeare in Performance: Macbeth*, 2nd ed., 44–61, Manchester: Manchester University Press.

Brecht, Bertolt (1969), *Texte für Filme II*, Frankfurt: Suhrkamp Verlag.

Brecht, Bertolt (1991), '*Vorrede zum 'Macbeth'*, in *Bertolt Brecht Schriften 4: Texte zu Stücken*, Frankfurt: Suhrkamp Verlag.

Brecht, Bertolt (1995), *Journale 2*, Frankfurt: Suhrkamp Verlag.

Brecht, Bertolt (1997a), *Prosa 5: Geschichten, Filmgeschichten, Drehbücher 1940–1956*, Frankfurt: Suhrkamp Verlag.

Brecht, Bertolt (1997b), *Stücke 10: Stückfragmente und Stückprojekte Teil 2*, Frankfurt: Suhrkamp Verlag.

Brown, John Russell, ed. (1982), *Focus on 'Macbeth'*, London: Routledge & Kegan Paul.

Brown, Mark (2011), 'David Greig Pushes beyond Macbeth with Dunsinane', *HeraldScotland*, 8 May. Available online: http://www. heraldscotland.com/arts-ents/stage-visual-arts/david-greig-pushes-beyond-macbeth-with-dunsinane-1.1099317 (accessed 9 July 2015).

Buc, George (1605), *Daphnis Polystephanos. An Eclog Treating of Crowns, and of Garlands*, London.

Buchanan, George (1690), *The History of Scotland* [*Rerum Scoticarum historia*, 1582], trans. T. Page, London.

Budden, Julian (2001), 'Lauro Rossi', *Grove Music Online*. https://doi-org.ezproxy.bu.edu/10.1093/gmo/9781561592630.article.23891 (accessed 28 March 2021).

Buhler, Stephen M. (2008), 'Politicizing *Macbeth* on U.S. Stages', in Nick Moschovakis (ed.), *Macbeth: New Critical Essays*, 258–75, New York: Routledge.

Bullough, Geoffrey, ed. (1975), *Narrative and Dramatic Sources of Shakespeare*, 8 vols, New York: Columbia University Press.

Burnett, Mark Thornton (2006), 'Figuring the Global/Historical in Filmic Shakespearean Tragedy', in Diana Henderson (ed.), *A Concise Companion to Shakespeare on Screen*, 133–54, Malden, MA: Blackwell.

Burnett, Mark Thornton (2008), 'Madagascan Will: Cinematic
    Shakespeares/Transnational Exchanges', *Shakespeare Survey*, 61:
    239–55.
Burnett, Mark Thornton (2013), *Shakespeare and World Cinema*,
    Cambridge: Cambridge University Press.
Bushnell, Rebecca (1990), *Tragedies of Tyrants*, Ithaca: Cornell University
    Press.
'Business Notables to Read from "Macbeth" in Exploration of
    Shakespeare and Leadership', http://www.suffolk.edu/college/14499.
    php#.WLhsL3-E2AU (accessed 2 March 2017).
C., I.W. (1825), 'On the Non-Appearance of the Ghost of Duncan, in
    the Banquet Scene of Macbeth', *The Drama: Or, Theatrical Pocket
    Magazine*, April: 334–6.
Cain, Bill (2014), *Equivocation*, New York: Dramatists Play Service.
Calbi, Maurizio (2013), *Spectral Shakespeares: Media Adaptations in the
    Twenty-First Century*, New York: Palgrave Macmillan.
Calderwood, James L. (1986), *If It Were Done: Macbeth and Tragic
    Action*, Amherst: University of Massachusetts Press.
Callaghan, Dympna (1992), 'Wicked Women in *Macbeth*: A Study of
    Power, Ideology, and the Production of Motherhood', in Mario A. Di
    Cesare (ed.), *Reconsidering the Renaissance: Papers from the Twenty-
    First Annual Conference*, 355–69, Binghamton: MRTS.
Callaghan, Dympna, Lorraine Helms, and Jyotsna Singh (1994),
    The Weyward Sisters: Shakespeare and Feminist Politics, Oxford:
    Blackwell.
Carlson, Marvin (1985), *The Italian Shakespearians: Performances by
    Ristori, Salvini, and Rossi in England and America*, Washington:
    Folger Books.
Carroll, William C. (2014), 'Spectacle, Representation, and Lineage in
    Macbeth 4.1', *Shakespeare Survey*, 67: 345–71.
Cartelli, Thomas (2012), 'Punchdrunk's *Sleep No More*: Masks,
    Unmaskings, One-on-Ones', *Borrowers and Lenders* 7.2, http://www.
    borrowers.uga.edu/7164/toc (accessed 6 April 2021).
Case, Sue-Ellen (1983), 'From Bertolt Brecht to Heiner Müller',
    Performing Arts Journal, 7.1: 94–102.
Chalmers, James (2015), *Lady Macbeth Her Early Life*, Kindle:
    CreateSpace Independent Publishing Platform.
Chambers, E. K. (1988), *William Shakespeare: A Study of Facts and
    Problems*, 2 vols, Oxford: Clarendon.
Chevrier-Bosseau, Adeline (2013), Personal Communication.
Clarke, Mary Cowden (1887), *The Girlhood of Shakespeare's Heroines*,
    New York: Armstrong.
Close, Ajay (2017), *The Daughter of Lady Macbeth*, Dingwall, UK:
    Sandstone Press.

Coduri, Maria (2013), 'A Travelling Tale: Shakespeare on the Italian Stage', MPhil. Thesis, School of European Languages, Culture and Society, University College London.

Coghill, Nevill (1975), 'Macbeth *at The Globe, 1606–1616 (?): Three Questions*', in Joseph G. Price (ed.), *The Triple Bond*, 223–39, University Park: Pennsylvania State University Press.

Cohn, Ruby (1976), *Modern Shakespeare Offshoots*, Princeton: Princeton University Press.

Cooney, Caroline B. (2007), *Enter Three Witches: A Story of Macbeth*, New York: Scholastic Press.

Cooper, Neil (2017), 'Theatre: The Macbeths, Citizens Theatre, Glasgow'. https://www.heraldscotland.com/arts_ents/15567537.theatre-the-macbeths-citizens-theatre-glasgowneil-cooper-four-stars/ (accessed 5 April 2021).

Copeland, Bonnie (1979), *Lady of Moray*, New York: Atheneum.

Coriat, Isador H. (1912), *The Hysteria of Lady Macbeth*, New York: Moffat, Yard and Company.

Coveney, Michael (2004), 'Shock Treatment', *The Guardian*, 6 August 2004. https://www.theguardian.com/music/2004/aug/07/classicalmusicandopera (accessed 13 March 2017).

Cowan, E. J. (1993), 'The Historical MacBeth', in W.D.H. Sellar (ed.), *Moray: Province and People*, 117–41, Edinburgh: Scottish Society for Northern Studies.

Cross, J. C. (1809), *The History, Murders, Life, and Death of Macbeth*, London: T. Page.

Davenant, William (1674), *Macbeth, A Tragaedy*, London.

Dawson, Anthony B. (2014), 'Notes and Queries Concerning the Text of *Macbeth*', in Ann Thompson (ed.), *Macbeth: The State of Play*, 11–30, London: Bloomsbury.

Dean, Winton (1964), 'Shakespeare and Opera', in Phyllis Hartnoll (ed.), *Shakespeare in Music*, 89–175, London: Macmillan.

DeLong, Kenneth (2008), 'Arthur Sullivan's Incidental Music to Henry Irving's Production of *Macbeth* (1888)', in Richard Foulkes (ed.), *Henry Irving: A Re-Evaluation of the Pre-Eminent Victorian Actor-Manager*, 149–84, Burlington, VT: Ashgate.

Dickson, Andrew (2012), *The Guardian*, 12 August 2012.

Distiller, Natasha (2004), '"The Zulu Macbeth": The Value of an "African" Shakespeare', *Shakespeare Survey*, 57: 159–68.

Dobin, Jr., Howard (1990), *Merlin's Disciples: Prophecy, Poetry, and Power in Renaissance England*, Stanford: Stanford University Press.

Donaldson, Peter S. (1990), *Shakespearean Films/Shakespearean Directors*, Boston: Unwin Hyman.

Donohue, Jr., Joseph W. (1967), 'Kemble's Production of *Macbeth* (1794)', *Theatre Notebook*, 21: 63–74.

Doran, Gregory (2006), 'As Performed: By the Royal Shakespeare Company at the Swan Theatre in Stratford-upon-Avon in 1999', in William Proctor Williams (ed.), *Macbeth*, 11–20, Naperville, IL: Sourcebooks.

Drábek, Pavel (2014), 'From the *General of the Scottish Army* to a Fattish Beer-Drinker: A Short History of Czech Translations of *Macbeth*', in Jana Bžochová-Wild (ed.), '*In Double trust*': *Shakespeare in Central Europe*, 52–72, Bratislava: VŠMU.

Drábek, Pavel (2016), 'Shakespearean Tragedy in Eastern Europe', in Michael Neill and David Schalkwyk (eds), *The Oxford Handbook of Shakespearean Tragedy*, 746–60, Oxford: Oxford University Press.

Drábek, Pavel (2017), '"Spirit, Fine Spirit, Ile free thee": Shakespeare's Spaces of Freedom on the Czech Stage', Shakespeare in Prague Conference, Ohio State University, 3–4 March, 1–42.

Dunnett, Dorothy (1982), *King Hereafter*, New York: Vintage Books.

Eagleton, Terry (1986), *William Shakespeare*, New York: Blackwell.

Empson, William (1986), *Essays on Shakespeare*, David B. Pirie (ed.), Cambridge: Cambridge University Press.

Farrow, Kenneth D. (1994), 'The Historiographical Evolution of the Macbeth Narrative', *Scottish Literary Journal*, 21: 5–23.

Fayard, Nicole (2006), *The Performance of Shakespeare in France since the Second World War: Re-Imagining Shakespeare*, Lewiston, NY: Edwin Mellen Press.

Fedderson, Kim, and J. Michael Richardson (2008), '*Macbeth*: Recent Migrations of the Cinematic Brand', in Nick Moschovakis (ed.), *Macbeth: New Critical Essays*, 300–17, New York: Routledge.

Fernie, Ewan and Simon Palfrey (2016), *Macbeth, Macbeth*, London: Bloomsbury.

Fisher, Burton D., ed. (2017), *Giuseppe Verdi Macbeth: Opera Study Guide and Libretto*, Boca Raton, FL: Opera Journeys Publishing.

Flaherty, Jennifer (2018), 'How Many Daughters Had Lady Macbeth?', in Andrew James Hartley, (ed.), *Shakespeare and Millennial Fiction*, 101–14, Cambridge: Cambridge University Press.

Floyd-Wilson, Mary (2006), 'English Epicures and Scottish Witches', *Shakespeare Quarterly*, 57.2: 131–61.

Ford, John R. (2005), '*Macbeth*: Presented by the Alabama Shakespeare Festival at the Festival Stage, Montgomery, Alabama', *Shakespeare Bulletin*, 23.1: 169–71.

Fordun, John (1872), *John of Fordun's Chronicle of the Scottish Nation*, in W. F. Skene (ed.), *The Historians of Scotlan*, vol 4, Edinburgh: Edmonston and Douglas.

Foucault, Michel (1979), *Discipline and Punish*, New York: Vintage.

Freeling, Nicolas (1993), *Lady Macbeth*, London: Warner Futura.

French, Marilyn (1992), '"Macbeth" and Masculine Values', in Alan Sinfield, ed., *Macbeth*, 14–24, Basingstoke: Macmillan.

Freud, Sigmund (1970), 'From "Some Character-Types Met with in
    Psycho-analytical Work"' in John Wain (ed.), *Shakespeare: Macbeth*,
    131–8, Nashville: Aurora Publishers.
Fuentes, Francisco, and Noemi Vera, eds (2014), 'Transcontinental
    Shakespeare: *Macbeth* and Tyranny in Glauber Rocha's *Severed
    Heads*', in Keith Gregor (ed.), *Shakespeare and Tyranny: Regimes
    of Reading in Europe and Beyond*, 259–76, Cambridge: Cambridge
    Scholars.
Gaines, Barbara (2019), *Macbeth: Teacher Handbook*, Chicago: Chicago
    Shakespeare Theater.
Galt, John (1812), *The Tragedies of Maddalen, Agamemnon, Lady
    Macbeth, Antonia and Clytemnestra*, London: Cadell and Davies.
Gambaro, Griselda (2003), *La Señora Macbeth*, Buenos Aires: Gruppo
    Editorial Norma.
Gamboa, Brett (2014), 'Dwelling "in Doubtful Joy": *Macbeth* and the
    Aesthetics of Disappointment', in Ann Thompson (ed.), *Macbeth: The
    State of Play*, 31–57, London: Bloomsbury.
Garber, Marjorie (1987), '*Macbeth*: The Male Medusa', in *Shakespeare's
    Ghost Writers*, New York: Routledge.
Gardner, Lyn (2012), '2008: Macbeth – Edinburgh Festival Review', *The
    Guardian*. https://www.theguardian.com/stage/2012/aug/12/2008-
    macbeth-edinburgh-festival-review (accessed 11 April 2021).
Garrick, David (1753), *The Historical Tragedy of Macbeth*, Edinburgh.
Garson, Barbara (1967), *MacBird!*, New York: Grove Press.
Gerwig, George William (1929), *Shakespeare's Lady Macbeth: A
    Shakespearian Story of Temptation*, East Aurora, NY: The Roycroft
    Shops.
Giese, Detlef (2018), *Macbeth* [Program, Staatsoper Unter den Linden],
    Berlin: Druckerei Conrad.
Gioia, Dana (2004), Alabama Shakespeare Festival Program. https://
    archive.org/details/macbeth00alab/mode/2up (accessed 12 January
    2021).
Goldberg, Jonathan (1987), 'Speculations: *Macbeth* and Source', in Jean
    E. Howard and Marion F. O'Connor (eds), *Shakespeare Reproduced:
    The Text in History and Ideology*, 242–64, London: Methuen.
Golder, John (1992), *Shakespeare for the Age of Reason: The Earliest
    Stage Adaptations of Jean-François Ducis, 1769–1792*, Oxford: The
    Voltaire Foundation.
Goodreads (2014), https://www.goodreads.com/book/show/280869.
    Light_Thicken
Gopnik, Adam (2016), 'Why Rewrite Shakespeare?', *The New Yorker*.
    https://www.newyorker.com/magazine/2016/10/17/why-rewrite-
    shakespeare (accessed 9 December 2020).

Gregor, Keith (2014), 'When the Tyrant Is a Despot: Jean-François Ducis's
  Adaptations of Shakespeare', in Keith Gregor (ed.), *Shakespeare
  and Tyranny: Regimes of Reading in Europe and Beyond*, 57–75,
  Cambridge: Cambridge Scholars.
Gregor, Keith (2010), *Shakespeare in the Spanish Theatre: 1772 to the
  Present*, London Continuum.
Greig, David (2010), *Dunsinane*, London: Faber and Faber.
Grimm, Reinhold (1989), 'Bertolt Brecht's Chicago – A German Myth?',
  in Siegfried Mews (ed.), *Critical Essays on Bertolt Brecht*, 223–35,
  Boston: G. K. Hall & Co.
Grunfeld, Sivan (2012), 'Fractured Realities: A Receptive Review of
  Punchdrunk's *Sleep No More*', *Borrowers and Lenders* 7.2. http://
  www.borrowers.uga.edu/7164/toc (accessed 6 April 2021).
Habicht, Werner (2012), 'German Shakespeare, the Third Reich, and the
  War', in Irena R. Makaryk and Marissa McHugh (eds), *Shakespeare
  and the Second World War: Memory, Culture, Identity*, 22–34,
  Toronto: University of Toronto Press.
Hadfield, Andrew (2005), *Shakespeare and Republicanism*, Cambridge:
  Cambridge University Press.
Hall, Peter (1982), 'Directing *Macbeth*', in John Russell Brown (ed.),
  Focus on 'Macbeth', 231–48, London: Routledge & Kegan Paul.
Handcock, Annette, Countess of Charlemont (1875), 'Gruach (Lady
  Macbeth)', in Ann Thompson and Sasha Roberts (eds.), *Women
  Reading Shakespeare, 1660–1900: An Anthology of Criticism*, 132–4,
  New York: Manchester University Press.
Hart, Jonathan L., ed. (2019), *Shakespeare and Asia*, New York:
  Routledge.
Hartley, Andrew, and David Hewson (2012), *Macbeth: A Novel*, Las
  Vegas, NV: Thomas & Mercer.
Hateley, Erica (2018), 'Criminal Adaptations: Gender, Genre, and
  Shakespearean Young Adult Literature', in Andrew James Hartley,
  (ed.), *Shakespeare and Millennial Fiction*, 129–44, Cambridge:
  Cambridge University Press.
Hattaway, Michael (2013), 'Tragedy and Political Authority', in Claire
  McEachern (ed.), *The Cambridge Companion to Shakespearean
  Tragedy*, 2nd ed., 110–31, Cambridge: Cambridge University Press.
Hazlitt, William (1845), *Characters of Shakspeare's Plays*, New York:
  Wiley and Putnam.
Henig, Stanley (2016), 'A Performance History of Bloch's Opera *Macbeth*:
  Paris 1910– Manhattan 2014', in Alexander Knapp and Norman
  Solomon (eds.), *Ernest Bloch Studies*, 150–70, Cambridge: Cambridge
  University Press.
Herring, Peg (2016), *Double Toil and Trouble: A Story of Macbeth's
  Nieces*, Kindle: Gwendolyn Books.

Hess, John L. (1972), 'Ionesco Talks of His Latest, "Macbett"', *New York Times*, 18 January.

Heylyn, Peter (1625), *Microcosmus, A Little Description of the Great World. Augmented and Revised*, Oxford.

Hodges, Bruce (2003), 'Salvatore Sciarrino, Macbeth *(U.S. Premiere)*', http://musicweb-international.com/SandH/2003/July03/Lincoln1.htm (accessed 2 April 2021).

Höfele, Andreas (2016a), *No Hamlets: German Shakespeare from Nietzsche to Carl Schmitt*, Oxford: Oxford University Press.

Höfele, Andreas (2016b), 'The Tragedies in Germany', in Michael Neill and David Schalkwyk (eds), *The Oxford Handbook of Shakespearean Tragedy*, 706–25, Oxford: Oxford University Press.

Holinshed, Raphael ([1587] 1808), *The Chronicles of England, Scotland, and Ireland*, 6 vols, London.

Holinshed, Raphael (1587), *The First and Second Volumes of Chronicles*, London. STC 2nd ed. 13569.

Homem, Rui Carvalho (2008), 'The Chore and the Passion: Shakespeare and Graduation in Mid- Twentieth-Century Portugal', *The Shakespearean International Yearbook*, 8: 15–31.

Hopkins, Lisa (2018), 'A Man with a Map: The Millennial Macbeth', in Andrew James Hartley, (ed.), *Shakespeare and Millennial Fiction*, 145–58, Cambridge: Cambridge University Press.

Hurley, Julia (2017), 'Review: "Macbeth" at Shakespeare Theatre Company'. https://dcmetrotheaterarts.com/2017/05/02/review-macbeth-shakespeare-theatre-company/ (accessed 3 March 2021).

Hutcheon, Linda (2013), *A Theory of Adaptation*, 2nd ed., New York: Routledge.

Ionesco, Eugene (1973), *Macbett*, trans. Charles Marowitz, New York: Grove Press.

Isherwood, Charles (2008), 'A Bunny, Too, Can Strut and Fret upon This Stage', *New York Times*: 23 June.

James VI, King (1597), *Daemonology, In Form of a Dialogue*, Edinburgh.

James VI, King (1598), *The True Lawe of Free Monarchies*, Edinburgh.

Jameson, Mrs. [Anna] (1901), *Shakespeare's Heroines*. London: Dent.

Jarry, Alfred (1961), *Ubu Roi*, trans. Barbara Wright, New York: New Directions.

Johnson, Douglas, Alan Tyson, and Robert Winter, eds (1985), *The Beethoven Sketchbooks: History, Reconstruction, Inventory*, Berkeley: University of California Press.

Jones, Kenneth (2009), 'Colm Feore Is *Macbeth* at Stratford'. https://www.playbill.com/article/colm-feore-is-macbeth-at-stratford-starting-may-22-mcanuff-directs-com-161143 (accessed 4 March 2021).

Jones, Melissa (2010), 'Education Notes for Out of Joint "Macbeth"', http://www.outofjoint.co.uk/wp-content/uploads/2010/09/Mac_pac1. doc (accessed 25 February 2021).

Jones, Stephen Philip (2001), *King of Harlem*, Bloomington, IN: iUniverse.

Joubin, Alexa Alice (2018), 'Shakespeare Theatre Company's *Macbeth* and the Limits of Multiculturalism', *Early Modern Culture*, 13: 240–6.

Joubin, Alexa Alice (2021), *Shakespeare and East Asia*, Oxford: Oxford University Press.

Kalb, Jonathan (2001), *The Theater of Heiner Müller*, rev. ed., New York: Limelight.

Kamenish, Paula K. (1991), 'Ionesco's Own *Ubu*', *Postscript*, Spring: 9–16.

Kantorowicz, Ernst (1957), *The King's Two Bodies*, Princeton: Princeton University Press.

Kavanagh, Sheila T. (2007), 'Tragic Humor: The Puppets Take *Macbeth*', in Lena Cowen Orlin and Miranda Johnson-Haddad (eds.), *Staging Shakespeare: Essays in Honor of Alan C. Dessen*, 227–43, Newark: University of Delaware Press.

Kaye, Marvin (2012), *Bullets for Macbeth*, New York: Mysterious Press. https://www.amazon.com/Bullets-Macbeth-Marvin-Kaye/dp/0841504245 (accessed 17 October 2020).

Kennedy, Dennis (2001), *Looking at Shakespeare: A Visual History of Twentieth-Century Performance*, 2nd ed., Cambridge: Cambridge University Press.

Kennedy, Dennis, and Yong Li Lan, eds. (2010), *Shakespeare in Asia: Contemporary Performance*, Cambridge: Cambridge University Press.

Kern, Edith (1974), 'Ionesco and Shakespeare: "Macbeth" on the Modern Stage', *South Atlantic Bulletin*, 39.1: 3–16.

Kernan, Alvin (1995), *Shakespeare, the King's Playwright*, New Haven: Yale University Press.

King, Susan Fraser (2008), *Lady Macbeth*, New York: Three Rivers Press.

Kingston, Sean (1999), 'Pidgin Arts', *Anthropology Today*, 15.2: 1–4.

Kinney, Arthur (2001), *Lies Like Truth: Shakespeare, Macbeth, and the Cultural Moment*, Detroit: Wayne State University Press.

Kirzinger, Robert (2015), 'The Program in Brief', in *Boston Symphony Orchestra Program Week 15*, 36, Boston.

Kiss, Attila (2013), '*Macbeth* as a Tragedy of Consciousness on the Hungarian Stage after 1989', *The Shakespearean International Yearbook*, 113–33.

Klein, Lisa (2009), *Lady Macbeth's Daughter*, London: Bloomsbury.

Kliman, Bernice W. (2004), *Shakespeare in Performance: Macbeth*, 2nd ed., Manchester: Manchester University Press.

Knights, L. C. (1946), 'How Many Children Had Lady Macbeth?'; *Explorations*, 1–39,London: Chatto and Windus,

Ko, Yu Jin (2014), '*Macbeth* behind Bars', *Borrowers and Lenders: The Journal of Shakespeare and Appropriation* 8.2 (accessed 2 February 2021).

Kott, Jan (1964), *Shakespeare, Our Contemporary*, New York: Doubleday.

Kushner, David Z. (2002), 'Macbeth (iii)', *Grove Music Online*. https://www-oxfordmusiconline-com.ezproxy.bu.edu/ grovemusic/view/10.1093/gmo/9781561592630.001.0001/omo-9781561592630-e-5000903140 (accessed 27 March 2021).

Lamb, Charles, and Mary Lamb (1909), *Tales from Shakespeare*, London: Dent.

Lamont, Rosette C. (1973), 'Ionesco, Eugène. *Macbett*', *The French Review*, 46.4: 858.

Lanier, Douglas (2002a), 'Shakescorp *Noir*', *Shakespeare Quarterly*, 53.2: 157–80.

Lanier, Douglas (2002b), *Shakespeare and Modern Popular Culture*, Oxford: Oxford University Press.

Lanier, Douglas (2006), '"Hours Dreadful and Things Strange": Macbeth in Popular Culture', in William Proctor Williams (ed.), *Macbeth. The SourceBooks Shakespeare*, 21–33, Chicago: SourceBooks.

Lanier, Douglas (2014), 'Shakespearean Rhizomatics: Adaptation, Ethics, Value', in Alexa Huang and Elizabeth Rivlin (eds), *Shakespeare and the Ethics of Appropriation*, 21–40, New York: Palgrave Macmillan.

Lanier, Douglas (2018) 'The Hogarth Shakespeare Series: Redeeming Shakespeare's Literariness', in Andrew James Hartley, (ed.), *Shakespeare and Millennial Fiction*, 230–50, Cambridge: Cambridge University Press.

Lear, Charles (2012), *Post-Apocalyptic Macbeth and the Girls*, Kindle: CreateSpace Independent Publishing Platform.

Lee, Adele (2018), *The English Renaissance and the Far East*, Madison, NJ: Fairleigh Dickinson University Press.

Lehmann, Courtney (2003), 'Out Damned Scot: Dislocating *Macbeth* in Transnational Film and Media Culture', in Richard Burt and Lynda E. Boose (eds), *Shakespeare, The Movie, II*, 231–51, London: Routledge.

Lei, Bi-qi Beatrice (2008), '*Macbeth* in Chinese opera', in Nick Moschovakis (ed.), *Macbeth: New Critical Essays*, 276–99, New York: Routledge.

Lei, Bi-qi Beatrice, Judy Celine Ick and Poonam Trivedi, eds. (2017), *Shakespeare's Asian Journeys*, New York: Routledge.

Leichtling, Avrohom (2004), 'Orchestral Prelude to Shakespeare's "Macbeth"', http://www.raff.org/support/download/mac_eng.htm (accessed 19 March 2021).

Leslie, John (1577), *De Origine, Moribus & Rebus gestis Scotorum*, London.

Leslie, Jhone [sic] (1888), *The Historie of Scotland*, trans. Father James Dalrymple, 2 vol, Edinburgh: Scottish Text Society.

'Let slip the dawgs' (2004), *The Economist*, 11 September.

Levin, Harry (1982), *Shakespeare's Craft: Eight Lectures*, ed. Philip H. Highfill, Jr., Carbondale: Southern Illinois University Press.

Lindfors, Bernth (2010), 'Ira Aldridge as Macbeth', in Scott L. Newstok and Ayanna Thompson (eds), *Weyward Macbeth: Intersections of Race and Performance*, 45–54, New York: Palgrave Macmillan.

Lockwood, Lewis (2003), *Beethoven: The Music and the Man*, New York: Norton.

Lopez, Jeremy (2017), *Constructing the Canon of Early Modern Drama*, Cambridge: Cambridge University Press.

Lucy, Margaret (1911), *Lady Macbeth, Read at a Meeting of Members of a Ladies Literary Circle at Stratford-upon-Avon*, Stratford-upon-Avon: E. Fox.

Lukeman, Noah (2008), *The Tragedy of Macbeth, Part II: The Seed of Banquo*, New York: Penguin.

Lyon, James K. (1980), *Bertolt Brecht in America*, Princeton: Princeton University Press.

Mack Jr., Maynard (1973), *Killing the King*, New Haven: Yale University Press.

Magnarelli, Sharon (2008), 'Staging Shadows/Seeing Ghosts: Ambiguity, Theatre, Gender, and History in Griselda Gambaro's *La señora Macbeth*', *Theatre Journal*, 60.3: 365–82.

Maguire, Laurie and Emma Smith (2013), *30 Great Myths about Shakespeare*, Oxford: Wiley- Blackwell.

Mahlke, Stefan (1999), 'Brecht ± Müller: German-German Brecht Images before and after 1989', *TDR*, 43.4: 40–9.

Mahon, J. W. (2007), 'The Elevator and the Smoke', *Shakespeare Bulletin*, 57.3: 81

Major, John (1892), *A History of Greater Britain*, trans. Archibald Constable, Edinburgh: Edinburgh University Press.

Makaryk, Irena R., (2006), 'Performance and Ideology: Shakespeare in 1920s Ukraine', in Irena R. Makaryk and Joseph G. Price (eds), *Shakespeare in the Worlds of Communism and Socialism*, 15–37, Toronto: University of Toronto Press.

Makaryk, Irena R. and Marissa McHugh, eds (2012), *Shakespeare and the Second World War: Memory, Culture, Identity*, Toronto: University of Toronto Press.

Mandel, Marc (2015), 'Richard Strauss', in *Boston Symphony Orchestra Program Week 15*, 37–41, Boston.

Marowitz, Charles (1978), *The Marowitz Shakespeare*, New York: Drama Book Specialists.

Marsh, Ngaio (1982), *Light Thickens*, Boston: Little Brown.

Matei-Chesnoiu, Monica (2006), *Shakespeare in the Romanian Cultural Memory*, Madison, NJ: Fairleigh Dickinson University Press.

McCarthy, Mary (1962), 'General Macbeth', in Sylvan Barnet (ed.), *Macbeth*, New York: New American Library.

McClure, J. Derrick (1999), 'When *Macbeth* Becomes Scots', *Ilha do Desterro*, 36: 29–51.

McDonald, Russ (2005), *Look to the Lady: Sarah Siddons, Ellen Terry, and Judi Dench on the Shakespearean Stage*, Athens: University of Georgia Press.

McIlwain, C. H., ed. (1918), *The Political Works of James I*, Cambridge, MA: Harvard University Press.

McKernan, Luke (2009), 'Bloody Dreams: Laurence Olivier's Macbeth and the Business of Filming Shakespeare', in Olwen Terris, Eve-Marie Oesterlen and Luke McKernan (eds), *Shakespeare on Film, Television and Radio: The Researcher's Guide*, 1–19, London: British Universities Film & Video Council.

McLuskie, Kate (1999), '*Macbeth/uMabatha*: Global Shakespeare in a Post-Colonial Market', *Shakespeare Survey*, 52: 154–65.

McLuskie, Kathleen E. (2009), *William Shakespeare: Macbeth*, Horndon UK: Northcote House.

McMillan, Joyce (2017), 'Theatre Reviews'. https://www.scotsman.com/arts-and-culture/theatre-and-stage/theatre-reviews-macbeths-spamalot-pleading-1438625 (accessed 5 April 2021).

Millen, Robbie (2018), 'Harry Hole Is Inspired by Macbeth', *The Times*, 7 April. https://www.thetimes.co.uk/article/jo-nesbo-harry-hole-is-inspired-by-macbeth-9d63z5r3m (accessed 20 March 2021).

Miller, Malcolm (2009), 'Bloomsbury Theatre: Bloch's "Macbeth"', *Tempo*, 63.249: 62–3.

Milosz, Czeslaw (1981), *The Captive Mind*, New York: Vintage.

Milton, John (1938), *The Works of John Milton*, ed. F. A. Patterson, vol. 18, New York: Columbia University Press.

Mitri, Paul T. (2007), 'Making Shakespeare Bi-Lingual', Paper delivered at International Association of Performing Language Conference, 11 November 2007.

Mitri, Paul T. (2008a), 'Director's Notes', *Macbeth Program*, University of Hawai'i at Mānoa.

Mitri, Paul T. (2008b), 'Working Script for *Macbeth*', University of Hawai'i at Mānoa. Provided by dramaturg Marie Charlson.

Mitri, Paul T. (2009), Personal Communication with William C. Carroll. 12 January.

Moretti, Franco (1982), '"A Huge Eclipse": Tragic Form and the Deconsecration of Sovereignty', in Stephen Greenblatt (ed.), *The Forms of Power and the Power of Forms in the Renaissance*, 7–40, Norman, OK: Pilgrim Books.

Morse, Ruth (2004), 'Monsieur Macbeth: From Jarry to Ionesco', *Shakespeare Survey*, 57: 112–25.

Moschovakis, Nick, ed. (2008), *Macbeth: New Critical Essays*, New York: Routledge.

Msomi, Welcome (2000), '*uMabatha*', in Daniel Fischlin and Mark Fortier (eds), *Adaptations of Shakespeare: A Critical Anthology*, 164–87, New York: Routledge.

Murray, Braham (2007), *The Worst It Can Be Is a Disaster*, London: Bloomsbury.

Murray, Ross (2020), 'A Letter from the Condo Association to Mr. and Mrs. Macbeth'. https://www.mcsweeneys.net/articles/a-letter-from-the-condo-association-to-mr-and-mrs-macbeth?utm_source=wordfly&utm_medium=email&utm_campaign=ShakespearePlus29Apr2020&utm_content=version_A&promo=12854 (accessed 20 March 2021).

Myklebost, Svenn-Arve (2013), 'Painted Devils and Samurai: *Macbeth* in Comics and Manga', in Stuart Sillars et al. (eds), *The Shakespearean International Yearbook: Volume 13: Special Section, Macbeth*, 93–112, New York: Routledge.

Nenner, Howard (1995), *The Right to Be King: The Succession to the Crown of England 1603– 1714*, Chapel Hill: University of North Carolina Press.

Nesbø, Jo (2018), *Macbeth*, London: Hogarth Shakespeare.

Newstok, Scott L. and Ayanna Thompson, eds (2010), *Weyward Macbeth: Intersections of Race and Performance*, New York: Palgrave Macmillan.

Ninagawa, Yukio (2015), 'Director's Note', in 'Program Notes', New York: Mostly Mozart Festival 2018.

Nietzsche, Friedrich ([1911] 1974), *The Dawn of Day*, in *The Complete Works of Friedrich Nietzsche*, trans. J. M. Kennedy, vol. 9, New York: Gordon Press.

Norbrook, David (1987), '*Macbeth* and the Politics of Historiography', in Kevin Sharpe and Steven N. Zwicker (eds), *Politics of Discourse: The Literature and History of Seventeenth-Century England*, 78–116, Berkeley: University of California Press.

Nottebohm, Gustav (1887), '*Aufzeichnungen zu einer Oper "Macbeth"*', in *Zweite Beethoveniana*, 225–7, Leipzig: Verlag Peters.

Orgel, Stephen (1999), 'Macbeth and the Antic Round', *Shakespeare Survey*, 52: 143–53.

Ouzounian, Richard (2009), 'Worse than Murder, This Macbeth's Dull'. https://www.thestar.com/entertainment/stage/2009/06/02/worse_than_murder_this_macbeths_dull.html (accessed 3 March 2021).

Passfield, John (2019), *Lord and Lady Macbeth: Full of Scorpions Is My Mind*, Oakville, ON: Rock's Mills Press.

Passfield, John (2019a), *The Making of Full of Scorpions Is My Mind*, www.johnpassfield.ca (accessed 7 July 2020).

Passfield, John (2019b), *Planning Full of Scorpions Is My Mind: A Notebook of the Development of a Novel*, www.johnpassfield.ca (accessed 7 July 2020).

Patterson, F. A. (1938), *The Works of John Milton*, New York: Columbia University Press.

Paul, Henry N. (1950), *The Royal Play of 'Macbeth'*, New York: Macmillan.

Peide, Zha, and Tian Jia (1988), 'Shakespeare in Traditional Chinese Operas', *Shakespeare Quarterly* 39.2: 204–11.

Pemble, John (2005), *Shakespeare Goes to Paris: How the Bard Conquered France*, London: Bloomsbury.

Pepys, Samuel (1908), *Diary of Samuel Pepys*, eds, Richard Braybrooke and John Smith, London: J. M. Dent.

Perry, Curtis (2000), 'Vaulting Ambitions and Killing Machines: Shakespeare, Jarry, Ionesco and the Senecan Absurd', in Donald Hedrick and Bryan Reynolds (eds), *Shakespeare without Class*, 85–106, New York: Palgrave.

Peterson, Kaara (2010), *Popular Medicine, Hysterical Disease, and Social Controversy in Shakespeare's England*, Burlington, VT: Ashgate.

Pfister, Manfred (1986), 'Germany Is Hamlet: The History of a Political Interpretation', *New Comparison*, 2: 106–26.

Pfister, Manfred (1994), 'Hamlets Made in Germany, East and West', in Michael Hattaway, Boika Sokolova, and Derek Roper (eds), *Shakespeare in the New Europe*, 76–91, Sheffield: Sheffield Academic Press.

Poniž, Denis (2014), 'Analyzing Shakespearean Models of Tyranny in a Communist Regime: Some Examples from the Slovene Theatre in the Period 1945–1983', in Keith Gregor (ed.), *Shakespeare and Tyranny: Regimes of Reading in Europe and Beyond*, 181–202, Cambridge: Cambridge Scholars.

Poole, Adrian (2004), *Shakespeare and the Victorians*, London: Thomson Learning.

Potter, Lois (1989), *Secret Rites and Secret Writing*, Cambridge: Cambridge University Press.

Power, Maggie (2008), *Lady Macbeth's Tale*, Charleston, SC: BookSurge Publishing.

Prescott, Paul (2004), 'Doing All That Becomes a Man: The Reception and Afterlife of the Macbeth Actor, 1744–1889', *Shakespeare Survey*, 57: 81–95.

Primmer, Brian (2001), 'Chelard', *Oxford Music Online*. https://doi-org. ezproxy.bu.edu/10.1093/gmo/9781561592630.article.05513 (accessed 28 March 2021).

Prochazka, Martin (1996), 'Shakespeare and Czech Resistance', in Heather Kerr, Robin Eaden, and Madge Mitton (eds), *Shakespeare: World Views*, 44–69, Newark: University of Delaware Press.

Pronko, Leonard (1993), '*The Chronicle of Macbeth*', *Theatre Journal*, 45.1: 110–12.

Purkiss, Diane (1996), *The Witch in History*, New York: Routledge.

Rackin, Phyllis (2005), *Shakespeare and Women*, Oxford: Oxford University Press.

Rampton, James (1997), 'Macbeth with Attitude', *Independent*, 5 April 1997. https://www.independent.co.uk/life-style/macbeth-with-attitude-1265408.html (accessed 11 June 2020).

Ray, Sid (2009), 'Finding Gruoch: The Hidden Genealogy of Lady Macbeth in Text and Cinematic Performance', in Martha W. Driver and Sid Ray (eds), *Shakespeare and the Middle Ages*, 116–34, London: McFarland.

Rayner, Francesca (2014), 'From the Snares of Watchful Tyranny to Post-Human Dictators: *Macbeth* under the Portugese Dictatorship and in Democracy', in Keith Gregor (ed.), *Shakespeare and Tyranny: Regimes of Reading in Europe and Beyond*, 127–44, Newcastle-upon-Tyne: Cambridge Scholars.

Reisert, Rebecca (2001), *The Third Witch*, New York: Washington Square Press.

Richardson, Sophia, and Lauren Shohet (2012), 'What's Missing in *Sleep No More*' *Borrowers and Lenders*, 7.2; http://www.borrowers.uga. edu/7164/toc (accessed 6 April 2021).

Richter, Stephen, and Mónica Andrade (2016), *Marqués – a narco-Macbeth*, n.p. Createspace Independent Publishing Platform.

Rippy, Marguerite (2010), 'Black Cast Conjures White Genius: Unraveling the Mystique of Orson Welles's "Voodoo" *Macbeth*', in Scott L. Newstok and Ayanna Thompson (eds), *Weyward Macbeth: Intersections of Race and Performance*', 83–90, New York: Palgrave Macmillan.

Rolls, Albert (2002), '*Macbeth* and the Uncertainties of the Succession Law', *Shakespeare Bulletin*, 52.2: 43–4, 48.

Rosen, David, and Andrew Porter, eds (1984), *Verdi's Macbeth: A Sourcebook*, New York: Norton.

Rosenberg, Marvin (1978), *The Masks of Macbeth*, Berkeley: University of California Press.

Rowe, Katherine (2004), 'The Politics of Sleepwalking: American Lady Macbeths', *Shakespeare Survey*, 57: 126–36.

Rozett, Martha Tuck (1994), *Talking Back to Shakespeare*, Newark, DE: University of Delaware Press.

Rutter, Carol Chillington (2004), 'Remind Me: How Many Children Had Lady Macbeth', *Shakespeare Survey*, 57: 38–53.

Ryan, Jessica (2002), 'The Welcome Msomi Company', *Shakespeare's Globe Research Bulletin*, 25: 1–13.

Rycroft, Eleanor (2020), 'Review of Shakespeare and Heiner Müller's *Macbeth*', *Shakespeare*, 16.3: 326–8. https://www.tandfonline.com/doi/full/10.1080/17450918.2020.1787497 (accessed 12 March 2021).

Salvini, Tommaso (1893), *Leaves from the Autobiography of Tommaso Salvini*, New York: The Century Co.

Scheil, Katherine West (2006), '*Macbeth*', *Shakespeare Bulletin*, 24.1: 115–18.

Schmidgall, Gary (1990), *Shakespeare & Opera*, Oxford: Oxford University Press.

Schuhmacher, Erich (1938), *Shakespeares Macbeth auf der deutschen Bühne*, Emsdetten: Verlags-Anstalt Heinr. & J. Lechte.

Sciarrino, Salvatore (2002), *Macbeth: Tre atti senza nome. Libretto di Salvatore Sciarrino da Shakespeare*; http://www.dicoseunpo.it/S_files/Macbeth.pdf (accessed 22 March 2021).

Seeff, Adele (2013), 'Shakespeare in Mzansi', in Sarah Hatchuel and Nathalie Vienne-Guerrin (eds), *Shakespeare on Screen: Macbeth*, 171–202, Rouen: Publications des Universités de Rouen et du Havre.

Seeff, Adele (2018), *South Africa's Shakespeare and the Drama of Language and Identity*, New York: Palgrave Macmillan.

Shirley, Rae (2010), *A Merry Regiment of Women*, Los Angeles: Baker's Plays.

Shurbanov, Alexander (1998), 'Politicized with a Vengeance: East European Uses of Shakespeare's Great Tragedies', in Jonathan Bate, Jill L. Levenson, and Dieter Mehl (eds), *Shakespeare and the Twentieth Century*, 137–47, Newark: University of Delaware Press.

Shurbanov, Alexander, and Boika Sokolova (1996), 'Macbeth in the Context of Twentieth- Century Totalitarianism', in Patricia Kennan and Mariangela Tempera (eds), *International Shakespeare: The Tragedies*, 105–11, Bologna: CLUEB.

Sinfield, Alan (1985), 'Introduction: Reproductions, Interventions', in Jonathan Dollimore and Alan Sinfield (eds), *Political Shakespeare: New Essays in Cultural Materialism*, 130–3, Ithaca: Cornell University Press.

Skinner, Quentin (1978), *The Foundations of Modern Political Thought*, 2 vols, Cambridge: Cambridge University Press.

Smith, Gay (2010), *Lady Macbeth in America: From the Stage to the White House*, New York: Palgrave Macmillan.

Smurthwaite, Nick (1999), 'Theater: Macbeth in Pidgin', *Asia Times Online*, 2 February 1999; www.atimes.com/oceania/AB02Ah01.html (accessed 4 December 2009).

Sorge, Thomas (1994), 'Buridan's Ass between Two Performances of *A Midsummer Night's Dream*, or Bottom's *Telos* in the GDR and After', in Michael Hattaway, Boika Sokolova, and Derek Roper (eds), *Shakespeare in the New Europe*, 54–74, Sheffield: Sheffield Academic Press.

South African History Online (2020), https://www.sahistory.org.za/people/shaka-zulu (accessed 20 February 2021).

Stafford-Clark, Max (2005), 'Murder Is Fine. It's the Witchcraft That's Dangerous', *The Guardian*. https://www.theguardian.com/stage/2005/dec/01/theatre.rsc (accessed 26 February 2021).

Stallybrass, Peter (1982), '*Macbeth* and Witchcraft', in John Russell Brown (ed.), *Focus on Macbeth*, 189–209, London: Routledge.

Stevenson, J. H. (1927), 'The Law of the Throne: Tanistry and the Introduction of the Law of Primogeniture: A Note on the Succession of the Kings of Scotland from Kenneth MacAlpin to Robert Bruce', *The Scottish Historical Review*, 25.97 (October): 1–12.

Stone, George Winchester Jr. (1941), 'Garrick's Handling of "Macbeth"', *Studies in Philology*, 38.4: 609–28.

Stoppard, Tom (1993), *Cahoot's Macbeth*, in *The Real Inspector Hound and Other Entertainments*, London: Faber and Faber.

Stříbrný, Zdeněk (1994), 'Shakespeare as Liberator: *Macbeth* in Czechoslovakia', in Tetsuo Kishi, Roger Pringle, and Stanley Wells (eds), *Shakespeare and Cultural Traditions*, 274–9, Newark, DE: University of Delaware Press.

Stříbrný, Zdeněk (2000), *Shakespeare and Eastern Europe*, Oxford: Oxford University Press.

Symington, Rodney (2005), *The Nazi Appropriation of Shakespeare: Cultural Politics in the Third Reich*, Lewiston, NY: Edwin Mellen Press.

Tate, Nahum (1731), *Macbeth*, London.

Taylor, Gary (2014), '*Macbeth* and Middleton', in Robert Miola (ed.), *Macbeth*, 296–305, New York: Norton.

Tempera, Mariangela (1993), 'The Art of Lying in *Macbeth*', *Testus*, 6: 57–76.

Thomas, Keith (1971), *Religion and the Decline of Magic*, New York: Scribner's.

Thomas, Mark (2017), *Joachim Raff Website*, http://www.raff.org/index. htm (accessed 19 March 2021).

Thomas, Sian (2006), 'Lady Macbeth', in Michael Dobson (ed.), *Performing Shakespeare's Tragedies Today*, 95–105, Cambridge: Cambridge University Press.

Thompson, George (1998), *A Documentary History of the African Theatre*, Evanston: Northwestern University Press.

Thurber, James (1942), 'The Macbeth Murder Mystery', in *My World – And Welcome to It*, 33–9, New York: Harcourt Brace & Co.

Töyrä, Kayleigh (2020), 'Dating Back', *Shakespeare Magazine*, http:// www.shakespearemagazine.com/2020/11/dating-back-to-the-first-half-of-the-nineteenth-century-the-earliest-finnish-language-translation-of-a-shakespeare-play-was-fated-to-fade-into-obscurity-almost-200-years-later-kayleigh-toyra-uneart/ (accessed 6 February 2021).

Tribble, Evelyn (2005), '"When Every Noise Appalls Me": Sound and Fear in *Macbeth* and Akira Kurosawa's *Throne of Blood*', *Shakespeare*, 1.1–2: 75–90.

Tuck, Richard (1974), '*Power* and *Authority* in Seventeenth-Century England,' *The Historical Journal*, 17: 43–61.

Valbuena, Olga L. (2003), *Subjects to the King's Divorce: Equivocation, Infidelity, and Resistance in Early Modern England*, Bloomington: Indiana University Press.

Vickers, Brian (2010), 'Disintegrated', *TLS*, 28 May: 13–14.

Wallace, Clare (2013), *The Theatre of David Greig*, London: Bloomsbury.

Wattenberg, Daniel (1992), 'The Lady Macbeth of Little Rock'. https:// spectator.org/64729_lady-macbeth-little-rock/ (accessed 5 May 2020).

Weaver, William (1984), 'Verdi, Shakespeare, and the Libretto', in David Rosen and Andrew Porter (eds), *Verdi's Macbeth: A Sourcebook*, 144–8, New York: Norton.

Weber, Carl, ed. (1984), *Hamletmachine and Other Texts for the Stage*, New York: PAJ.

Weber, Carl (1990), 'Heiner Müller in East Berlin', *Performing Arts Journal*, 12.2/3: 29–35.

Weber, Carl, and Paul David Young, eds (2012), *Heiner Müller: After Shakespeare*, New York: PAJ.

Wells, Stanley, ed. (1978), *Nineteenth-Century Shakespeare Burlesques*, vols. 2 and 3 Wilmington, DE: Michael Glazier.

Wells, Stanley (2001), 'Shakespeare in Max Beerbohm's Theatre Criticism', *Shakespeare Survey*, 29 (2001): 133–45.

Whitney, Hilary (2010), 'Interview with Hilary Whitney', *theartsdesk Q&A: Playwright David Greig*; theartsdesk.com; 6 February 2010 (accessed 7 July 2015).

Wilders, John (2004), *Shakespeare in Production: Macbeth*, Cambridge: Cambridge University Press.

Williams, Katarzyna Kwapisz (2012), 'Appropriating Shakespeare in Defeat: *Hamlet* and the Contemporary Polish Vision of War', in Irena R. Makaryk and Marissa McHugh (eds), *Shakespeare and the Second World War: Memory, Culture, Identity*, 286–307, Toronto: University of Toronto Press.

Williams, Simon (2004), 'Taking Macbeth Out of Himself: Davenant, Garrick, Schiller and Verdi', *Shakespeare Survey*, 57: 54–78.

Williams, Tony (2006), '*Macbeth*', *Senses of Cinema*, 38. https://www.sensesofcinema.com/2006/cteq/macbeth-2/ (accessed 29 March 2021).

Wills, Garry (2011), *Verdi's Shakespeare: Men of the Theater*, New York: Viking.

Wilson, Arthur (1719), *The Life and Reign of James the First, King of Great Britain*, ed. White Kennett, London.

Wilson, R. A. (2012), *The Tragedy of Macbeth: A Novel*, Kindle: AlyMur Productions.

Wong, Katrine K. (2017), 'Witches and Their Power and Agency in Brett Bailey's *Macbeth*', *Adaptation*, 10.2: 262–83.

Woolcock, Penny (n.d.), https://pennywoolcock.com/macbethontheestate (accessed 11 June 2020).

Worthen, Anna (2007), 'Within and beyond: Pavel Kohout's *Play Makbeth* and Its Audiences', *Gramma: Journal of Theory and Criticism*, 15: 111–32.

Worthen, W. B. (2010), 'Jan Kott, Shakespeare Our Contemporary', *Forum Modernes Theater*, 25.2: 91–7.

Worthen, W. B. (2012), '"The Written Troubles of the Brain": *Sleep No More* and the Space of Character', *Theatre Journal*, 64.1: 79–97.

Wray, Ramona (2011), 'The Morals of *Macbeth* and Peace as Process: Adapting Shakespeare in Northern Ireland's Maximum Security Prison', *Shakespeare Quarterly*, 62.3: 340–63.

Wyntoun, Andrew (1872), *The Orygynale Cronykil of Scotland by Andrew of Wyntoun*, ed. David Laing 3 vols, Edinburgh: Edmonston and Douglas.

Xingxing, Li (2020), 'When "Macbeth" Meets Chinese Opera: A Crossroad of Humanity', *Multicultural Shakespeare: Translation, Appropriation and Performance*, 21.1: 55–68.

Yoshihara, Yukari (2007), 'Popular Shakespeare in Japan', *Shakespeare Survey*, 60: 130–40.

Yost, Michelle K. (2018), 'Stratford-Upon-Web: Shakespeare in Twenty-First-Century Fanfiction', in Andrew James Hartley (ed.), *Shakespeare and Millennial Fiction*, 193–212, Cambridge: Cambridge University Press.

Ziegler, Georgianna (1999), 'Accommodating the Virago: Nineteenth-Century Representations of Lady Macbeth', in Christy Desmet and Robert Sawyer (eds), *Shakespeare and Appropriation*, 119–41, London: Routledge.

Zimmerman, Heiner O. (1994), 'Is Hamlet Germany? On the Political
  Reception of *Hamlet*', in Mark Thornton Burnett and John Manning
  (eds), *New Essays on Hamlet*, 293–318, New York: AMS Press.
Zimmerman, Susan (2005), *The Early Modern Corpse and Shakespeare's
  Theatre*, Edinburgh: Edinburgh University Press.

INDEX

Milton Keynes UK
Ingram Content Group UK Ltd.
UKHW020346070823
426434UK00009B/303